THE
LAW

THE
Mental Health Act
explained BRIDGET DOLAN & DEBRA POWELL

London: The Stationery Office

Applications for reproduction should be made in writing to The Stationery Office Limited, St Crispins, Duke Street, Norwich NR3 1PD.

The information contained in this publication is believed to be correct at the time of manufacture. Whilst care has been taken to ensure that the information is accurate, the publisher can accept no responsibility for any errors or commissions or for changes to the detailed given. Every effort has been made to trace copyright holders and to obtain permission for the use of copyright material. The publishers will gladly receive any information enabling them to rectify any errors or omissions in subsequent editions.

Bridget Dolan and Debra Powell have asserted their moral rights under the Copyright, Designs and Patents Act 1988, to be identified as the author of this work.

Crown copyright material reproduced with permission of Her Majesty's Stationery Office.

A CIP catalogue record for this book is available from the British Library.
A Library of Congress CIP catalogue record has been applied for.

First published 2000

ISBN 0 11 702345 0

Printed in the United Kingdom by The Stationery Office
J0094458   01/00   C10   454412   19585

Mental Health Act 1983 c. 20

Contents

Duration of detention or guardianship and discharge

Aftercare under supervision

Functions of relatives of patients

Supplemental

Supplemental

PART IV: CONSENT TO TREATMENT

PART V: MENTAL HEALTH REVIEW TRIBUNALS

Constitution of Mental Health Review Tribunals etc.

Applications and references concerning Part II patients

Applications and references concerning Part III patients

PART VI: REMOVAL AND RETURN OF PATIENTS WITHIN UNITED KINGDOM, ETC.

Removal to Scotland

Removal to and from Northern Ireland

Removal to and from Channel Islands and Isle of Man

PART VIII: MISCELLANEOUS FUNCTIONS OF LOCAL AUTHORITIES AND THE SECRETARY OF STATE

Approved social workers

Visiting patients

After-care

Functions of the Secretary of State

PART IX: OFFENCES

PART X: MISCELLANEOUS AND SUPPLEMENTARY

Miscellaneous provisions

Supplemental

SCHEDULES:

Schedule 1

The 1983 Mental Health Act Explained

Bridget Dolan & Debra Powell

The "Mental Health Act 1983 explained" was written by Bridget Dolan and Debra Powell, both barristers in private practice at 3 Serjeants' Inn, London, EC4Y 1BQ, a chambers specialising in all aspects of medical law and ethics. (Tel: 0207 427 5000; fax: 0207 353 0425; email: clerks@3serjeantsinn.com)

Bridget Dolan, Ph.D., C.Psychol. Before being called to the Bar in 1997 Bridget Dolan worked for 13 years at St. George's Hospital Medical School, London, where, as a forensic psychologist, she specialised in working with patients with personality disorders. Her current practice entails all aspects of mental health law and medical law, including a recent inquiry into homicide by a psychiatric patient. She is author of *Psychopathic and Anti-social Personality Disorders: Treatment and Research Issues.*[1]

Debra Powell, B.A. (Law) Before her call to the Bar in 1995 Debra Powell worked at the Law Commission where she was involved in the report on *Mental Incapacity.*[2] She specialises primarily in medical law and mental health law and has been junior counsel in the long running GMC inquiry into Bristol Paediatric Cardiac Surgery and the subsequent public inquiry.

Disclaimer

This publication is intended as a brief commentary on the Mental Health Act 1983 and should not be relied upon by any party without taking further legal advice.

The authors have attempted to state the law as it was on 1st August 1999 but bear no responsibility for the accuracy or currency of information contained in this book nor for any reliance placed upon it.

Readers should use this book in conjunction with the most recent Mental Health Act Code of Practice[3] *and the Memorandum on Parts I to VI, VIII and X of the Mental Health Act*[4]. *Those requiring more detailed analysis of the Act may wish to refer to the Mental Health Act Manual*[5].

[1](1993) Dolan B. & Coid J., London, Gaskell

[2](1995) Law Commission No. 231, London, HMSO.

[3](1999) Dept. Health and Welsh Office, London, The Stationery Office.

[4](1998) Dept. Health and Welsh Office, London, The Stationery Office.

[5](1999) 6th edition, R.Jones, London, Sweet and Maxwell.

Mental Health Act 1983

1983 Chapter 20

1. Application of Act: "Mental Disorder"

(1) The provisions of this Act shall have effect with respect to the reception, care and treatment of mentally disordered patients, the management of their property and other related matters.

Section 1(1)

The Act applies to the treatment and care of mentally disordered patients and the management of their affairs.

(2) In this Act–

"mental disorder" means mental illness, arrested or incomplete development of mind, psychopathic disorder and any other disorder or disability of mind and "mentally disordered" shall be construed accordingly;

"severe mental impairment" means a state of arrested or incomplete development of mind which includes severe impairment of intelligence and social functioning and is associated with abnormally aggressive or seriously irresponsible conduct on the part of the person concerned and "severely mentally impaired" shall be construed accordingly;

"mental impairment" means a state of arrested or incomplete development of mind (not amounting to severe mental impairment) which includes significant impairment of intelligence and social functioning and is associated with abnormally aggressive or seriously irresponsible conduct on the part of the person concerned and "mentally impaired" shall be construed accordingly;

"psychopathic disorder" means a persistent disorder or disability of mind (whether or not including significant impairment of intelligence) which results in abnormally aggressive or seriously irresponsible conduct on the part of the person concerned;

and other expressions shall have the meanings assigned to them in section 145 below.

Section 1(2)

Defines 'mental disorder' 'mental impairment' 'severe mental impairment' and 'psychopathic disorder' for the purposes of the Act.

'mental disorder' is broadly defined to encompass mental illness, developmental disorders, psychopathic disorder and any other disorder or disability of mind.

Note: for some purposes within the Act only a the broad 'diagnosis' of 'mental disorder' is required (eg s.2, s.4, s.135, s.136). Other sections (eg s. 3, s.7, s.37, s.38, s.47) require one of the four specific types of mental disorder to be present, that is either 'mental illness', 'mental impairment', 'severe mental impairment' or 'psychopathic disorder'.

'Mental illness' is not further defined within the Act or the Mental Health Act Code of Practice (1999 ed.)[1].

The 'mental impairment' and 'severe mental impairment' must be associated with, and the 'psychopathic disorder' must result in, 'abnormally aggressive or seriously irresponsible conduct'.

Note: the Code of Practice (at 30.5) suggests that "<u>abnormally aggressive behaviour</u>" occurs where actions "are outside the usual range of aggressive behaviour and cause actual damage and/or real distress occurring recently or persistently or with excessive severity". "<u>Irresponsible conduct</u>" is described as "behaviour which shows a lack of responsibility, a disregard of action taken, and where results cause actual damage or real distress, either recently or persistently or with excessive severity". The Court of Appeal have recently found that a mentally impaired child's desire to return to a home where she would be exposed to sexual abuse was not "seriously irresponsible conduct" so as to justify proceedings under the Act[2].

[1] Dept. Health and Welsh Office, Code of Practice, Mental Health Act 1983, Published March 1999, pursuant to s.118 of the Act. London, The Stationery Office.

[2] *In ReF (A child) (Care Order: Sexual Abuse)* Court of Appeal 30th September 1999, TLR 19th October 1999.

(3) Nothing in subsection (2) above shall be construed as implying that a person may be dealt with under this Act as suffering from mental disorder, or from any form of mental disorder described in this section, by reason only of promiscuity or other immoral conduct, sexual deviancy or dependence on alcohol or drugs.

Section 1(3)

A person may not be classified as 'mentally disordered', 'mentally ill', 'mentally impaired' 'severely mentally impaired' or as having 'psychopathic disorder' only on the basis of their sexual deviancy, promiscuity, immoral conduct or alcohol or drug dependance.

Note: s.1(3) does not exclude those who display symptoms or characteristics such as sexual deviancy or substance abuse which are associated with their mental disorder provided that there is other independent evidence of that mental disorder.

PART II

PROCEDURE FOR HOSPITAL ADMISSION

2. Admission for assessment

(1) A patient may be admitted to a hospital and detained there for the period allowed by subsection (4) below in pursuance of an application (in this Act referred to as "an application for admission for assessment") made in accordance with subsections (2) and (3) below.

> **Section 2(1)**
> *Allows a person to be detained in hospital for a period not exceeding 28 days for assessment provided that the grounds set out in section 2(2) below are met and the procedure set out in section 2(3) is followed.*

(2) An application for admission for assessment may be made in respect of a patient on the grounds that-

   (a) he is suffering from mental disorder of a nature or degree which warrants the detention of the patient in a hospital for assessment (or for assessment followed by medical treatment) for at least a limited period; and

   (b) he ought to be so detained in the interests of his own health or safety or with a view to the protection of other persons.

> **Section 2(2)**
> *Sets out the grounds on which an application for admission may be made, a person may only be detained if both subsections (a) and (b) apply.*

> **Section 2(2)(a)**
> *The patient is suffering from a mental disorder of a <u>nature or degree which warrants detention in hospital for assessment</u>.*
>
> Note: the nature or degree of the disorder must be sufficient to justify detention. This is sometimes referred to as '<u>the diagnosis test</u>'. Thus if the nature or degree of the disorder are such that a patient could be adequately assessed in the community this section should not be used.
>
> It has been suggested that '<u>nature</u>' refers to the specific diagnosis including aspects of its history, prognosis and chronicity (type of disorder) whilst '<u>degree</u>' refers to the present manifestation of the disorder and the extent to which it is currently active (its current severity)[3]
>
> '<u>nature or degree</u>' is to be read disjunctively, thus if a patient is suffering with a chronic mental condition which is stable or asymptomatic at the present time this may nevertheless be of a <u>nature</u> which fulfills this criterion.

---

[3]R v S. Thames MHRT. ex parte Smith [1998] TLR 9th December (1999) 47 BMLR 104.

Section 2(2)(b)

The patient ought to be detained in the interests of his/her own health or safety or to protect others.

Note: detention must be necessary to protect the mental or physical health of the patient or others. This is sometimes referred to as 'the necessity test' . The patient need not yet be a danger; averting a deterioration to a state in which s/he would be dangerous is sufficient to justify detention.

(3) An application for admission for assessment shall be founded on the written recommendations in the prescribed form of two registered medical practitioners, including in each case a statement that in the opinion of the practitioner the conditions set out in subsection (2) above are complied with.

Section 2(3)

The applicant will be an Approved Social Worker (ASW) or the patient's nearest relative (see s.11). Two doctors must also make written recommendations in support of the application for admission for assessment one of whom must be approved by the Secretary of State for Health for these purposes (under s.12 i.e. "a s.12 approved doctor").

The medical recommendations must state that the 'diagnosis' and 'necessity' conditions for detention for assessment (above) are met.

(4) Subject to the provisions of section 29(4) below, a patient admitted to hospital in pursuance of an application for admission for assessment may be detained for a period not exceeding 28 days beginning with the day on which he is admitted, but shall not be detained after the expiration of that period unless before it has expired he has become liable to be detained by virtue of a subsequent application, order or direction under the following provisions of this Act.

Section 2(4)

Provides that a patient can not be detained for assessment for longer than 28 days.

The only exception to this 28 day time limit is that in s.29(4), which allows further detention under s.2 where an application has been made to the court to displace the patient's nearest relative.

Note: the use of consecutive s.2 assessment sections is unlawful. The correct procedure if further hospital detention is deemed necessary is to apply for admission for treatment under s.3.

The Code of Practice (1999 ed.) (at chapter 5) gives pointers for deciding whether s.2 or s.3 should be used to admit a patient. Chapter 2 of the Code of Practice sets out the roles and responsibilities of ASWs and doctors in assessing patients who may be admitted under the Act.

3. Admission for treatment

(1) A patient may be admitted to a hospital and detained there for the period allowed by the following provisions of this Act in pursuance of an application (in this Act referred to as "an application for admission for treatment") made in accordance with this section.

Section 3(1)

Allows the compulsory admission of a patient for treatment for an initial period of six months (which is renewable under s.20) provided that the grounds set out in s.3(2) are met and the procedure set out in s.3(3) is followed.

Note: a patient can lawfully be admitted under s.3 immediately following a s.2 admission, even where the patient has been very recently discharged from a s.2 detention by a Mental Health Review Tribunal (MHRT)[4].

[4] R v Managers of South Western Hospital ex parte M [1994] 1 All ER 161.

(2) An application for admission for treatment may be made in respect of a patient on the grounds that-
   (a) he is suffering from mental illness, severe mental impairment, psychopathic disorder or mental impairment and his mental disorder is of a nature or degree which makes it appropriate for him to receive medical treatment in a hospital; and
   (b) in the case of psychopathic disorder or mental impairment, such treatment is likely to alleviate or prevent a deterioration of his condition; and
   (c) it is necessary for the health or safety of the patient or for the protection of other persons that he should receive such treatment and it cannot be provided unless he is detained under this section.

Section 3(2)

The three grounds for detention for treatment, which must all be met, are that:

(a)   the patient is suffering with one of the four specified forms of disorder, i.e. mental illness, mental impairment, severe mental impairment or psychopathic disorder, of either a type or current severity which justifies his/her treatment in a hospital as an in-patient;

(b)   in the case of both mental impairment and psychopathic disorder an additional 'treatability test' must be met: treatment must be likely either to improve or to prevent a worsening of the condition;

Note: 'likely to' in this context means probable and not merely possible. 'Alleviation' does not require cure, merely improvement. It does not matter if the condition is very unlikely to improve with admission for treatment, so long as it is likely that deterioration will be prevented. The treatability test can even be satisfied if there is likely to be initial worsening of the patient's condition, so long as either improvement or stabilisation is likely to follow[5].

(c)   not only must it be necessary for the health or safety of the patient or the protection of others that s/he receives treatment but it must also be shown that treatment can not be provided unless the patient is compulsorily detained in hospital.

[5] R v Canons Park MHRT ex parte A [1994] 2 All ER 659.

(3) An application for admission for treatment shall be founded on the written recommendations in the prescribed form of two registered medical practitioners, including in each case a statement that in the opinion of the practitioner the conditions set out in subsection (2) above are complied with; and each such recommendation shall include-

(a) such particulars as may be prescribed of the grounds for that opinion so far as it relates to the conditions set out in paragraphs (a) and (b) of that subsection; and

(b) a statement of the reasons for that opinion so far as it relates to the conditions set out in paragraph (c) of that subsection, specifying whether other methods of dealing with the patient are available and, if so, why they are not appropriate.

Section 3(3)

The applicant will be an ASW or the patient's nearest relative (see s.11). Two doctors must make written recommendations in support of the application for admission for treatment, one of whom must be approved by the Secretary of State for Health for these purposes (under s.12).

(a) The doctors' recommendations must state the grounds for their opinion that:

(i) the patient is suffering from mental illness, (severe) mental impairment or psychopathic disorder;

(ii) the disorder is of a type or current severity which makes it appropriate to be treated in hospital; and

(iii) in the case of mental impairment or psychopathic disorder, that treatment will either improve or prevent a worsening of the condition.

(b) The two doctors who recommend admission for treatment must also state:

(i) why they are of the opinion that it is necessary for the health or safety of the patient or the protection of others that the patient receives treatment in hospital; and

(ii) whether other methods of treating or managing the patient are available; and,

(iii) if so, why they are of the opinion that those other available methods are not appropriate.

Note: the Code of Practice (1999 ed.) (at chapter 5) gives pointers for deciding whether s.2 or s.3 should be used to admit a patient.

Chapter 2 of the Code of Practice sets out the roles and responsibilities of ASWs and doctors in assessing patients who may be admitted under the Act.

4. Emergency admission for assessment

(1) In any case of urgent necessity, an application for admission for assessment may be made in respect of a patient in accordance with the following provisions of this section, and any application so made is in this Act referred to as "an emergency application".

Section 4(1)

Allows for emergency admission of a patient for assessment for up to 72 hours provided that the procedures within this section are followed.

(2) An emergency application may be made either by an approved social worker or by the nearest relative of the patient; and every such application shall include a statement that it is of urgent necessity for the patient to be admitted and detained under section 2 above, and that compliance with the provisions of this Part of this Act relating to applications under that section would involve undesirable delay.

Section 4(2)

Emergency applications can be made by an ASW or the patient's nearest relative. The applicant must state that it is urgent and necessary for the patient to be compulsorily admitted for assessment and that it would involve undesirable delay if the provisions of s.2 of the Act (i.e. obtaining a second doctor's opinion) were complied with.

(3) An emergency application shall be sufficient in the first instance if founded on one of the medical recommendations required by section 2 above, given, if practicable, by a practitioner who has previous acquaintance with the patient and otherwise complying with the requirements of section 12 below so far as applicable to a single recommendation, and verifying the statement referred to in subsection (2) above.

Section 4(3)

In cases of emergency admission only one doctor's recommendation is required and, although if practicable the doctor should have previous knowledge of the patient and be approved under s.12 of the Act, this need not be so.

The doctor must however verify the ASW's or nearest relative's statement that it is urgent and necessary for the patient to be compulsorily admitted for assessment and obtaining a second doctor's recommendation (in compliance with the provisions of s.2) would involve undesirable delay.

(4) An emergency application shall cease to have effect on the expiration of a period of 72 hours from the time when the patient is admitted to the hospital unless-

(a) the second medical recommendation required by section 2 above is given and received by the managers within that period; and

(b) that recommendation and the recommendation referred to in subsection (3) above together comply with all the requirements of section 12 below (other than the requirement as to the time of signature of the second recommendation).

Section 4(4)

72 hours after admission under s.4 the authority to detain the patient will expire unless:

(a) the s.4 emergency detention is converted to a s.2 detention (for assessment) by the receipt of a second medical recommendation within 72 hours; and

(b) both medical recommendations comply fully with the general provisions as to medical recommendations contained in s.12, save that the second recommendation can be signed after the date of the initial application.

Note: the s.4 detention is converted to a s.2 detention by adding the second doctor's recommendation. A s.4 detention can not be converted to a s.3 detention in this way.

---

(5) In relation to an emergency application, section 11 below shall have effect as if in subsection (5) of that section for the words "the period of 14 days ending with the date of the application" there were substituted the words "the previous 24 hours".

Section 4(5)

For the purposes of s.4 applications the usual 14 day time limit within which the patient must be seen by the applicant (see s.11(5)) does not apply: the person making an emergency application must have seen the patient within the previous 24 hours.

Note: chapter 6 of the Code of Practice (1999 ed.) gives further guidance on admissions under s.4.

---

5. Application in respect of patients who are already in hospital

This section creates temporary holding powers which allow nurses and doctors to prevent voluntary in-patients from leaving hospital whilst a s.2 or s.3 application is completed.

(1) An application for the admission of a patient to a hospital may be made under this Part of this Act notwithstanding that the patient is already an in-patient in that hospital or, in the case of an application for admission for treatment, that the patient is for the time being liable to be detained in the hospital in pursuance of an application for admission for assessment; and where an application is so made the patient shall be treated for the purposes of this Part of this Act as if he had been admitted to the hospital at the time when that application was received by the managers.

Section 5(1)

Applications under Part II of the Act can be made to detain patients who are already voluntary in-patients in hospital. Those already compulsorily detained in hospital for assessment (under s.2) may be further detained for treatment.

For the purposes of calculating time limits when a patient is detained by virtue of an application made when the patient was already in hospital the admission period is deemed to have begun when the application was received by the hospital managers.

Note: admission time periods (save for those beginning under s.4(4) and s.5(4)) are to be calculated from the time of receipt of the application by hospital managers and not from the time when the patient was actually admitted to the hospital – which for a previously informal patient may have been much earlier.

(2) If, in the case of a patient who is an in-patient in a hospital, it appears to the registered medical practitioner in charge of the treatment of the patient that an application ought to be made under this Part of this Act for the admission of the patient to hospital, he may furnish to the managers a report in writing to that effect; and in any such case the patient may be detained in the hospital for a period of 72 hours from the time when the report is so furnished.

Section 5(2)

If it appears to the doctor in charge of treating a patient who is already in hospital that they ought to be detained under s.2 or s.3 of the Act s/he can apply for detention by reporting this opinion to the hospital managers in writing. The patient may then be detained for up to 72 hours from when the report is received.

Note: chapter 8 of the Code of Practice (1999 ed.) gives further guidance on admissions under s.5(2).

Although this sub-section does not explicitly preclude the use of s.4 following a s.5(2) detention this may, in practice, be difficult to justify. In particular, as the patient is already in a hospital, it should be possible to comply with normal s.2 procedures within the 72 hours detention allowed under s.5(2).

(3) The registered medical practitioner in charge of the treatment of a patient in a hospital may nominate one (but not more than one) other registered medical practitioner on the staff of that hospital to act for him under subsection (2) above in his absence.

Section 5(3)

The doctor in charge of treating an in-patient can nominate one other doctor on the hospital staff to act for him/her in his/her absence under s.5(2).

(4) If, in the case of a patient who is receiving treatment for mental disorder as an in-patient in a hospital, it appears to a nurse of the prescribed class-

    (a) that the patient is suffering from mental disorder to such a degree that it is necessary for his health or safety or for the protection of others for him to be immediately restrained from leaving the hospital; and

    (b) that it is not practicable to secure the immediate attendance of a practitioner for the purpose of furnishing a report under subsection (2) above,

the nurse may record that fact in writing; and in that event the patient may be detained in the hospital for a period of six hours from the time when that fact is so recorded or until the earlier arrival at the place where the patient is detained of a practitioner having power to furnish a report under that subsection.

Section 5(4)

A nurse can detain a voluntary in-patient for up to six hours (or until a doctor arrives who can provide a report under s.5(2), whichever is the sooner) if it appears to the nurse that:

(a)   the patient is suffering with mental disorder of such a degree that, in order to safeguard the patient or to protect others, it is necessary to immediately prevent him/her from leaving hospital; and

(b)   it is not practicable to get a doctor to attend immediately and make a report, as required under s.5(2).

This must be recorded in writing and the six hour period begins to run when the written record is made by the nurse.

Note: chapter 9 of the Code of Practice gives further guidance on use of the holding power under s.5(4). The type of nurse who can authorise detention of a patient is prescribed in s.5(7).

---

(5) A record made under subsection (4) above shall be delivered by the nurse (or by a person authorised by the nurse in that behalf) to the managers of the hospital as soon as possible after it is made; and where a record is made under that subsection the period mentioned in subsection (2) above shall begin at the time when it is made.

Section 5(5)

The written record made by the nurse under s.5(4) must be delivered to the hospital managers by the nurse (or by someone to whom he/she has delegated the task), as soon as possible after it is made.

When a patient is initially detained under the nurse's holding power (s.5(4)) and then is further detained under the doctor's holding power (s.5(2)) the 72 hour period of detention described within s.5(2) begins to run from the time the nurse makes the s.5(4) written record and not from when the doctor makes the report to managers.

Note: there is a prescribed form for the making of the nurse's written record[6].

[6] Form 13 as prescribed within the Mental Health (Hospital, Guardianship and Consent to Treatment) Regulations 1983/893 as amended by S.I. 1998/2624.

---

(6) The reference in subsection (1) above to an in-patient does not include an in-patient who is liable to be detained in pursuance of an application under this Part of this Act and the references in subsections (2) and (4) above do not include an in-patient who is liable to be detained in a hospital under this Part of this Act.

Section 5(6)

This subsection excludes those who are already compulsorily detained from the provisions for short term detention under s.5(2) and 5(4).

Note: the combined effect of this subsection and s.5(1) is that doctors' and nurses' short term holding powers can only be used in respect of voluntary in-patients.

(7) In subsection (4) above "prescribed" means prescribed by an order made by the Secretary of State.

Section 5(7)

The type of nurse who can make an application under s.5(4) is prescribed by the Secretary of State for Health.

Note: the current regulations state this is a Registered Nurse trained in mental illness or learning disabilities (specifically under parts 3,4,5,6,13 or 14 of the nursing register)[7].

[7] The Mental Health (Nurses) Order 1998 (S.I. 1998/2625).

6. Effect of Application for Admission

(1) An application for the admission of a patient to a hospital under this Part of this Act, duly completed in accordance with the provisions of this Part of this Act, shall be sufficient authority for the applicant, or any person authorised by the applicant, to take the patient and convey him to the hospital at any time within the following period, that is to say-

   (a) in the case of an application other than an emergency application, the period of 14 days beginning with the date on which the patient was last examined by a registered medical practitioner before giving a medical recommendation for the purposes of the application;

   (b) in the case of an emergency application, the period of 24 hours beginning at the time when the patient was examined by the practitioner giving the medical recommendation which is referred to in section 4(3) above, or at the time when the application is made, whichever is the earlier.

Section 6(1)

Once an application for admission has been correctly completed as prescribed within the Act the applicant, or another person authorised by him/her, can lawfully take the patient to a hospital where s/he may be lawfully detained against his/her will.

The time limits for exercise of this power are:

(a)   when the application is not an emergency application, 14 days from the day on which the patient was last examined by the doctor making the recommendation in support of the application;

(b)   when the application is an emergency application (under s.4), 24 hours from either (1) when the application was made, or (2) when the doctor making the medical recommendation in support examined the patient, whichever is the earlier.

Note: the patient may be conveyed to hospital using no more force than is reasonably necessary.

Chapter 11 of the Code of Practice (1999 ed.) gives further guidance on the conveyance of patients.

(2) Where a patient is admitted within the said period to the hospital specified in such an application as is mentioned in subsection (1) above, or, being within that hospital, is treated by virtue of section 5 above as if he had been so admitted, the application shall be sufficient authority for the managers to detain the patient in the hospital in accordance with the provisions of this Act.

Section 6(2)

An application for admission (including a s.5 application for the 'technical' admission of someone who is already an in-patient) provides lawful authority for the detention of the patient by the hospital managers.

(3) Any application for the admission of a patient under this Part of this Act which appears to be duly made and to be founded on the necessary medical recommendations may be acted upon without further proof of the signature or qualification of the person by whom the application or any such medical recommendation is made or given or of any matter of fact or opinion stated in it.

Section 6(3)

If on the face of the application it appears to be correctly made and the appropriate number of medical recommendations are provided with it the hospital managers may act upon the documents without further proof of the truth of their contents.

Note: in s.6(1) 'duly completed' is an objective requirement. The application must state that the relevant provisions have been complied with and they must actually have been complied with. If the application is not 'duly completed' the detention will be unlawful. However, if on the face of the application it appears to be duly completed the hospital managers are entitled to act upon it and they (but not the applicant) will be protected from liability for false imprisonment even if the facts stated on the form subsequently turn out to be untrue[8].

Defective or incorrect applications and medical recommendations can be amended under s.15.

[8] Re S-C (Mental patient: habeus corpus) [1996] 1 All ER 532.

(4) Where a patient is admitted to a hospital in pursuance of an application for admission for treatment, any previous application under this Part of this Act by virtue of which he was liable to be detained in a hospital or subject to guardianship shall cease to have effect.

Section 6(4)
When a patient is admitted for treatment any pre-existing authority for either compulsory detention or guardianship under Part II of the Act lapses.

GUARDIANSHIP

7. Application for guardianship

(1) A patient who has attained the age of 16 years may be received into guardianship, for the period allowed by the following provisions of this Act, in pursuance of an application (in this Act referred to as "a guardianship application" made in accordance with this section.

Section 7(1)
A guardianship application may only be made for those aged 16 or over. Guardianship will be for an initial period of six months which is renewable thereafter (under s.20).

(2) A guardianship application may be made in respect of a patient on the grounds that-

(a) he is suffering from mental disorder, being mental illness, severe mental impairment, psychopathic disorder or mental impairment and his mental disorder is of a nature or degree which warrants his reception into guardianship under this section; and
(b) it is necessary in the interests of the welfare of the patient or for the protection of other persons that the patient should be so received.

Section 7(2)

The two grounds for making a guardianship application, both of which must be met, are that:

(a) the patient is suffering with one of the four forms of mental disorder (mental illness, mental impairment, severe mental impairment or psychopathic disorder) of a type or current severity which justifies guardianship; and

(b) it is necessary for the welfare of the patient or protection of others that s/he be placed under guardianship.

Note: 'welfare' of the patient in this context is wide enough to encompass matters such as the avoidance of exploitation by others.

Unlike the grounds for detention for treatment there is no requirement that the guardianship should improve or prevent a worsening of the patient's condition.

As this section of the Act requires the person to be suffering from one of the four specific types of disorder (rather than using the broad term 'mental disorder') it would not be lawful to place under guardianship a mentally impaired person whose impairment is not associated with either abnormally aggressive or seriously irresponsible conduct (see s.1(2)).

(3) A guardianship application shall be founded on the written recommendations in the prescribed form of two registered medical practitioners, including in each case a statement that in the opinion of the practitioner the conditions set out in subsection (2) above are complied with; and each such recommendation shall include-

(a) such particulars as may be prescribed of the grounds for that opinion so far as it relates to the conditions set out in paragraph (a) of that subsection; and

(b) a statement of the reasons for that opinion so far as it relates to the conditions set out in paragraph (b) of that subsection.

Section 7(3)

The applicant will be an ASW or the patient's nearest relative (see s.11). However two doctors must also make written recommendations in support of the application for guardianship, one of whom must be approved by the Secretary of State for Health for these purposes (under s.12(7)).

Section 7(3)(a) to (b)

The doctors' recommendations must state the grounds for their opinion that:

(i) the patient is suffering from mental illness, mental impairment, severe mental impairment or psychopathic disorder;

(ii) the disorder is of a type or current severity which makes it appropriate for him/her to be received into guardianship;

(iii) it is necessary for the welfare of the patient or protection of others that the patient be received into guardianship.

(4) A guardianship application shall state the age of the patient or, if his exact age is not known to the applicant, shall state (if it be the fact) that the patient is believed to have attained the age of 16 years.

Section 7(4)
The guardianship application must give the patient's age or, if this is unknown, must state that he is believed to be over 16 years.

(5) The person named as guardian in a guardianship application may be either a local social services authority or any other person (including the applicant himself); but a guardianship application in which a person other than a local social services authority is named as guardian shall be of no effect unless it is accepted on behalf of that person by the local social services authority for the area in which he resides, and shall be accompanied by a statement in writing by that person that he is willing to act as guardian.

Section 7(5)
The guardian must be either a local social services authority or a person who has put in writing that s/he is willing to act as a guardian and is deemed acceptable by the local social services to act in that capacity.

Note: chapter 13 of the Code of Practice (1999 ed.) gives further guidance on guardianship[9].

[9]Further regulations governing guardianship procedures are provided in the Mental Health (Hospital, Guardianship and Consent to Treatment) Regulations 1983/89 (as amended by S.I.s 1996/540, 1997/801, 1998/2624).

8. Specific powers of guardians

(1) Where a guardianship application, duly made under the provisions of this Part of this Act and forwarded to the local social services authority within the period allowed by subsection (2) below is accepted by that authority, the application shall, subject to regulations made by the Secretary of State, confer on the authority or person named in the application as guardian, to the exclusion of any other person-

(a) the power to require the patient to reside at a place specified by the authority or person named as guardian;
(b) the power to require the patient to attend at places and times so specified for the purpose of medical treatment, occupation, education or training;
(c) the power to require access to the patient to be given, at any place where the patient is residing, to any registered medical practitioner, approved social worker or other person so specified.

Section 8(1)

A properly completed guardianship application which is forwarded to the local social services authority within 14 days and is accepted gives the guardian (and only the guardian) the power to require:

(a)   the person to live in a place specified by the guardian;

Note: there is no power to require a person to live with a particular person, only at a particular place. Although the 'place' could be a hospital, guardianship is intended to be an alternative to hospital detention and if compulsory detention in hospital is deemed necessary an application for hospital admission ought to be made.

(b)   the person to attend for treatment, work, education or training at place specified by the guardian;

Note: although there is power to require a person to attend at a hospital for treatment there is no power within this section to take a patient there or to treat a patient under guardianship without his/her consent.

(c)   access to the person to be given to any doctor, ASW or other person specified by the guardian.

Note: guardianship powers are mainly persuasive, carrying no sanctions. As such a person can not be forced to comply with the guardian's 'requirements' save that if a patient subject to guardianship absents him/herself without leave from the place at which s/he is required to reside, s/he may be taken into custody and returned to that place under s.18 (below).

(2) The period within which a guardianship application is required for the purposes of this section to be forwarded to the local social services authority is the period of 14 days beginning with the date on which the patient was last examined by a registered medical practitioner before giving a medical recommendation for the purposes of the application.

Section 8(2)

A guardianship application must be forwarded to the local social services authority within 14 days beginning with the day that the patient was last seen by a doctor in order to make the medical recommendation for guardianship.

(3) A guardianship application which appears to be duly made and to be founded on the necessary medical recommendations may be acted upon without further proof of the signature or qualification of the person by whom the application or any such medical recommendation is made or given, or of any matter of fact or opinion stated in the application.

Section 8(3)
If on the face of the guardianship application it seems to be correctly made and the appropriate number of medical recommendations are provided the documents may be acted upon without further proof of the truth of their contents.

(4) If within the period of 14 days beginning with the day on which a guardianship application has been accepted by the local social services authority the application, or any medical recommendation given for the purposes of the application, is found to be in any respect incorrect or defective, the application or recommendation may, within that period and with the consent of that authority, be amended by the person by whom it was signed; and upon such amendment being made the application or recommendation shall have effect and shall be deemed to have had effect as if it had been originally made as so amended.

Section 8(4)
If either the guardianship application or a doctor's recommendation accompanying it is found to be incorrect or defective within 14 days of receipt it may be amended by the author with the consent of the local social services authority. Once amended the application is treated as if it had been correctly made from the outset.

Note: this section is intended for amending slips and clerical errors and ought not to be used for righting incorrect procedures such as lack of a medical recommendation or failure to see the patient within 14 days of making the application.

(5) Where a patient is received into guardianship in pursuance of a guardianship application, any previous application under this Part of this Act by virtue of which he was subject to guardianship or liable to be detained in a hospital shall cease to have effect.

Section 8(5)
When a patient is received into guardianship any pre-existing authority for detention in hospital or guardianship made under Part II of the Act lapses.

Note: guardianship remains in place if a patient is subsequently admitted voluntarily to hospital or is admitted compulsorily for assessment under s.2 or s.4 of the Act. However (by virtue of s.6(4) above) guardianship ceases if the patient is compulsorily admitted for treatment.

9. Regulations as to Guardianship

(1) Subject to the provisions of this Part of this Act, the Secretary of State may make regulations-

    (a) for regulating the exercise by the guardians of patients received into guardianship under this Part of this Act of their powers as such; and

    (b) for imposing on such guardians, and upon local social services authorities in the case of patients under the guardianship of persons other than local social services authorities, such duties as he considers necessary or expedient in the interests of the patients.

Section 9(1)

The Secretary of State for Health may make regulations[10] to:

(a) regulate the exercise of guardian's powers;

(b) impose duties upon guardians and local social service authorities in the interests of patients.

---

[10] The current regulations are found within the Mental Health (Hospital, Guardianship and Consent to Treatment) Regulations 1983 (as amended by S.I.s 1996/540, 1997/801, 1998/2624).

---

(2) Regulations under this section may in particular make provision for requiring the patients to be visited, on such occasions or at such intervals as may be prescribed by the regulations, on behalf of such local social services authorities as may be so prescribed, and shall provide for the appointment, in the case of every patient subject to the guardianship of a person other than a local social services authority, of a registered medical practitioner to act as the nominated medical attendant of the patient.

Section 9(2)

The regulations may provide for the visiting of patients on behalf of local social services authorities and must provide for the appointment of a nominated doctor to every patient whose guardian is not the local social services authority.

Note: this section also applies to guardianship ordered by the court under s.37(6).

---

10. Transfer of guardianship in case of death, incapacity, etc., of guardian

(1) If any person (other than a local social services authority) who is the guardian of a patient received into guardianship under this Part of this Act-

    (a) dies; or

    (b) gives notice in writing to the local social services authority that he desires to relinquish the functions of guardian,

the guardianship of the patient shall thereupon vest in the local social services authority, but without prejudice to any power to transfer the patient into the guardianship of another person in pursuance of regulations under section 19 below.

Section 10(1)

Provides for guardianship to be transferred to the local social services authority should the guardian die or inform the local social services authority in writing that s/he wishes to cease acting as guardian.

The local social services authority may then transfer the guardianship to another person in line with regulations made by the Secretary of State for Health (see s.19(1)(b) below)

(2) If any such person, not having given notice under subsection (1)(b) above, is incapacitated by illness or any other cause from performing the functions of guardian of the patient, those functions may, during his incapacity, be performed on his behalf by the local social services authority or by any other person approved for the purposes by that authority.

Section 10(2)

Provides for guardianship to be transferred to the local social services authority or person approved by the local social services authority should the guardian become incapacitated through illness or otherwise. The transfer is temporary, for the period of the guardian's incapacity.

(3) If it appears to the county court, upon application made by an approved social worker, that any person other than a local social services authority having the guardianship of a patient received into guardianship under this Part of this Act has performed his functions negligently or in a manner contrary to the interests of the welfare of the patient, the court may order that the guardianship of the patient be transferred to the local social services authority or to any other person approved for the purpose by that authority.

Section 10(3)

Empowers an ASW to apply to a county court for an order that guardianship be transferred to the local social services authority (or person approved by the local social services authority) if the court considers that the current guardian has performed his/her duties negligently or acted in any way against the welfare of the patient.

(4) Where the guardianship of a patient is transferred to a local social services authority or other person by or under this section, subsection (2)(c) of section 19 below shall apply as if the patient had been transferred into the guardianship of that authority or person in pursuance of regulations under that section.

Section 10(4)

Provides that s.19(2)(c) (regulations on transfer of guardianship - see below) applies where transfer of guardianship is effected under s.10.

Where transfer of guardianship is effected under s.10 the 'new' guardianship is deemed to have begun at the time of the initial guardianship application being accepted.

GENERAL PROVISIONS AS TO APPLICATIONS AND RECOMMENDATIONS

11. General provisions as to applications

(1) Subject to the provisions of this section, an application for admission for assessment, an application for admission for treatment and a guardianship application may be made either by the nearest relative of the patient or by an approved social worker; and every such application shall specify the qualification of the applicant to make the application.

Section 11(1)

Provides that applications for admission either for assessment or treatment and for guardianship may be made by either an ASW or the nearest relative of the patient.

All applications must state the qualification of the person to make the application.

Note: the process for deciding which person is the "nearest relative" is prescribed in s.26 below.

The Code of Practice (1999 ed.) states that the ASW is "usually the right applicant" and the nearest relative should be advised of this (para 2.35).

(2) Every application for admission shall be addressed to the managers of the hospital to which admission is sought and every guardianship application shall be forwarded to the local social services authority named in the application as guardian, or, as the case may be, to the local social services authority for the area in which the person so named resides.

Section 11(2)

All applications for admission must be delivered to the relevant hospital managers (in practice the officer delegated to accept the application) and all guardianship applications must be made to the relevant local social services authority.

Note: a guardianship application does not take effect until either accepted by the local social services authority or the local social services authority's consent is given for an individual to act as the guardian.

(3) Before or within a reasonable time after an application for the admission of a patient for assessment is made by an approved social worker, that social worker shall take such steps as are practicable to inform the person (if any) appearing to be the nearest relative of the patient that the application is to be or has been made and of the power of the nearest relative under section 23(2)(a) below.

Section 11(3)

Before making a s.2 application for admission for assessment an ASW must take all practicable steps to inform the patient's nearest relative of their intended actions (or, at least, to inform them of their actions within a reasonable time of the application being made).

The nearest relative should also be informed of his/her power to order discharge of the detained patient (under s.23(2)(a) below).

Note: unlike applications for treatment or guardianship (below), the nearest relative can not prevent an assessment application from continuing by objecting to it.

(4) Neither an application for admission for treatment nor a guardianship application shall be made by an approved social worker if the nearest relative of the patient has notified that social worker, or the local social services authority by whom that social worker is appointed, that he objects to the application being made and, without prejudice to the foregoing provision, no such application shall be made by such a social worker except after consultation with the person (if any) appearing to be the nearest relative of the patient unless it appears to that social worker that in the circumstances such consultation is not reasonably practicable or would involve unreasonable delay.

Section 11(4)

The ASW can only make an application for admission for treatment or guardianship if s/he has consulted the nearest relative, unless such a consultation is not reasonably practicable or would involve unreasonable delay.

Applications for admission for treatment or for guardianship can not go ahead if the nearest relative notifies the ASW or local social services authority that s/he objects to the application.

Note: the nearest relative need not approve of the ASW's proposed actions, s/he must simply not object. Should the nearest relative object, the ASW may apply under s.29 to have the nearest relative displaced.

Although the consultation can be carried out through a third party or by correspondence, any consultation with the nearest relative must be "full and effective". Simply informing the nearest relative of the intended action will not suffice nor will any consultation after the application has been made.[11]

---

[11] R v Managers of South Western Hospital, ex part M [1994] 1 All ER 161 (at 175) and In the matter of Briscoe (Application for *habeus corpus ad subjuciendum*) QB [1998] C.O.D. 402.

(5) None of the applications mentioned in subsection (1) above shall be made by any person in respect of a patient unless that person has personally seen the patient within the period of 14 days ending with the date of the application.

Section 11(5)
The person making an application for a patient to be admitted to hospital or for guardianship must have personally seen the patient within the previous 14 days.

(6) An application for admission for treatment or a guardianship application, and any recommendation given for the purposes of such an application, may describe the patient as suffering from more than one of the following forms of mental disorder, namely mental illness, severe mental impairment, psychopathic disorder or mental impairment; but the application shall be of no effect unless the patient is described in each of the recommendations as suffering from the same form of mental disorder, whether or not he is also described in either of those recommendations as suffering from another form.

Section 11(6)
Applications for admission to hospital or for guardianship and the doctors' recommendations accompanying those applications may describe the patient as suffering with one or more of the four forms of mental disorder (i.e. mental illness, psychopathic disorder, mental impairment and severe mental impairment). However the two medical recommendations must agree on the presence of at least one of these forms of disorder.

(7) Each of the applications mentioned in subsection (1) above shall be sufficient if the recommendations on which it is founded are given either as separate recommendations, each signed by a registered medical practitioner, or as a joint recommendation signed by two such practitioners.

Section 11(7)
The doctors' recommendations accompanying applications may be in the form of either two separate signed recommendations or of a single joint recommendation signed by both doctors.

12. General provisions as to Medical Recommendations

(1) The recommendations required for the purposes of an application for the admission of a patient under this Part of this Act (in this Act referred to as "medical recommendations") shall be signed on or before the date of the application, and shall be given by practitioners who have personally examined the patient either together or separately, but where they have examined the patient separately not more than five days must have elapsed between the days on which the separate examinations took place.

Section 12(1)

Medical recommendations accompanying applications for admission or guardianship must be signed on or before the day the application is made.

Note: there is an exception under s.4 where, on converting from a s.4 detention to a s.2 detention, the second doctor's recommendation may be signed after the application for admission has been made.

Doctors making these recommendations must have personally examined the patient (either together or separately). If separate examinations are made these must be not more than five clear days apart (e.g. Monday and Sunday).

(2) Of the medical recommendations given for the purposes of any such application, one shall be given by a practitioner approved for the purposes of this section by the Secretary of State as having special experience in the diagnosis or treatment of mental disorder; and unless that practitioner has previous acquaintance with the patient, the other such recommendation shall, if practicable, be given by a registered medical practitioner who has such previous acquaintance.

Section 12(2)

One of the medical recommendations accompanying applications for admission or guardianship must be made by a doctor specially approved by the Secretary of State for Health as having psychiatric expertise (known as a "s.12 approved" doctor).[12]

Unless the s.12 approved doctor has previous knowledge of the patient the other recommendation must, if practicable, be given by a doctor who knows the patient.

Note: only one of the recommending doctors need be s.12 approved. It is preferable but not essential that at least one of the doctors has previous knowledge of the patient.

[12] The granting of 'Section 12 approval' is now delegated to Health Authorities by virtue of the NHS (Functions of Health Authorities and Administrations) Regulations 1996 (S.I. 1996/708).

(3) Subject to subsection (4) below, where the application is for the admission of the patient to a hospital which is not a mental nursing home, one (but not more than one) of the medical recommendations may be given by a practitioner on the staff of that hospital, except where the patient is proposed to be accommodated under section 65 or 66 of the National Health Service Act 1977 or paragraph 14 of Schedule 2 to the National Health Service and Community Care Act 1990(which relate to accommodation for private patients).

Section 12(3)

When the patient is to be admitted to a hospital as an NHS patient no more than one of the doctors' recommendations accompanying the application can be made by a doctor employed in or by that hospital.

Note: this would not appear to preclude the recommendations being made by two doctors employed by the same NHS Trust but working in different 'hospitals'.

If the patient is admitted to a private hospital or registered nursing home then neither recommendation may come from doctors employed in or by that institution.

Note: chapter 4 of the Code of Practice (1999 ed.) sets out guidance for the provision of medical recommendations by doctors in private practice.

(4) Subsection (3) above shall not preclude both the medical recommendations being given by practitioners on the staff of the hospital in question if-

    (a) compliance with that subsection would result in delay involving serious risk to the health or safety of the patient; and

    (b) one of the practitioners giving the recommendations works at the hospital for less than half of the time which he is bound by contract to devote to work in the health service; and

    (c) where one of those practitioners is a consultant, the other does not work (whether at the hospital or elsewhere) in a grade in which he is under that consultant's directions.

Section 12(4)

The s.12(3) requirement that the two recommending doctors are not employed in or by the same hospital can be dispensed with if <u>all</u> of the three following conditions are met:

(a)   compliance with s.12(3) would cause delay which would involve serious risk to the health or safety of the patient; and

(b)   one of the recommending doctors works at the hospital for less than half of his/her NHS contract time; and

(c)   if one of the doctors is a consultant, the other doctor is not a junior doctor under his/her direction at this hospital or elsewhere.

Note: condition (b) only concerns a doctor who has a contract to spend more than half of his/her NHS working time in another institution. Thus those on a part-time contract who do not work elsewhere in the NHS would not satisfy the condition.

(5) A medical recommendation for the purposes of an application for the admission of a patient under this Part of this Act shall not be given by:

(a) the applicant;

(b) a partner of the applicant or of a practitioner by whom another medical recommendation is given for the purposes of the same application;

(c) a person employed as an assistant by the applicant or by any such practitioner;

(d) a person who receives or has an interest in the receipt of any payments made on account of the maintenance of the patient; or

(e) except as provided by subsection (3) or (4) above, a practitioner on the staff of the hospital to which the patient is to be admitted,
or by the husband, wife, father, father-in-law, mother, mother-in-law, son, son-in-law, daughter, daughter-in-law, brother, brother-in-law, sister or sister-in-law of the patient, or of any person mentioned in paragraphs (a) to (e) above, or of a practitioner by whom another medical recommendation is given for the purposes of the same application.

Section 12(5)

The recommending doctor may not be:

(a) the applicant;

(b) the partner of either the applicant or the other recommending doctor;

(c) employed as an assistant to either the applicant or the other recommending doctor;

(d) anyone with interest in payments made for the maintenance of the patient;

(e) a practitioner on the staff of the hospital admitting the patient (unless the conditions in s.12(3) and s.12(4) above apply),

Or a close relative of either the patient, the applicant, other recommending doctor or anyone else mentioned in this section.

Note: 'partner' means 'professional partner' such as GPs from the same practice.

(6) A general practitioner who is employed part-time in a hospital shall not for the purposes of this section be regarded as a practitioner on its staff.

Section 12(6)

A GP who works part-time in a hospital is not considered to be a member of staff. Thus a GP may act as a recommending doctor even if s/he works at the hospital where the patient is to be admitted as the exclusion under s.12(3) will not apply.

(7) Subsections (1),(2) and (5) above shall apply to applications for guardianship as they apply to applications for admission but with the substitution for paragraph (e) of subsection (5) above of the following paragraph-

"(e) the person named as guardian in the application.".

Section 12(7)
Provides that relevant parts of this section also apply to medical recommendations accompanying guardianship applications.

Note: chapter 2 of the Code of Practice (1999 ed.) sets out the roles and responsibilities of doctors in assessing patients and making medical recommendations under the Act.

13. Duty of Approved Social Workers to make applications for admission or guardianship

(1) It shall be the duty of an approved social worker to make an application for admission to hospital or a guardianship application in respect of a patient within the area of the local social services authority by which that officer is appointed in any case where he is satisfied that such an application ought to be made and is of the opinion, having regard to any wishes expressed by relatives of the patient or any other relevant circumstances, that it is necessary or proper for the application to be made by him.

Section 13(1)
If an ASW considers that an application for admission or guardianship ought to be made and, having consulted relatives and taken any relevant circumstances into account, is of the opinion that it is necessary, s/he is under a duty to make that application.

Note: this is a personal obligation of the social worker and thus s/he and not his/her employing authority is liable for his/her actions. It exists despite any earlier decision of a MHRT, however recent, to discharge the patient.[13]

There is no corresponding duty on a nearest relative to make an application for admission or guardianship.

---

[13] R v Managers of South Western Hospital ex parte M [1994] 1 All ER 161 (at 171).

(2) Before making an application for the admission of a patient to hospital an approved social worker shall interview the patient in a suitable manner and satisfy himself that detention in a hospital is in all the circumstances of the case the most appropriate way of providing the care and medical treatment of which the patient stands in need.

Section 13(2)
The ASW must have interviewed the patient and be satisfied that admission to hospital is the most appropriate way to provide the care and treatment the patient needs before making an application for admission.

Note: the social worker must have personally seen the patient within 14 days of making the application for admission (see s.11(5) above).

If the patient refuses to allow access for an interview the ASW can consider the use of powers under s.135 (applying for a warrant to search for and remove patients).

(3) An application under this section by an approved social worker may be made outside the area of the local social services authority by which he is appointed.

Section 13(3)
Is self explanatory.

(4) It shall be the duty of a local social services authority, if so required by the nearest relative of a patient residing in their area, to direct an approved social worker as soon as practicable to take the patient's case into consideration under subsection (1) above with a view to making an application for his admission to hospital; and if in any such case that approved social worker decides not to make an application he shall inform the nearest relative of his reasons in writing.

Section 13(4)
If the nearest relative of a patient asks for consideration to be given to making an application for admission to hospital the local social services authority must, as soon as practicable, direct an ASW to take the case into consideration.

If the ASW then decides not to make the application s/he, not the local authority, must inform the patient's nearest relative in writing of the reasons for this decision.

Note: this sub-section does not apply to applications for guardianship.

(5) Nothing in this section shall be construed as authorising or requiring an application to be made by an approved social worker in contravention of the provisions of section 11(4) above, or as restricting the power of an approved social worker to make any application under this Act.

Section 13(5)

The ASW must still comply with s.11(4) (above) in that the ASW can only make an application for admission for treatment or guardianship if s/he has consulted the nearest relative, unless such a consultation is not reasonably practicable or would involve unreasonable delay.

An application for admission for treatment or for guardianship may then not be made if the nearest relative notifies the ASW that s/he objects (see s.11(4) above).

Note: chapter 2 of the Code of Practice (1999 ed.) sets out the roles and responsibilities of ASWs in assessing patients under the Act.

14. Social Reports

Where a patient is admitted to a hospital in pursuance of an application (other than an emergency application) made under this Part of this Act by his nearest relative, the managers of the hospital shall as soon as practicable give notice of that fact to the local social services authority for the area in which the patient resided immediately before his admission; and that authority shall as soon as practicable arrange for a social worker of their social services department to interview the patient and provide the managers with a report on his social circumstances.

Section 14

If a patient is admitted under s.2 or s.3 following an application made by the patient's nearest relative the hospital managers must inform the patient's local social services authority of the admission as soon as practicable.

Once informed the local social services authority must, as soon as practicable, arrange for a social worker to interview the patient and provide a social work report on the patient's social circumstances to the hospital managers.

Note: the social worker providing this report need not be an ASW.

15. Rectification of applications and recommendations

(1) If within the period of 14 days beginning with the day on which a patient has been admitted to a hospital in pursuance of an application for admission for assessment or for treatment the application, or any medical recommendation given for the purposes of the application, is found to be in any respect incorrect or defective, the application or recommendation may, within that period and with the consent of the managers of the hospital, be amended by the person by whom it was signed; and upon such amendment being made the application or recommendation shall have effect and shall be deemed to have had effect as if it had been originally made as so amended.

Section 15(1)

If, within 14 days of the admission of a patient to hospital (including the day of admission), it is found that the application or accompanying medical recommendation is incorrectly completed it may be amended by the author with the consent of the hospital managers.

Once so amended the application or recommendation will be treated as if it had been correctly made from the outset.

Note: this section is intended to correct administrative errors on the face of documents and not to inaccurately present a factual situation, cover up procedural errors or retrospectively validate a fundamentally defective application.[14]

---

[14] R v Managers of South Western Hospital ex parte M [1994] 1 All ER 161.

(2) Without prejudice to subsection (1) above, if within the period mentioned in that subsection it appears to the managers of the hospital that one of the two medical recommendations on which an application for the admission of a patient is founded is insufficient to warrant the detention of the patient in pursuance of the application, they may, within that period, give notice in writing to that effect to the applicant; and where any such notice is given in respect of a medical recommendation, that recommendation shall be disregarded, but the application shall be, and shall be deemed always to have been, sufficient if–

   (a) a fresh medical recommendation complying with the relevant provisions of this Part of this Act (other than the provisions relating to the time of signature and the interval between examinations) is furnished to the managers within that period; and

   (b) that recommendation, and the other recommendation on which the application is founded, together comply with those provisions.

Section 15(2)

If, within 14 days of the admission of a patient to hospital (including the day of admission), it appears to the hospital managers that one of the doctors' recommendations is insufficient to justify the detention of the patient they may, within that 14 day period, inform the applicant of this in writing. On giving such a notice the recommendation will be disregarded.

The application may nevertheless be rectified and will be deemed sufficient if:

(a)   a fresh medical recommendation is provided to the hospital managers within 14 days of admission which complies with the provisions of the Act (save for those which relate to the time of signing and the five day interval between examinations);

(b)   the recommendation taken together with the other medical recommendation and the application itself now comply with all the provisions of the Act.

Note: the fresh recommendation may be by the same or a different doctor. It must be supplied to the hospital managers within 14 days of the patient's admission.

(3) Where the medical recommendations upon which an application for admission is founded are, taken together, insufficient to warrant the detention of the patient in pursuance of the application, a notice under subsection (2) above may be given in respect of either of those recommendations; but this subsection shall not apply in a case where the application is of no effect by virtue of section 11(6) above.

Section 15(3)

The rectification procedure in s.15(2) above may be used where both medical recommendations are good in themselves but when taken together do not comply with requirements.

*However the rectification procedure may **not** be used if the recommendations are deficient because the doctors disagree about the form of the patient's mental disorder (in contravention of s.11(6) above).*

(4) Nothing in this section shall be construed as authorising the giving of notice in respect of an application made as an emergency application, or the detention of a patient admitted in pursuance of such an application, after the period of 72 hours referred to in section 4(4) above, unless the conditions set out in paragraphs (a) and (b) of that section are complied with or would be complied with apart from any error or defect to which this section applies.

Section 15(4)

The rectification procedure in s.15(2) above may not be used to rectify an emergency application made under s.4 after 72 hours (when it expires) unless it has been 'converted' to a longer admission by the provision of a second medical recommendation as required under s.2(3) (for this 'conversion' procedure see s.4(4)(a) and (b) above).

POSITION OF PATIENTS SUBJECT TO DETENTION OR GUARDIANSHIP

16. Reclassification of patients

(1) If in the case of a patient who is for the time being detained in a hospital in pursuance of an application for admission for treatment, or subject to guardianship in pursuance of a guardianship application, it appears to the appropriate medical officer that the patient is suffering from a form of mental disorder other than the form or forms specified in the application, he may furnish to the managers of the hospital, or to the guardian, as the case may be, a report to that effect; and where a report is so furnished, the application shall have effect as if that other form of mental disorder were specified in it.

Section 16(1)

If a patient is detained in hospital for treatment or is under guardianship and it appears to the doctor in charge of the patient's treatment that the patient is now suffering from a form of mental disorder different from that which was specified when the original application was made, the doctor may provide a report to that effect to the hospital managers or guardian and the patient's mental disorder will be reclassified accordingly.

Note: the report may either add an additional form of disorder or substitute an entirely different form of disorder from that given in the original application. There is no limit placed upon the number of times this reclassification may occur.

Reclassification can also take place under s.20(9) when a report renewing the authority to detain a patient is provided.

(2) Where a report under subsection (1) above in respect of a patient detained in a hospital is to the effect that he is suffering from psychopathic disorder or mental impairment but not from mental illness or severe mental impairment the appropriate medical officer shall include in the report a statement of his opinion whether further medical treatment in hospital is likely to alleviate or prevent a deterioration of the patient's condition; and if he states that in his opinion such treatment is not likely to have that effect the authority of the managers to detain the patient shall cease.

Section 16(2)

Where the re-classification substitutes psychopathic disorder or mental impairment as the form of mental disorder in the absence of mental illness or severe mental impairment the doctor must include a statement as to whether detention in hospital is likely to alleviate or prevent deterioration of that disorder. If s/he states that it will not do so there will be no longer any authority to detain the patient in hospital.

Note: this in essence requires that the 'treatability' criterion in s.3(2)(b) be met (where relevant) if detention is to continue when a patient's disorder is reclassified. Where the patient is simultaneously classified as suffering with mental illness or severe mental impairment authority to detain continues as these two disorders do not need to be 'treatable' for detention to be lawful.

(3) Before furnishing a report under subsection (1) above the appropriate medical officer shall consult one or more other persons who have been professionally concerned with the patient's medical treatment.

> **Section 16(3)**
> *Before providing a reclassification report the doctor must consult at least one other person who has been professionally involved in the patient's treatment.*

(4) Where a report is furnished under this section in respect of a patient, the managers or guardian shall cause the patient and the nearest relative to be informed.

> **Section 16(4)**
> *The hospital managers or guardian must ensure that the patient and his/her nearest relative are informed about the receipt of a reclassification report.*
>
> Note: reclassification of a patient's mental disorder gives rise to a right of the patient and the patient's nearest relative to make an application to a MHRT under s.66(1)(d).

(5) In this section "appropriate medical officer" means–
    (a) in the case of a patient who is subject to the guardianship of a person other than a local social services authority, the nominated medical attendant of the patient; and
    (b) in any other case, the responsible medical officer.

> **Section 16(5)**
> *Defines 'appropriate medical officer' for the purposes of this sections as:*
>
> *(a) for a patient under guardianship, the nominated medical attendant (see s.9(2));*
>
> *(b) in any other case, the responsible medical officer (RMO).*
>
> Note: RMO is in turn defined in s.34(1)(a) as "the registered medical practitioner in charge of the treatment of the patient".

17. Leave of absence from the hospital

(1) The responsible medical officer may grant to any patient who is for the time being liable to be detained in a hospital under this Part of this Act leave to be absent from the hospital subject to such conditions (if any) as that officer considers necessary in the interests of the patient or for the protection of other persons.

Section 17(1)

The RMO is empowered to grant leave of absence to a detained patient. This leave may be subject to any conditions which the RMO deems necessary either in the interests of the patient of for the protection of others.

Note: only the RMO may authorise leave of absence. The RMO's power to grant leave is not delegable thus no other clinical staff may authorise leave. Staff should be aware of s.128(1) below which makes it an offence to induce or help a patient to absent himself without leave.

This section applies unamended to patients detained under hospital orders (s.37) and, subject to the consent of the Home Secretary, to patients under a restriction order (see s. 41(3)(c)(i) and Schedule 1 Part 2 below). In the case of restricted patient the permission of the Home Secretary is also required before leave is given (see s. 41(3)(c)(i) below).

Despite being on s.17 leave outside hospital a patient remains "liable to be detained" in hospital and thus all relevant provisions of the Act will apply (eg Part IV Consent to Treatment provisions).

Chapter 20 of the Code of Practice (1999 ed.) gives further guidance on leave of absence.

(2) Leave of absence may be granted to a patient under this section either indefinitely or on specified occasions or for any specified period; and where leave is so granted for a specified period, that period may be extended by further leave granted in the absence of the patient

Section 17(2)

Leave of absence may be granted for any specified time period or granted indefinitely. Any period of leave may be extended by the RMO in the absence of the patient.

Note: contrary to previously accepted practice the Court of Appeal have recently decided that a person need not be returned from leave in order for his/her period of detention to be renewed [15] (see s.20 below).

[15] Barker v Barking Havering and Brentwood Community Healthcare NHS Trust and another [1999] Lloyd's Rep Med 101.

(3) Where it appears to the responsible medical officer that it is necessary so to do in the interests of the patient or for the protection of other persons, he may, upon granting leave of absence under this section, direct that the patient remain in custody during his absence; and where leave of absence is so granted the patient may be kept in the custody of any officer on the staff of the hospital, or of any other person authorised in writing by the managers of the hospital or, if the patient is required in accordance with conditions imposed on the grant of leave of absence to reside in another hospital, of any officer on the staff of that other hospital.

> **Section 17(3)**
>
> *Provides for escorted leave from hospital i.e. the RMO may direct that the patient remains 'in custody' of another person during the leave period.*
>
> *If the custody escort is not a member of staff of the hospital s/he must have the written authorisation of the hospital managers to act as escort.*

(4) In any case where a patient is absent from a hospital in pursuance of leave of absence granted under this section, and it appears to the responsible medical officer that it is necessary so to do in the interests of the patient's health or safety or for the protection of other persons, that officer may, subject to subsection (5) below, by notice in writing given to the patient or to the person for the time being in charge of the patient, revoke the leave of absence and recall the patient to the hospital.

> **Section 17(4)**
>
> *The RMO may revoke any leave of absence previously authorised and recall the patient to hospital by giving written notice to him/her or to the person in charge of the patient.*
>
> *Such action can only be taken if it appears to the RMO that it is necessary in the interests of the health or safety of the patient or for the protection of others.*
>
> Note: in the case of restricted patients the Home Secretary may also exercise the power to revoke leave (see s. 41(3)(c) below).

(5) A patient to whom leave of absence is granted under this section shall not be recalled under subsection (4) above after he has ceased to be liable to be detained under this Part of this Act.

> **Section 17(5)**
>
> *The RMO may not recall a patient once their liability to be detained in hospital has expired.*
>
> Note: a patient will thus cease to be liable to be detained twelve months after his/her first day of leave (by virtue of s.20(2)(b)) or when the authority to detain him/her lapses, whichever is sooner.

18. Return and re-admission of patients absent without leave

> This section (and s.21, s.21A-B) provide the authority to return and re-admit patients who have absented themselves without permission.

(1) Where a patient who is for the time being liable to be detained under this Part of this Act in a hospital–

(a) absents himself from the hospital without leave granted under section 17 above; or

(b) fails to return to the hospital on any occasion on which, or at the expiration of any period for which, leave of absence was granted to him under that section, or upon being recalled under that section; or

(c) absents himself without permission from any place where he is required to reside in accordance with conditions imposed on the grant of leave of absence under that section,

he may, subject to the provisions of this section, be taken into custody and returned to the hospital or place by any approved social worker, by any officer on the staff of the hospital, by any constable, or by any person authorised in writing by the managers of the hospital.

Section 18(1)

If a patient:

(a)   absconds;

(b)   fails to return from authorised s.17 leave; or

(c)   absents himself from a place where s/he is required to reside as a condition of s.17 leave,

s/he may be taken into custody and returned to the hospital or place by any ASW, staff member of the hospital, police officer or any person authorised in writing by the hospital managers to do so.

---

(2) Where the place referred to in paragraph (c) of subsection (1) above is a hospital other than the one in which the patient is for the time being liable to be detained, the references in that subsection to an officer on the staff of the hospital and the managers of the hospital shall respectively include references to an officer on the staff of the first-mentioned hospital and the managers of that hospital.

Section 18(2)

If, as a condition of s.17 leave, a patient is required to reside in a hospital other than that at which s/he is liable to be detained, a staff member of that hospital or any person authorised in writing by the managers of that hospital may exercise the powers described in s.18(1).

Note: s.18(1) and s.18(2) do not apply to patients under guardianship.

---

(3) Where a patient who is for the time being subject to guardianship under this Part of this Act absents himself without the leave of the guardian from the place at which he is required by the guardian to reside, he may, subject to the provisions of this section, be taken into custody and returned to that place by any officer on the staff of a local social services authority, by any constable, or by any person authorised in writing by the guardian or a local social services authority.

Section 18(3)
If a patient subject to guardianship absents him/herself without leave from the place at which s/he is required to reside, s/he may be taken into custody and returned to that place by any staff member of the local social services authority (i.e. not necessarily a social worker), police officer or any person authorised in writing by the guardian or local social services authority to do so.

(4) A patient shall not be taken into custody under this section after the later of–

   (a) the end of the period of six months beginning with the first day of his absence without leave; and

   (b) the end of the period for which (apart from section 21 below) he is liable to be detained or subject to guardianship;

and, in determining for the purposes of paragraph (b) above or any other provision of this Act whether a person who is or has been absent without leave is at any time liable to be detained or subject to guardianship, a report furnished under section 20 or 21B below before the first day of his absence without leave shall not be taken to have renewed the authority for his detention or guardianship unless the period of renewal began before that day.

Section 18(4)
A patient can not be taken into custody under s.18 after:
(a)   six months from the first day of absence without leave; or
(b)   the end of the period for which s/he is liable to be detained, whichever is the later.
Any report under s.20 or s.21B purporting to renew the authority for detention will be ineffective if the renewal date is after the day when the patient went absent without leave.

Note: detention can however be renewed under s.20 whilst a patient is absent with leave.[16]

---

[16] Barker v Barking Havering and Brentwood Community NHS Trust and another [1999] Lloyd's Rep Med 101.

(5) A patient shall not be taken into custody under this section if the period for which he is liable to be detained is that specified in section 2(4), 4(4) or 5(2) or (4) above and that period has expired.

Section 18(5)
A patient who is absent without permission can not be taken into custody if the period for which s/he is liable to be detained is either:
(a)   the 28 days specified under s.2(4);
(b)   the 72 hours specified under s.4(4) or s.5(2); or
(c)   the 6 hours specified under s.5(4),
and that period of time has expired.

(6) In this Act "absent without leave" means absent from any hospital or other place and liable to be taken into custody and returned under this section, and related expressions shall be construed accordingly.

> **Section 18(6)**
> *Is self explanatory.*
> Note: chapter 21 of the Code of Practice (1999 ed.) gives further guidance on absence without leave.

19. Regulations as to transfer of patients

(1) In such circumstances and subject to such conditions as may be prescribed by regulations made by the Secretary of State–

   (a) a patient who is for the time being liable to be detained in a hospital by virtue of an application under this Part of this Act may be transferred to another hospital or into the guardianship of a local social services authority or of any person approved by such an authority;

   (b) a patient who is for the time being subject to the guardianship of a local social services authority or other person by virtue of an application under this Part of this Act may be transferred into the guardianship of another local social services authority or person, or be transferred to a hospital.

> **Section 19(1)**
> *The Secretary of State for Health may make regulations[17] for the transfer of patients between hospitals, between guardians or between a guardian and a hospital.*
> Note: transfers to and from special hospitals are made under s.123 (below).
>
> ---
> [17] Regs 7 to 9 of the Mental Health (Hospital Guardianship and Consent to Treatment) Regulations 1983 (SI 1983/893).

(2) Where a patient is transferred in pursuance of regulations under this section, the provisions of this Part of this Act (including this subsection) shall apply to him as follows, that is to say:

   (a) in the case of a patient who is liable to be detained in a hospital by virtue of an application for admission for assessment or for treatment and is transferred to another hospital, as if the application were an application for admission to that other hospital and as if the patient had been admitted to that other hospital at the time when he was originally admitted in pursuance of the application;

   (b) in the case of a patient who is liable to be detained in a hospital by virtue of such an application and is transferred into guardianship, as if the application were a guardianship application duly accepted at the said time;

   (c) in the case of a patient who is subject to guardianship by virtue of a guardianship application and is transferred into the guardianship of another authority or person, as if the application were for his reception into the guardianship of that authority or person and had been accepted at the time when it was originally accepted;

(d) in the case of a patient who is subject to guardianship by virtue of a guardianship application and is transferred to a hospital, as if the guardianship application were an application for admission to that hospital for treatment and as if the patient had been admitted to the hospital at the time when the application was originally accepted.

Section 19(2)
Stipulates when guardianship and hospital admission is deemed to begin in respect of transferred patients for the purpose of calculating time periods under the Act.
In the case of transfer of a patient liable to be detained in hospital:
(a) any new admission to hospital is deemed to have commenced at the time of admission to the first hospital and not at the time of transfer and admission to the new hospital;
(b) guardianship is deemed to have commenced at the time of the transfer.
In the case of transfer of a patient subject to guardianship:
(c) any new guardianship is deemed to have commenced at the time of the initial guardianship application and not at the time of transfer of guardianship;
(d) admission to hospital is deemed to have commenced at the time of the initial guardianship application and not at the time of transfer.

(3) Without prejudice to subsections (1) and (2) above, any patient who is for the time being liable to be detained under this Part of this Act in a hospital vested in the Secretary of State for the purposes of his functions under the National Health Service Act 1977 or any accommodation used under Part I of that Act by the managers of such a hospital or in a hospital vested in a National Health Service trust, may at any time be removed to any other such hospital or accommodation which is managed by the managers of, or is vested in the National Health Service trust for, the first-mentioned hospital; and paragraph (a) of subsection (2) above shall apply in relation to a patient so removed as it applies in relation to a patient transferred in pursuance of regulations made under this section.

Section 19(3)
Allows for a patient to be transferred to another hospital which is managed by the same managers.
The new admission to hospital is deemed to have commenced at the time of admission to the first hospital and not at the time of transfer to the new hospital.

(4) Regulations made under this section may make provision for regulating the conveyance to their destination of patients authorised to be transferred or removed in pursuance of the regulations or under subsection (3) above.

Section 19(4)
Regulations made under this section of the Act can regulate the means used to transfer patients between hospitals.

DURATION OF DETENTION OR GUARDIANSHIP AND DISCHARGE

20. Duration of authority

This section provides for the renewal of the authority to detain a patient. The renewed authority arises from the act of the RMO in providing a report complying with the requirements of the section. Although the authority must be recorded by hospital managers it does not arise from any managerial decision.

This section also applies to hospital or guardianship orders made by the courts under s.37.

(1) Subject to the following provisions of this Part of this Act, a patient admitted to hospital in pursuance of an application for admission for treatment, and a patient placed under guardianship in pursuance of a guardianship application, may be detained in a hospital or kept under guardianship for a period not exceeding six months beginning with the day on which he was so admitted, or the day on which the guardianship application was accepted, as the case may be, but shall not be so detained or kept for any longer period unless the authority for his detention or guardianship is renewed under this section.

Section 20(1)

A patient may be detained in hospital for treatment or placed under guardianship for a maximum period of six months, unless that authority is further renewed.

The six month period includes the day of admission or acceptance into guardianship.

(2) Authority for the detention or guardianship of a patient may, unless the patient has previously been discharged, be renewed-

(a) from the expiration of the period referred to in subsection (1) above, for a further period of six months;
(b) from the expiration of any period of renewal under paragraph (a) above, for a further period of one year,

and so on for periods of one year at a time.

Section 20(2)

The authority for detention or guardianship can be renewed for:

(a)   six months in the first instance; and then

(b)   one year periods thereafter,

so long as the patient has not been discharged in the meantime.

(3) Within the period of two months ending on the day on which a patient who is liable to be detained in pursuance of an application for admission for treatment would cease under this section to be so liable in default of the renewal of the authority for his detention, it shall be the duty of the responsible medical officer-

    (a) to examine the patient; and

    (b) if it appears to him that the conditions set out in subsection (4) below are satisfied, to furnish to the managers of the hospital where the patient is detained a report to that effect in the prescribed form; and where such a report is furnished in respect of a patient the managers shall, unless they discharge the patient, cause him to be informed.

Section 20(3)

In the two months prior to the expiry of any authority for detention for treatment the RMO is under a duty to:

(a)   examine the patient; and

(b)   if in his/her opinion the conditions for further detention set out in s.20(4) below are fulfilled, provide a report to this effect to the hospital managers[18].

On receiving a report from the RMO the managers must either discharge the patient or ensure s/he is informed that a renewal report has been received.

Note: 'furnishing' a report means 'providing a report that complies with the requirements of the subsection'. Authority to renew detention arises when the form is completed and is provided to the managers. The authority then runs from the expiration of the previous period of detention.

Authority to detain arises from the actions of the doctor and not the actions of the managers, thus, although the form must be completed _and_ provided to managers _before_ the previous detention period expires, there is no requirement for the managers to have either read the report or reached a decision upon it before the previous detention period expires[19].

---

[18] Regulation 10(1) of the Mental Health (Hospital, Guardianship and Consent to Treatment) Regulations 1983 (SI 1983/893) requires that the RMO's report should be on the specified form - Form 30.

[19] R v Managers of Warlingham Park Hospital ex parte B. (1994) 22 BMLR 1.

---

(4) The conditions referred to in subsection (3) above are that-

    (a) the patient is suffering from mental illness, severe mental impairment, psychopathic disorder or mental impairment, and his mental disorder is of a nature or degree which makes it appropriate for him to receive medical treatment in a hospital; and

    (b) such treatment is likely to alleviate or prevent a deterioration of his condition; and

    (c) it is necessary for the health or safety of the patient or for the protection of other persons that he should receive such treatment and that it cannot be provided unless he continues to be detained;

but, in the case of mental illness or severe mental impairment, it shall be an alternative to the condition specified in paragraph (b) above that the patient, if discharged, is unlikely to be able to care for himself, to obtain the care which he needs or to guard himself against serious exploitation.

Section 20(4)
Before authority for detention is renewed it must appear to the doctor that:

(a) *the patient is suffering with one of the four specified forms of mental disorder of either a type or severity which justifies his/her treatment in a hospital as an in-patient; and*

(b) *treatment must be likely to either improve or prevent worsening of the condition;*
or
only in the case of 'mental illness' or 'severe mental impairment', that if discharged the patient is unlikely to be able to care for him/herself or obtain care or to guard him/herself from serious exploitation; and

(c) *it is necessary for the health and safety of himself/herself or the protection of others that the patient receive treatment and such treatment can not be provided unless the patient is compulsorily detained in hospital.*

Note: the 'treatability test' applies to all four forms of mental disorder at the time of renewal of detention. However a patient suffering with mental illness or severe mental impairment who is not deemed treatable may nevertheless be detained if there is a likelihood that they will be uncared for or exploited.

In an earlier court judgment it was said that detention could not be renewed whilst the patient was on s.17 leave of absence. This case has recently been overruled by the Court of Appeal and it is now clear that detention can be renewed under s.20 when a patient is absent with leave from a hospital. However there must be a continuing need for the patient to receive in-patient treatment as a part of his/her ongoing treatment package [20].

---

[20] Barker v Barking Havering and Brentwood Community NHS Trust and another [1999] Lloyd's Rep Med. 101.

(5) Before furnishing a report under subsection (3) above the responsible medical officer shall consult one or more other persons who have been professionally concerned with the patient's medical treatment.

Section 20(5)
Before providing a report to hospital managers the RMO must consult at least one other professional who has been involved in treating the patient.

(6) Within the period of two months ending with the day on which a patient who is subject to guardianship under this Part of this Act would cease under this section to be so liable in default of the renewal of the authority for his guardianship, it shall be the duty of the appropriate medical officer-

(a) to examine the patient; and

(b) if it appears to him that the conditions set out in subsection (7) below are satisfied, to furnish to the guardian and, where the guardian is a person other than a local social services authority, to the responsible local social services authority a report to that effect in the prescribed form;

and where such a report is furnished in respect of a patient, the local social services authority shall, unless they discharge the patient, cause him to be informed.

Section 20(6)

Allows for the renewal of authority for guardianship. In the two months preceding expiry of guardianship the appropriate medical officer (AMO) (see section s.20 (10)) must examine the patient and, if satisfied that the conditions for renewal of guardianship (in section 20(7)) are met, must report this to the guardian or local social services authority.

On receiving a report from the AMO the local social services authority must either discharge the patient from guardianship or ensure s/he is informed that a renewal report has been received.

(7) The conditions referred to in subsection (6) above are that-

(a) the patient is suffering from mental illness, severe mental impairment, psychopathic disorder or mental impairment and his mental disorder is of a nature or degree which warrants his reception into guardianship; and

(b) it is necessary in the interests of the welfare of the patient or for the protection of other persons that the patient should remain under guardianship.

Section 20(7)

Before guardianship is renewed it must appear to the AMO that:

(a) the patient is suffering with one of the four specified forms of mental disorder of either a type or severity which justifies his/her continued guardianship; and

(b) it is necessary for the guardianship to continue for either the welfare of the patient or the protection of others.

(8) Where a report is duly furnished under subsection (3) or (6) above, the authority for the detention or guardianship of the patient shall be thereby renewed for the period prescribed in that case by subsection (2) above.

Section 20(8)

On providing the report the authority for further detention or guardianship is automatically renewed.

Note: the authority to continue detention/guardianship arises at the time the report is provided to the hospital managers/ local social services authority and not when they read or consider it (see note to s.20(3)). That authority will then run from the expiration of the previous period of detention/guardianship.

(9) Where the form of mental disorder specified in a report furnished under subsection (3) or (6) above is a form of disorder other than that specified in the application for admission for treatment or, as the case may be, in the guardianship application, that application shall have effect as if that other form of mental disorder were specified in it; and where on any occasion a report specifying such a form of mental disorder is furnished under either of those subsections the appropriate medical officer need not on that occasion furnish a report under section 16 above.

Section 20(9)

If the form of mental disorder specified on the renewal application is different from that specified on the original detention/guardianship application the effect is that the patient is reclassified without the need for a further 'reclassification report' under s.16.

(10) In this section "appropriate medical officer" has the same meaning as in section 16(5) above.

Section 20(10)

The appropriate medical officer is:

(a)   for a patient under guardianship, the doctor nominated by the local social services authority to be the medical attendant (see s.9(2));

(b)   in any other case, the responsible medical officer (RMO).

21. Special provisions as to patients absent without leave

(1) Where a patient is absent without leave-

(a) on the day on which (apart from this section) he would cease to be liable to be detained or subject to guardianship under this Part of this Act; or

(b) within the period of one week ending with that day,

he shall not cease to be so liable or subject until the relevant time.

(2) For the purposes of subsection (1) above the relevant time-

(a) where the patient is taken into custody under section 18 above, is the end of the period of one week beginning with the day on which he is returned to the hospital or place where he ought to be;

(b) where the patient returns himself to the hospital or place where he ought to be within the period during which he can be taken into custody under section 18 above, is the end of the period of one week beginning with the day on which he so returns himself; and

(c) otherwise, is the end of the period during which he can be taken into custody under section 18 above.

Section 21(1)

Where a patient is absent without leave on the day his/her detention or guardianship is due to expire (or in the one week before the expiration date) s/he will remain under the detention/guardianship until:

Section 21(2)

the end of the week following the day on which s/he is returned to hospital if either:

(a)   s/he was taken into custody within six months of absconding and returned to hospital (under s.18); or

(b)   s/he returns to hospital voluntarily within six months of absconding;

otherwise:

(c)   six months from the day s/he absconded.

21A. Patients taken into custody or who return within 28 days

This section allows for the usual s.20 procedures for renewal of detention/guardianship to be followed if a patient has absconded for less than four weeks.

(1) This section applies where a patient who is absent without leave is taken into custody under section 18 above, or returns himself to the hospital or place where he ought to be, not later than the end of the period of 28 days beginning with the first day of his absence without leave.

(2) Where the period for which the patient is liable to be detained or subject to guardianship is extended by section 21 above, any examination and report to be made and furnished in respect of the patient under section 20(3) or (6) above may be made and furnished within the period as so extended.

(3) Where the authority for the detention or guardianship of the patient is renewed by virtue of subsection (2) above after the day on which (apart from section 21 above) that authority would have expired, the renewal shall take effect as from that day.

> **Section 21A (1) to (3)**
> *If a patient who absconds is taken into custody under s.18, or returns to hospital voluntarily, within 28 days of absconding and the authority to detain (or for guardianship) expired during the patient's absence the renewal period is extended by a week from the date of return by virtue of s.21.*
>
> *In such cases the RMO may examine the patient and provide a valid renewal report under s.20 at any time within that extension period of a week.*
>
> *Any such report will have retrospective effect so as to be effective from the initial day of expiration of authority to detain and not the date on which it is made.*

21B. Patients taken into custody or who return after more than 28 days

> *This section ensures that anyone absent from detention or guardianship for more than four weeks is re-assessed before their detention/guardianship is continued irrespective of whether their detention/guardianship has time left to run on their return.*

(1) This section applies where a patient who is absent without leave is taken into custody under section 18 above, or returns himself to the hospital or place where he ought to be, later than the end of the period of 28 days beginning with the first day of his absence without leave.

(2) It shall be the duty of the appropriate medical officer, within the period of one week beginning with the day on which the patient is returned or returns himself to the hospital or place where he ought to be-

(a) to examine the patient; and
(b) if it appears to him that the relevant conditions are satisfied, to furnish to the appropriate body a report to that effect in the prescribed form;

and where such a report is furnished in respect of the patient the appropriate body shall cause him to be informed.

> **Section 21B(1) & (2)**
> *If a patient who absconds is taken into custody under s.18 (or returns voluntarily) more than 28 days after absconding the AMO (under s.21B (10)) must, within one week, examine the patient and, if it appears the relevant conditions for continued detention/ guardianship (under s.20(4) or s.20(7) above) are satisfied, report this to the hospital managers or the local social services authority (as appropriate).*

The hospital managers or the local social services authority (as appropriate) must then ensure that the patient is informed that the report has been received.

Note: regulation 10A of the Mental Health (Hospital, Guardianship and Consent to Treatment) Regulations 1983 (SI 1983/893 - as amended by SI 1997/801) requires that the RMO's report should be on the specified form – Form 31A in the case of detained patients and 31B in the case of patients subject to guardianship.

(3) Where the patient is liable to be detained (as opposed to subject to guardianship), the appropriate medical officer shall, before furnishing a report under subsection (2) above, consult-

   (a) one or more other persons who have been professionally concerned with the patient's medical treatment; and

   (b) an approved social worker.

Section 21B(3)
In the case of detention in hospital, but not guardianship, before providing a report the RMO must consult:

(a)   at least one other professional who has been involved in treating the patient;

and

(b)   an Approved Social Worker.

(4) Where the patient would (apart from any renewal of the authority for his detention or guardianship on or after the day on which he is returned or returns himself to the hospital or place where he ought to be) be liable to be detained or subject to guardianship after the end of the period of one week beginning with that day, he shall cease to be so liable or subject at the end of that period unless a report is duly furnished in respect of him under subsection (2) above.

Section 21B(4)
If a report is not provided within a week of return the patient's liability for detention or guardianship will end even if the original detention/guardianship period has not expired.

(5) Where the patient would (apart from section 21 above) have ceased to be liable to be detained or subject to guardianship on or before the day on which a report is duly furnished in respect of him under subsection (2) above, the report shall renew the authority for his detention or guardianship for the period prescribed in that case by section 20(2) above.

Section 21B(5)
Even if the patient's liability for detention or guardianship would have expired before the end of the additional week allowed by s.21, providing a report nevertheless has the effect of renewing the detention/guardianship for the period specified in s.20(2) (ie. six months for the first renewal and one year thereafter).

(6) Where the authority for the detention or guardianship of the patient is renewed by virtue of subsection (5) above-

   (a) the renewal shall take effect as from the day on which (apart from section 21 above and that subsection) the authority would have expired; and

   (b) if (apart from this paragraph) the renewed authority would expire on or before the day on which the report is furnished, the report shall further renew the authority, as from the day on which it would expire, for the period prescribed in that case by section 20(2) above.

Section 21B(6)
Renewal of otherwise expired detention/guardianship under s.21B(5) takes effect from the day on which the detention or guardianship would have originally expired and not when the report is provided.

(7) Where the authority for the detention or guardianship of the patient would expire within the period of two months beginning with the day on which a report is duly furnished in respect of him under subsection (2) above, the report shall, if it so provides, have effect also as a report duly furnished under section 20(3) or (6) above; and the reference in this subsection to authority includes any authority renewed under subsection (5) above by the report.

Section 21B(7)
If the original detention/guardianship is due to expire within the next two months the report will have the same effect as a renewal report under s.20(3) or s.20(6).

Note: this subsection obviates the need for two reports to be made within less than two months by allowing the report following absconding to function also as a s.20 renewal report in relevant circumstances.

(8) Where the form of mental disorder specified in a report furnished under subsection (2) above is a form of disorder other than that specified in the application for admission for treatment or guardianship application concerned (and the report does

not have effect as a report furnished under section 20(3) or (6) above), that application shall have effect as if that other form of mental disorder were specified in it.

(9) Where on any occasion a report specifying such a form of mental disorder is furnished under subsection (2) above the appropriate medical officer need not on that occasion furnish a report under section 16 above.

> ### Section 21B(8) & (9)
> *If the form of mental disorder specified on the report following absconding is different from that specified on the original detention/guardianship application the effect is that the patient is reclassified without the need for a separate 'reclassification' report under s.16.*

(10) In this section-

"appropriate medical officer" has the same meaning as in section 16(5) above;

"the appropriate body" means-
- (a) in relation to a patient who is liable to be detained in a hospital, the managers of the hospital; and
- (b) in relation to a patient who is subject to guardianship, the responsible local social services authority; and

"the relevant conditions" means-
- (a) in relation to a patient who is liable to be detained in a hospital, the conditions set out in subsection (4) of section 20 above; and
- (b) in relation to a patient who is subject to guardianship, the conditions set out in subsection (7) of that section

> ### Section 21B(10)
> *The appropriate medical officer is:*
> *(a) for a patient under guardianship, the nominated medical attendant (see s.9(2));*
> *(b) in any other case, the responsible medical officer (RMO).*
> *The remainder of the sub-section is self-explanatory.*

22. Special provisions as to patients sentenced to imprisonment etc.

(1) Where a patient who is liable to be detained by virtue of an application for admission for treatment or is subject to guardianship by virtue of a guardianship application is detained in custody in pursuance of any sentence or order passed or made by a court in the United Kingdom (including an order committing or remanding him in custody), and is so detained for a period exceeding, or for successive periods exceeding in the aggregate, six months, the application shall cease to have effect at the expiration of that period.

Section 22(1)

If a detained patient or patient subject to guardianship is detained in custody by a court order (e.g. sentenced, remanded) for more than six months the authority for detention/guardianship will cease to have effect on release.

(2) Where any such patient is so detained in custody but the application does not cease to have effect under subsection (1) above, then-

(a) if apart from this subsection the patient would have ceased to be liable to be so detained or subject to guardianship on or before the day on which he is discharged from custody, he shall not cease and shall be deemed not to have ceased to be so liable or subject until the end of that day; and

(b) in any case, sections 18, 21 and 21A above, shall apply in relation to the patient as if he had absented himself without leave on that day.

Section 22(2)

If a detained patient or patient subject to guardianship is detained in custody by a court order (e.g. sentenced, remanded) for less than six months, but his/her liability for detention/guardianship would have expired on or before his/her release day, s/he does not cease to be liable for detention/guardianship until the end of his/her release day.

On release from custody the patient can be treated as if s/he is absent without leave and if returned to hospital (or relevant place for guardianship) within 28 days of release (s.18 above) his/her detention/guardianship may be renewed providing the requisite formalities are complied with within seven days of return (under s.21 and 21A above).

(3) In its application by virtue of subsection (2) above section 18(4) above shall have effect with the substitution of the words "end of the period of 28 days beginning with the first day of his absence without leave" for the words from "later of" onwards.

Section 22(3)

The time limits in s.18(4) is reduced to 28 days for the purposes of this section instead of the six months otherwise provided for in respect of patients who have absconded.

Note: this section also applies (with modifications) to patients under s.37 and s.41 (see below).

23. Discharge of Patients

Note: the Code of Practice (1999 ed.) (at chapter 23) provides guidance on the hospital managers' powers of discharge.

(1) Subject to the provisions of this section and section 25 below, a patient who is for the time being liable to be detained or subject to guardianship under this Part of this Act shall cease to be so liable or subject if an order in writing discharging him from detention or guardianship (in this Act referred to as "an order for discharge") is made in accordance with this section.

Section 23(1)
Provides for detention or guardianship to end when an order for discharge is made. The order must be in writing.

(2) An order for discharge may be made in respect of a patient–

   (a) where the patient is liable to be detained in a hospital in pursuance of an application for admission for assessment or for treatment by the responsible medical officer, by the managers or by the nearest relative of the patient;

   (b) where the patient is subject to guardianship, by the responsible medical officer, by the responsible local social services authority or by the nearest relative of the patient.

Section 23(2)
An order for discharge may be made by the RMO, the nearest relative and the hospital managers (in the case of hospital detention) or the RMO, the nearest relative or the local social services authority (in the case of guardianship).

(3) Where the patient is liable to be detained in a mental nursing home in pursuance of an application for admission for assessment or for treatment, an order for his discharge may, without prejudice to subsection (2) above, be made by the Secretary of State and, if the patient is maintained under a contract with a National Health Service trust, Health Authority or Special Health Authority, by that National Health Service trust, Health Authority or Special Health Authority.

Section 23(3)
Where a patient is detained in a mental nursing home an order for discharge may also be made by the Secretary of State for Health , or the relevant NHS Trust or Health Authority.

(4) The powers conferred by this section on any authority trust or body of persons may be exercised subject to subsection (5) below by any three or more members of that authority trust or body authorised by them in that behalf or by three or more members of a committee or sub-committee of that authority trust or body which has been authorised by them in that behalf.

> **Section 23(4)**
> *The power to discharge can be delegated to three or more people authorised by hospital managers or members of the authority or Trust to act in that respect.*

(5) The reference in subsection (4) above to the members of an authority, trust or body or the members of a committee or sub-committee of an authority, trust or body,–
   (a) in the case of a Health Authority or Special Health Authority or a committee or sub-committee of a Health Authority or Special Health Authority, is a reference only to the chairman of the authority and such members (of the authority, committee or sub-committee, as the case may be) as are not also officers of the authority, within the meaning of the National Health Service Act 1977; and
   (b) in the case of a National Health Service trust or a committee or sub-committee of such a trust, is a reference only to the chairman of the trust and such directors or (in the case of a committee or sub-committee) members as are not also employees of the trust.

> **Section 23(5)**
> *The delegated members under s.23(4) must not be officers of the Health Authority or employees of the Trust.*
>
> Note: no criteria are set for the exercise of the power of discharge but the Code of Practice (1999 ed.) at 23.11 suggests that (in relation to hospital managers) the review panel should consider whether: (1) the patient is still suffering from mental disorder; (2) the disorder is of a nature or degree which makes hospital treatment appropriate; (3) detention is still necessary in the interests of the health or safety of the patient or protection of others and (4) where the RMO has made a report under s.25 barring the nearest relative's order to discharge, whether the patient is indeed likely to act in a dangerous manner if discharged.[21]
>
> ---
> [21] R v Riverside Mental Health Trust ex parte Huzzey (1998) 43 BMLR 167.

24. Visiting and Examination of Patients

(1) For the purpose of advising as to the exercise by the nearest relative of a patient who is liable to be detained or subject to guardianship under this Part of this Act of any power to order his discharge, any registered medical practitioner authorised by or on behalf of the nearest relative of the patient may, at any reasonable time, visit the patient and examine him in private.

Section 24(1)

A doctor may visit and examine a patient in private on behalf of the nearest relative at any reasonable time for the purpose of advising the nearest relative in respect of his/her powers to order discharge.

(2) Any registered medical practitioner authorised for the purposes of subsection (1) above to visit and examine a patient may require the production of and inspect any records relating to the detention or treatment of the patient in any hospital or to any after-care services provided for the patient under section 117 below.

Section 24(2)

Any such doctor may inspect any records relating to the patient's detention, treatment and after-care.

(3) Where application is made by the Secretary of State or a Health Authority, Special Health Authority or National Health Service trust to exercise, in respect of a patient liable to be detained in a mental nursing home, any power to make an order for his discharge, the following persons, that is to say–

   (a) any registered medical practitioner authorised by the Secretary of State or, as the case may be, that Health Authority, Special Health Authority or National Health Service trust; and

   (b) any other person (whether a registered medical practitioner or not) authorised under Part II of the Registered Homes Act 1984 to inspect the home;

may at any reasonable time visit the patient and interview him in private.

Section 24(3)

Where the patient is detained in a mental nursing home the Secretary of State for Health, a Health Authority or a Trust may authorise either a doctor or another person (who may or may not be a doctor but must be authorised under the Registered Homes Act 1984) to visit and interview the patient in private.

(4) Any person authorised for the purposes of subsection (3) above to visit a patient may require the production of and inspect any documents constituting or alleged to constitute the authority for the detention of the patient under this Part of this Act; and any person so authorised, who is a registered medical practitioner, may examine the patient in private, and may require the production of and inspect any other records relating to the treatment of the patient in the home or to any after-care services provided for the patient under section 117 below.

Section 24(4)

Any person authorised under subsection (3) above may inspect the documents relating to the patient's detention, but only a doctor may examine the patient or see their records relating to treatment and aftercare.

Note: a person may commit an offence (by virtue of s.129 below) if s/he fails to allow access to the patient or his/her records in accordance with this section or refuses to leave should a doctor request that an interview be conducted in private.

25. Restrictions on discharge by nearest relative

This section allows the RMO to prevent a nearest relative's order for discharge from being effected.

(1) An order for the discharge of a patient who is liable to be detained in a hospital shall not be made by his nearest relative except after giving not less than 72 hours' notice in writing to the managers of the hospital; and if, within 72 hours after such notice has been given, the responsible medical officer furnishes to the managers a report certifying that in the opinion of that officer the patient, if discharged, would be likely to act in a manner dangerous to other persons or to himself,–

    (a) any order for the discharge of the patient made by that relative in pursuance of the notice shall be of no effect; and

    (b) no further order for the discharge of the patient shall be made by that relative during the period of six months beginning with the date of the report.

Section 25(1)

A nearest relative must give 72 hours notice in writing to the hospital managers of his/her intention to order discharge of a patient from hospital.

If within 72 hours of receipt of that notice the RMO reports that in his/her opinion the patient would probably act in a way that would endanger him/herself or others if discharged the nearest relative's order for discharge will have no effect.

In these circumstances the nearest relative may not exercise his/her power of discharge for a further six months from the date of the RMO's report.

Note: the Mental Health (Hospital, Guardianship and Consent to Treatment) Regulations 1983 (SI 1983/893) require that a nearest relative's notice is given to "an officer of the managers authorised to receive it" or sent by prepaid post. If the written order is otherwise delivered (e.g. by handing it to a ward receptionist) the 72 hour period will run from the time that the written order for discharge is actually received by the hospital managers.[22]

[22] In the matter of Gary Kinsey. High Court, 21st June 1999 (unreported).

(2) In any case where a report under subsection (1) above is furnished in respect of a patient who is liable to be detained in pursuance of an application for admission for treatment the managers shall cause the nearest relative of the patient to be informed.

Section 25(2)

The hospital managers must ensure that the nearest relative is informed if the RMO makes a report barring the patient's discharge.

Note: this section does not apply to patients under guardianship.

The Code of Practice (1999 ed.) (at 23.8 and 23.12) states that the managers must consider holding a review of the patient's detention when the RMO bars the nearest relative's order for discharge.

Despite the RMO's opposition the managers retain a general discretion to discharge the patient and, in addition to the criteria for admission/continued detention (see note to s.23(5) above), the managers should consider whether or not they are persuaded that the patient, if discharged, would be likely to act in a manner dangerous to him or herself or others.[23]

---

[23] <u>R v Riverside Mental Health Trust ex p. Huzzey</u> (1998) 43 BMLR 167.

AFTER CARE UNDER SUPERVISION

Note: The current regulations in respect of after-care under supervision are the Mental Health (After-care under Supervision) Regulations 1996 (SI 1996/294).

Chapter 28 of the current Code of Practice (1999 ed.) provides limited further guidance on after-care under supervision. However more extensive guidance is found in the supplement to the 1993 Code of Practice which was published in February 1996 and remains extant despite not being published within the new Code of Practice.

25A. Application for supervision

(1) Where a patient–

    (a) is liable to be detained in a hospital in pursuance of an application for admission for treatment; and

    (b) has attained the age of 16 years, an application may be made for him to be supervised after he leaves hospital, for the period allowed by the following provisions of this Act, with a view to securing that he receives the after-care services provided for him under section 117 below.

Section 25A(1)

Applications for after-care under supervision can only be made for patients over 16 who are (or are liable to be) detained in hospital for treatment.

The purpose of this formal supervision is to ensure that the patient receives after-care services under s.117 (below).

(2) In this Act an application for a patient to be so supervised is referred to as a "supervision application"; and where a supervision application has been duly made and accepted under this Part of this Act in respect of a patient and he has left hospital, he is for the purposes of this Act "subject to after-care under supervision" (until he ceases to be so subject in accordance with the provisions of this Act).

Section 25A(2)
Sets out terms used in the Act.

Applications for after-care under supervision are termed 'supervision applications'. Patients to whom these provisions apply are described as 'subject to after-care under supervision'.

(3) A supervision application shall be made in accordance with this section and sections 25B and 25C below.

Section 25A(3)
Is self explanatory.

(4) A supervision application may be made in respect of a patient only on the grounds that–

(a) he is suffering from mental disorder, being mental illness, severe mental impairment, psychopathic disorder or mental impairment;

(b) there would be a substantial risk of serious harm to the health or safety of the patient or the safety of other persons, or of the patient being seriously exploited, if he were not to receive the after-care services to be provided for him under section 117 below after he leaves hospital; and

(c) his being subject to after-care under supervision is likely to help to secure that he receives the after-care services to be so provided.

Section 25A(4)
A supervision application can only be made if:

(a)   the patient is suffering with one of the four forms of mental disorder;

(b)   there would be a <u>substantial</u> risk of <u>serious</u> harm to the patient's health or safety or others' safety or others or of <u>serious</u> exploitation of the patient if s/he did not receive after-care services on leaving hospital; and

(c)   supervision of the patient will make it more likely that s/he will actually receive after-care.

(5) A supervision application may be made only by the responsible medical officer.

(6) A supervision application in respect of a patient shall be addressed to the Health Authority which will have the duty under section 117 below to provide after-care services for the patient after he leaves hospital.

Sections 25A(5) & 25A(6)
Are self explanatory.

(7) Before accepting a supervision application in respect of a patient a Health Authority shall consult the local social services authority which will also have that duty.

Section 25A(7)
Requires consultation (but not agreement) between health and local social services authorities.

(8) Where a Health Authority accept a supervision application in respect of a patient the Health Authority shall–

(a) inform the patient both orally and in writing–
   (i) that the supervision application has been accepted; and
   (ii) of the effect in his case of the provisions of this Act relating to a patient subject to after-care under supervision (including, in particular, what rights of applying to a Mental Health Review Tribunal are available);
(b) inform any person whose name is stated in the supervision application in accordance with sub-paragraph (i) of paragraph (e) of section 25B(5) below that the supervision application has been accepted; and
(c) inform in writing any person whose name is so stated in accordance with sub-paragraph (ii) of that paragraph that the supervision application has been accepted.

Section 25A(8)
On accepting a supervision application the Health Authority are required to inform the following people that the application has been accepted:

(a)   the patient (orally and in writing);

(b)   any non-professional involved in the after-care of the patient who has been consulted and named on the supervision application (by any means);

(c)   the patient's nearest relative (if s/he was consulted and named on the supervision application) (in writing).

The patient must also be told orally and in writing of the effect of the application and his/her rights to apply to a MHRT.

(9) Where a patient in respect of whom a supervision application is made is granted leave of absence from a hospital under section 17 above (whether before or after the supervision application is made), references in–

    (a) this section and the following provisions of this Part of this Act; and

    (b) Part V of this Act, to his leaving hospital shall be construed as references to his period of leave expiring (otherwise than on his return to the hospital or transfer to another hospital).

Section 25A(9)

For a patient granted leave of absence, any reference in this section, in the remainder of Part II of the Act and in Part V of the Act (provisions relating to MHRT's) to 'leaving hospital' also means 'when s.17 leave of absence expires'.

Note: this section permits patients granted leave of absence from hospital to be made subject to supervised discharge in the community as soon as their leave of absence expires without any need to return to hospital.

25B. Making of supervision application

(1) The responsible medical officer shall not make a supervision application unless–

    (a) subsection (2) below is complied with; and

    (b) the responsible medical officer has considered the matters specified in subsection (4) below.

Section 25B(1)

The RMO can only make a supervision application if:

(a)   there has been consultation with those people named in subsection 25B(2) below and the RMO has taken account of their views; and

(b)   the RMO has considered both the after-care to be provided under s.117 and any requirements (of residence, attendance or access) to be imposed in order to ensure that the patient receives that after-care (see s.25B(4) below).

(2) This subsection is complied with if-

    (a) the following persons have been consulted about the making of the supervision application-

        (i) the patient;

        (ii) one or more persons who have been professionally concerned with the patient's medical treatment in hospital;

        (iii) one or more persons who will be professionally concerned with the after-care services to be provided for the patient under section 117 below; and

(iv) any person who the responsible medical officer believes will play a substantial part in the care of the patient after he leaves hospital but will not be professionally concerned with any of the after-care services to be so provided;

(b) such steps as are practicable have been taken to consult the person (if any) appearing to be the nearest relative of the patient about the making of the supervision application; and

(c) the responsible medical officer has taken into account any views expressed by the persons consulted.

Section 25B(2)

The following people must be consulted (not necessarily by the RMO) and any views expressed taken into account by the RMO before a supervision application is made:

(a) (i)   the patient;

(ii) at least one person professionally involved in the patient's treatment in hospital;

(iii) at least one person who is to be professionally involved in the patient's after-care under s.117;

(iv) any non-professional it seems will be substantially involved in the care of the patient outside hospital;

(b)   the nearest relative of the patient (so far as is practicable).

---

(3) Where the patient has requested that paragraph (b) of subsection (2) above should not apply, that paragraph shall not apply unless-

(a) the patient has a propensity to violent or dangerous behaviour towards others; and

(b) the responsible medical officer considers that it is appropriate for steps such as are mentioned in that paragraph to be taken.

Section 25B(3)

The patient may request that his/her nearest relative is not consulted about the making of a supervision application and that request must be complied with unless:

(a)   the patient has a propensity for violence or dangerousness to others; and

(b)   the RMO considers consultation with the nearest relative to be appropriate.

Note: if the nearest relative is also the person named under s.25B(2)(a)(iv) - i.e. a non-professional who will play a substantial part in the care of the patient outside hospital, then there is an obligation to consult with him/her under that paragraph.

---

(4) The matters referred to in subsection (1)(b) above are-

    (a) the after-care services to be provided for the patient under section 117 below; and

    (b) any requirements to be imposed on him under section 25D below.

Section 25B(4)

The following matters must be considered by the RMO before a supervision application is made:

(a)   the after-care to be provided under s.117;

(b)   any requirements which may be imposed in order to ensure that the patient receives that after-care, i.e. that:

    (i)   the patient lives at a specific place;

    (ii) the patient attends a specific place for treatment, occupation, education or training;

    (iii) access is given to the patient.

---

(5) A supervision application shall state-

    (a) that the patient is liable to be detained in a hospital in pursuance of an application for admission for treatment;

    (b) the age of the patient or, if his exact age is not known to the applicant, that the patient is believed to have attained the age of 16 years;

    (c) that in the opinion of the applicant (having regard in particular to the patient's history) all of the conditions set out in section 25A(4) above are complied with;

    (d) the name of the person who is to be the community responsible medical officer, and of the person who is to be the supervisor, in relation to the patient after he leaves hospital; and

    (e) the name of-

        (i) any person who has been consulted under paragraph (a)(iv) of subsection (2) above; and

        (ii) any person who has been consulted under paragraph (b) of that subsection.

Section 25B(5)

The following must be stated on the supervision application:

(a)   that the patient is liable to be detained in hospital for treatment;

(b)   the patient's age (or, if unknown, that s/he is believed to be over 16);

(c)   that the applicant's opinion is that the patient fulfils the criteria for supervised discharge set out in s.25A(4), i.e.:

> (a) *the patient is suffering with one of the four forms of mental disorder;*
>
> (b) *there would be a substantial risk of serious harm to the patient or others or of serious exploitation of the patient if s/he did not receive after-care services on leaving hospital; and*
>
> (c) *supervision of the patient will make it more likely that s/he will actually receive after-care.*
>
> (d) *the name of the community RMO and supervisor on discharge (who may or may not be the same person);*
>
> (e) *the name of anyone who was consulted about the making of the supervision application.*

(6) A supervision application shall be accompanied by-

   (a) the written recommendation in the prescribed form of a registered medical practitioner who will be professionally concerned with the patient's medical treatment after he leaves hospital or, if no such practitioner other than the responsible medical officer will be so concerned, of any registered medical practitioner; and

   (b) the written recommendation in the prescribed form of an approved social worker.

> **Section 25B(6)**
>
> *The supervision application must be accompanied by two written recommendations, one from a doctor and the other from an ASW.*
>
> *This 'second recommending doctor' should be professionally involved in the patient's aftercare, but, if there is no such person, any doctor will suffice.*
>
> Note: the second doctor may not be the RMO, anyone who has a financial interest in the patient's aftercare or a close relative of the patient (see s.25C(9) below).

(7) A recommendation under subsection (6)(a) above shall include a statement that in the opinion of the medical practitioner (having regard in particular to the patient's history) all of the conditions set out in section 25A(4) above are complied with.

> **Section 25B(7)**
>
> *The second doctor's recommendation must state that:*
>
> (a) *the patient is suffering with one of the four forms of mental disorder;*
>
> (b) *there would be a substantial risk of serious harm to the patient or others or of serious exploitation of the patient if s/he did not receive after-care services on leaving hospital; and*
>
> (c) *supervision of the patient will make it more likely that s/he will actually receive after-care.*

(8) A recommendation under subsection (6)(b) above shall include a statement that in the opinion of the social worker (having regard in particular to the patient's history) both of the conditions set out in section 25A(4)(b) and (c) above are complied with.

> **Section 25B(8)**
>
> *The ASW's recommendation must state that:*
>
> (a) *there would be a substantial risk of serious harm to the patient or others or of serious exploitation of the patient if s/he did not receive after-care services on leaving hospital; and*
>
> (b) *supervision of the patient will make it more likely that s/he will actually receive after-care.*

(9) A supervision application shall also be accompanied by-

(a) a statement in writing by the person who is to be the community responsible medical officer in relation to the patient after he leaves hospital that he is to be in charge of the medical treatment provided for the patient as part of the after-care services provided for him under section 117 below;

(b) a statement in writing by the person who is to be the supervisor in relation to the patient after he leaves hospital that he is to supervise the patient with a view to securing that he receives the after-care services so provided;

(c) details of the after-care services to be provided for the patient under section 117 below; and

(d) details of any requirements to be imposed on him under section 25D below.

> **Section 25B(9)**
>
> *The supervision application must also be accompanied by:*
>
> (a) *a written statement of the community RMO stating that s/he is to be in charge of the patient's medical after-care provided under s.117;*
>
> (b) *a written statement of the community supervisor stating that s/he is to supervise the patient with the intention of ensuring that s/he receives the s.117 after-care provided;*
>
> (c) *details of the s.117 after-care plan;*
>
> (d) *details of any requirements of residence, attendance or access to be imposed in order to ensure that the patient receives that after-care.*

(10) On making a supervision application in respect of a patient the responsible medical officer shall-

(a) inform the patient both orally and in writing;

(b) inform any person who has been consulted under paragraph (a)(iv) of subsection (2) above; and

(c) inform in writing any person who has been consulted under paragraph (b) of that subsection,

of the matters specified in subsection (11) below.

(11) The matters referred to in subsection (10) above are-

(a) that the application is being made;

(b) the after-care services to be provided for the patient under section 117 below;

(c) any requirements to be imposed on him under section 25D below; and

(d) the name of the person who is to be the community responsible medical officer, and of the person who is to be the supervisor, in relation to the patient after he leaves hospital.

Section 25B(10) & 25B(11)

On making a supervision application the RMO is required to inform the following people (a) that the application has been made; (b) of the after-care services planned; (c) of any requirements attached to the supervised discharge; (d) of the name of the community RMO and community supervisor:

(a)   the patient (orally and in writing);

(b)   any non-professional involved in the after-care of the patient who has been consulted about the application (by any means);

(c)   the patient's nearest relative (if they were consulted about the application) (in writing).

25C. Supervision applications: supplementary

(1) Subject to subsection (2) below, a supervision application, and the recommendation under section 25B(6)(a) above accompanying it, may describe the patient as suffering from more than one of the following forms of mental disorder, namely, mental illness, severe mental impairment, psychopathic disorder and mental impairment.

Section 25C(1)

The supervision application and the second doctor's recommendation may describe the patient as suffering from one or more of the four forms of mental disorder.

(2) A supervision application shall be of no effect unless the patient is described in the application and the recommendation under section 25B(6)(a) above accompanying it as suffering from the same form of mental disorder, whether or not he is also described in the application or the recommendation as suffering from another form.

Section 25C(2)
The supervision application and the second doctor's recommendation must agree on the presence of at least one of those forms of mental disorder.

(3) A registered medical practitioner may at any reasonable time visit a patient and examine him in private for the purpose of deciding whether to make a recommendation under section 25B(6)(a) above.

Section 25C(3)
A doctor may, at any reasonable time, visit and privately examine a patient when considering making a 'second doctor's recommendation' in support of supervised discharge.

(4) An approved social worker may at any reasonable time visit and interview a patient for the purpose of deciding whether to make a recommendation under section 25B(6)(b) above.

Section 25C(4)
An ASW may, at any reasonable time, visit and privately interview a patient when considering making a recommendation in support of supervised discharge.

(5) For the purpose of deciding whether to make a recommendation under section 25B(6) above in respect of a patient, a registered medical practitioner or an approved social worker may require the production of and inspect any records relating to the detention or treatment of the patient in any hospital or to any after-care services provided for the patient under section 117 below.

Section 25C(5)
The second recommending doctor or ASW may ask to see any records relating to the patient's detention, treatment or after-care when considering making a recommendation in support of supervised discharge.

(6) If, within the period of 14 days beginning with the day on which a supervision application has been accepted, the application, or any recommendation accompanying it, is found to be in any respect incorrect or defective, the application or recommendation may, within that period and with the consent of the Health Authority which accepted the application, be amended by the person by whom it was made or given.

Section 25C(6)

If the supervision application or accompanying recommendations are incorrectly completed they may be amended by the author within 14 days of acceptance, with the consent of the Health Authority.

(7) Where an application or recommendation is amended in accordance with subsection (6) above it shall have effect, and shall be deemed to have had effect, as if it had been originally made or given as so amended.

Section 25C(7)

If the supervision application or accompanying recommendation is amended it will be treated as if it had been correctly completed from the outset.

(8) A supervision application which appears to be duly made and to be accompanied by recommendations under section 25B(6) above may be acted upon without further proof of-

(a) the signature or qualification of the person by whom the application or any such recommendation was made or given; or

(b) any matter of fact or opinion stated in the application or recommendation.

Section 25C(8)

If the supervision application appears correctly completed and includes the required accompanying recommendations it may be acted upon without any further verification of the identity or credentials of the people completing the documents or verification of the contents of the documents.

(9) A recommendation under section 25B(6) above accompanying a supervision application in respect of a patient shall not be given by-

(a) the responsible medical officer;

(b) a person who receives or has an interest in the receipt of any payments made on account of the maintenance of the patient; or

(c) a close relative of the patient, of any person mentioned in paragraph (a) or (b) above or of a person by whom the other recommendation is given under section 25B(6) above for the purposes of the application.

Section 25C(9)

The second doctor's recommendation must not be made by the RMO, anyone who has a financial interest in the patient's aftercare or a close relative of the patient, RMO, second doctor, ASW, or person with a financial interest in the aftercare.

(10) In subsection (9)(c) above "close relative" means husband, wife, father, father-in-law, mother, mother-in-law, son, son-in-law, daughter, daughter-in-law, brother, brother-in-law, sister or sister-in-law.

> **Section 25C(10)**
> *Defines 'close relative' and is self explanatory.*

Section 25D. Requirements to secure receipt of after-care under supervision

(1) Where a patient is subject to after-care under supervision (or, if he has not yet left hospital, is to be so subject after he leaves hospital), the responsible after-care bodies have power to impose any of the requirements specified in subsection (3) below for the purpose of securing that the patient receives the after-care services provided for him under section 117 below.

(2) In this Act "the responsible after-care bodies", in relation to a patient, means the bodies which have (or will have) the duty under section 117 below to provide after-care services for the patient.

> **Section 25D(1) and 25D(2)**
> *The Health Authority and local social services authority responsible for s.117 after-care may impose requirements on the supervised discharge in order to ensure that the patient receives that after-care.*

(3) The requirements referred to in subsection (1) above are-

    (a) that the patient reside at a specified place;

    (b) that the patient attend at specified places and times for the purpose of medical treatment, occupation, education or training; and

    (c) that access to the patient be given, at any place where the patient is residing, to the supervisor, any registered medical practitioner or any approved social worker or to any other person authorised by the supervisor.

> **Section 25D(3)**
> *The requirements which may be imposed are that:*
>
> *(a)   the patient lives at a specific place;*
>
> *(b)   the patient attends a specific place for treatment, occupation, education or training;*
>
> *(c)   the patient's community supervisor, any doctor, any ASW or person authorised by the community supervisor is given access to the patient at the place where s/he lives.*
>
> Note: this section can not be used to compel medical treatment in the community. The power is to require attendance for treatment not acceptance of that treatment.

(4) A patient subject to after-care under supervision may be taken and conveyed by, or by any person authorised by, the supervisor to any place where the patient is required to reside or to attend for the purpose of medical treatment, occupation, education or training.

Section 25D(4)

The patient's community supervisor, or a person authorised by the supervisor may take the patient to any place s/he is require to live, or attend for treatment, occupation, education or training.

Note: the power to 'take and convey' does not give rise to any authority to detain a patient against his/her wishes once s/he arrives at the specified place.

(5) A person who demands-

(a) to be given access to a patient in whose case a requirement has been imposed under subsection (3)(c) above; or

(b) to take and convey a patient in pursuance of subsection (4) above,

shall, if asked to do so, produce some duly authenticated document to show that he is a person entitled to be given access to, or to take and convey, the patient.

Section 25D(5)

Anyone who asks to be given access to the patient (pursuant to a requirement of s.25D(3)(c) above) or to take and convey the patient to a specified place must, if asked, show a document authenticated by the community supervisor to show that s/he is authorised to act in that way.

25E. Review of after-care under supervision

(1) The after-care services provided (or to be provided) under section 117 below for a patient who is (or is to be) subject to after-care under supervision, and any requirements imposed on him under section 25D above, shall be kept under review, and (where appropriate) modified, by the responsible after-care bodies.

Section 25E(1)

The after-care provided and any requirements attached to the supervised discharge must be kept under review and, if appropriate, modified by the responsible health authority and local social services authority.

Modifications may be made to the original after-care plan and associated requirements before the patient leaves hospital.

(2) This subsection applies in relation to a patient who is subject to after-care under supervision where he refuses or neglects-

    (a) to receive any or all of the after-care services provided for him under section 117 below; or

    (b) to comply with any or all of any requirements imposed on him under section 25D above.

(3) Where subsection (2) above applies in relation to a patient, the responsible after-care bodies shall review, and (where appropriate) modify-

    (a) the after-care services provided for him under section 117 below; and

    (b) any requirements imposed on him under section 25D above.

(4) Where subsection (2) above applies in relation to a patient, the responsible after-care bodies shall also-

    (a) consider whether it might be appropriate for him to cease to be subject to after-care under supervision and, if they conclude that it might be, inform the community responsible medical officer; and

    (b) consider whether it might be appropriate for him to be admitted to a hospital for treatment and, if they conclude that it might be, inform an approved social worker.

Section 25E(2)
Should a patient refuse (or neglect to receive) any part of the planned after-care or to comply with the requirements of supervised discharge the responsible health authority and social services authority must:

Section 25E(3)
review and, if appropriate, modify the after-care plan and any associated requirements;

Section 25E(4)
consider whether the supervised discharge order should end and inform the community RMO if this might be appropriate;

consider whether the patient should be admitted to hospital and inform an ASW if this might be appropriate.

(5) The responsible after-care bodies shall not modify-

    (a) the after-care services provided (or to be provided) under section 117 below for a patient who is (or is to be) subject to after-care under supervision; or

    (b) any requirements imposed on him under section 25D above, unless subsection (6) below is complied with.

(6) This subsection is complied with if-

   (a) the patient has been consulted about the modifications;

   (b) any person who the responsible after-care bodies believe plays (or will play) a substantial part in the care of the patient but is not (or will not be) professionally concerned with the after-care services provided for the patient under section 117 below has been consulted about the modifications;

   (c) such steps as are practicable have been taken to consult the person (if any) appearing to be the nearest relative of the patient about the modifications; and

   (d) the responsible after-care bodies have taken into account any views expressed by the persons consulted.

Section 25E(5)

The after-care plan and any requirements attached to the supervised discharge can only be modified by the responsible health authority and local social services authority if ...

Section 25E(6)

...the following people have been consulted about the modifications and their views taken into account:

(a)   the patient

(b)   any non-professional it seems will be substantially involved in the care of the patient outside hospital;

(c)   the nearest relative of the patient (so far as is practicable).

---

(7) Where the patient has requested that paragraph (c) of subsection (6) above should not apply, that paragraph shall not apply unless-

   (a) the patient has a propensity to violent or dangerous behaviour towards others; and

   (b) the community responsible medical officer (or the person who is to be the community responsible medical officer) considers that it is appropriate for steps such as are mentioned in that paragraph to be taken.

Section 25E(7)

The patient may request that his/her nearest relative is not consulted about modifications to his/her supervised discharge and that request must be complied with unless:

(a)   the patient has a propensity to violent or dangerous behaviour to others; and

(b)   the community RMO considers consultation with the nearest relative to be appropriate.

(8) Where the responsible after-care bodies modify the after-care services provided (or to be provided) for the patient under section 117 below or any requirements imposed on him under section 25D above, they shall-

(a) inform the patient both orally and in writing;

(b) inform any person who has been consulted under paragraph (b) of subsection (6) above; and

(c) inform in writing any person who has been consulted under paragraph (c) of that subsection,

that the modifications have been made.

Section 25E(8)

On making modifications to the after-care plan or requirements the health authority and local social services authority are required to inform the following people that the modifications have been made:

(a)   the patient (orally and in writing);

(b)   any non-professional involved in the after-care of the patient who has been consulted about the application (by any means);

(c)   the patient's nearest relative (if s/he was consulted about the application) (in writing).

---

(9) Where-

(a) a person other than the person named in the supervision application becomes the community responsible medical officer when the patient leaves hospital; or

(b) when the patient is subject to after-care under supervision, one person ceases to be, and another becomes, the community responsible medical officer,

the responsible after-care bodies shall comply with subsection (11) below.

(10) Where-

(a) a person other than the person named in the supervision application becomes the supervisor when the patient leaves hospital; or

(b) when the patient is subject to after-care under supervision, one person ceases to be, and another becomes, the supervisor,

the responsible after-care bodies shall comply with subsection (11) below.

(11) The responsible after-care bodies comply with this subsection if they-

(a) inform the patient both orally and in writing;

(b) inform any person who they believe plays a substantial part in the care of the patient but is not professionally concerned with the after-care services provided for the patient under section 117 below; and

(c) unless the patient otherwise requests, take such steps as are practicable to inform in writing the person (if any) appearing to be the nearest relative of the patient,

of the name of the person who becomes the community responsible medical officer or the supervisor.

Sections 25E(9) and 25E(10)
Should the identity of the community RMO or community supervisor change at any time the responsible health authority and local social services authority must give the name of the new community RMO/supervisor to:

and 25E(11)
(a)   the patient (orally and in writing);

(b)   any non-professional involved in the after-care of the patient who has been consulted about the application (by any means);

(c)   the patient's nearest relative (unless the patient asks for him/her not to be informed) (in writing).

25F. Reclassification of patient subject to after-care under supervision.

(1) If it appears to the community responsible medical officer that a patient subject to after-care under supervision is suffering from a form of mental disorder other than the form or forms specified in the supervision application made in respect of the patient, he may furnish a report to that effect to the Health Authority which have the duty under section 117 below to provide after-care services for the patient.

(2) Where a report is so furnished the supervision application shall have effect as if that other form of mental disorder were specified in it.

Section 25F(1)
If it appears to the community RMO that a patient is now suffering from a form of mental disorder different from that which was specified when the supervision application was made the doctor may provide a report to that effect to the health authority.

Section 25F(2)
The effect of providing such a report is that the patient's disorder is considered retrospectively changed for the purposes of the supervision application.

Note: the report may either add an additional form of disorder or substitute an entirely different form of disorder from that given in the original supervision application. If the reclassification occurs at the same time as the renewal of the supervised discharge a further reclassification report is not required (see 25G(10) below).

Reclassification will give rise to the right of both the patient and his/her nearest relative to apply to a MHRT under s.66.

(3) Unless no-one other than the community responsible medical officer is professionally concerned with the patient's medical treatment, he shall consult one or more persons who are so concerned before furnishing a report under subsection (1) above.

(4) Where a report is furnished under subsection (1) above in respect of a patient, the responsible after-care bodies shall-

(a) inform the patient both orally and in writing; and
(b) unless the patient otherwise requests, take such steps as are practicable to inform in writing the person (if any) appearing to be the nearest relative of the patient,

that the report has been furnished.

Section 25F(3)
The community RMO must consult with at least one other professional (if such a person exists) who is involved in the patient's after-care under supervision before providing a reclassification report.

Section 25F(4)
When a reclassification report is provided the responsible health authority and local social services authority must inform the patient of this orally and in writing and also take steps to inform the patient's nearest relative (unless the patient asks them not to do so).

25G. Duration and renewal of after-care under supervision

(1) Subject to sections 25H and 25I below, a patient subject to after-care under supervision shall be so subject for the period-

(a) beginning when he leaves hospital; and
(b) ending with the period of six months beginning with the day on which the supervision application was accepted,

but shall not be so subject for any longer period except in accordance with the following provisions of this section.

Section 25G(1)
Supervised discharge will commence when a patient leaves hospital (or when s.17 leave expires (see s.25A(9)) and end six months after the supervision application is accepted.

(2) A patient already subject to after-care under supervision may be made so subject-

(a) from the end of the period referred to in subsection (1) above, for a further period of six months; and
(b) from the end of any period of renewal under paragraph (a) above, for a further period of one year,

and so on for periods of one year at a time.

> **Section 25G(2)**
> *Supervised discharge may be renewed:*
> (a) *for a further six months after the initial period expires;*
> (b) *for further periods of one year thereafter.*

(3) Within the period of two months ending on the day on which a patient who is subject to after-care under supervision would (in default of the operation of subsection (7) below) cease to be so subject, it shall be the duty of the community responsible medical officer-

    (a) to examine the patient; and

    (b) if it appears to him that the conditions set out in subsection (4) below are complied with, to furnish to the responsible after-care bodies a report to that effect in the prescribed form.

> **Section 25G(3)**
> *Within the two month period prior to the expiration of a supervised discharge order the community RMO must:*
> (a) *examine the patient; and*
> (b) *if it appears that the conditions for continuation of supervised discharge are met, provide a report (on form 5S) to this effect for the responsible health authority and local social services authority.*

(4) The conditions referred to in subsection (3) above are that-

    (a) the patient is suffering from mental disorder, being mental illness, severe mental impairment, psychopathic disorder or mental impairment;

    (b) there would be a substantial risk of serious harm to the health or safety of the patient or the safety of other persons, or of the patient being seriously exploited, if he were not to receive the after-care services provided for him under section 117 below;

    (c) his being subject to after-care under supervision is likely to help to secure that he receives the after-care services so provided.

> **Section 25G(4)**
> *The conditions which must be met before continuation of a supervised discharge order are:*
> (a) *the patient is suffering with one of the four forms of mental disorder;*
> (b) *there would be a substantial risk of serious harm to the patient's health or safety or others' safety or others or of serious exploitation of the patient if s/he did not receive after-care services on leaving hospital; and*
> (c) *supervision of the patient will make it more likely that s/he will actually receive after-care.*
> Note: the grounds for renewal are exactly the same as those for making the initial supervision application.

(5) The community responsible medical officer shall not consider whether the conditions set out in subsection (4) above are complied with unless-

   (a) the following persons have been consulted-
     (i) the patient;
     (ii) the supervisor;
     (iii) unless no-one other than the community responsible medical officer is professionally concerned with the patient's medical treatment, one or more persons who are so concerned;
     (iv) one or more persons who are professionally concerned with the after-care services (other than medical treatment) provided for the patient under section 117 below; and
     (v) any person who the community responsible medical officer believes plays a substantial part in the care of the patient but is not professionally concerned with the after-care services so provided;
   (b) such steps as are practicable have been taken to consult the person (if any) appearing to be the nearest relative of the patient; and
   (c) the community responsible medical officer has taken into account any relevant views expressed by the persons consulted.

Section 25G(5)
The community RMO must not consider whether the conditions for renewal of supervised discharge are met until the following people have been consulted and their views taken into account:

(a) (i)   the patient;

    (ii) the community supervisor;

    (iii) at least one person professionally involved in the patient's medical treatment (if such persons exist);

    (iv) at least one other person professionally involved in the patient's after-care under s.117;

    (v) any non-professional it seems is substantially involved in the care of the patient outside hospital;

(b) the nearest relative of the patient (so far as is practicable).

(6) Where the patient has requested that paragraph (b) of subsection (5) above should not apply, that paragraph shall not apply unless-

   (a) the patient has a propensity to violent or dangerous behaviour towards others; and
   (b) the community responsible medical officer considers that it is appropriate for steps such as are mentioned in that paragraph to be taken.

Section 25G(6)

The patient may request that his /her nearest relative is not consulted about renewal of the supervised discharge and that request must be complied with unless:

(a)   the patient has a propensity to violent or dangerous behaviour to others; and

(b)   the community RMO considers consultation with the nearest relative to be appropriate.

(7) Where a report is duly furnished under subsection (3) above, the patient shall be thereby made subject to after-care under supervision for the further period prescribed in that case by subsection (2) above.

Section 25G(7)

The provision of a report has the effect of renewing the patient's supervised discharge for the specified period (i.e. either six months in the first instance and one year thereafter).

(8) Where a report is furnished under subsection (3) above, the responsible after-care bodies shall-

   (a) inform the patient both orally and in writing-

   (i) that the report has been furnished; and

   (ii) of the effect in his case of the provisions of this Act relating to making a patient subject to after-care under supervision for a further period (including, in particular, what rights of applying to a Mental Health Review Tribunal are available);

   (b) inform any person who has been consulted under paragraph (a)(v) of subsection (5) above that the report has been furnished; and

   (c) inform in writing any person who has been consulted under paragraph (b) of that subsection that the report has been furnished.

Section 25G(8)

On receiving a renewal report the responsible health authority and local social services authority are required to inform the following people that the report has been received:

(a)   the patient (orally and in writing);

(b)   any non-professional involved in the after-care of the patient who has been consulted and named on the supervision application (by any means);

(c)   the patient's nearest relative (if s/he was consulted about the renewal) (in writing).

The patient must also be told orally and in writing of the effect of the renewal and his/her rights to apply to a MHRT.

(9) Where the form of mental disorder specified in a report furnished under subsection (3) above is a form of disorder other than that specified in the supervision application, that application shall have effect as if that other form of mental disorder were specified in it.

> **Section 25G(9)**
> *If the form of mental disorder specified in the renewal report is different from that which was specified when the supervision application was made the form of the patient's disorder will be considered retrospectively changed for the purposes of the supervision application.*

(10) Where on any occasion a report specifying such a form of mental disorder is furnished under subsection (3) above the community responsible medical officer need not on that occasion furnish a report under section 25F above.

> **Section 25G(10)**
> *Having reclassified the form of mental disorder in the renewal report there is no need for a further reclassification report to be provided by the community RMO under section 25F.*

25H. Ending of after-care under supervision

(1) The community responsible medical officer may at any time direct that a patient subject to after-care under supervision shall cease to be so subject.

(2) The community responsible medical officer shall not give a direction under subsection (1) above unless subsection (3) below is complied with.

(3) This subsection is complied with if-
- (a) the following persons have been consulted about the giving of the direction-
  - (i) the patient;
  - (ii) the supervisor;
  - (ii) unless no-one other than the community responsible medical officer is professionally concerned with the patient's medical treatment, one or more persons who are so concerned;
  - (iv) one or more persons who are professionally concerned with the after-care services (other than medical treatment) provided for the patient under section 117 below; and
  - (v) any person who the community responsible medical officer believes plays a substantial part in the care of the patient but is not professionally concerned with the after-care services so provided;
- (b) such steps as are practicable have been taken to consult the person (if any) appearing to be the nearest relative of the patient about the giving of the direction; and
- (c) the community responsible medical officer has taken into account any views expressed by the persons consulted.

Section 25H(1)
The community RMO may direct that a patient's supervised discharge should end at any time.

Section 25H(2) and 25H(3)
The community RMO can only make such a direction if the following persons have been consulted and their views taken into account:

(a)   *(i)*   *the patient;*

      (ii)   *the community supervisor;*

      (iii)   *at least one person professionally involved in the patient's medical treatment (if such persons exist);*

      (iv)   *at least one person professionally involved in the patient's after-care under s.117;*

      (v)   *any non-professional it seems is substantially involved in the care of the patient outside hospital;*

(b)   *the nearest relative of the patient (so far as is practicable).*

(4) Where the patient has requested that paragraph (b) of subsection (3) above should not apply, that paragraph shall not apply unless-

     (a) the patient has a propensity to violent or dangerous behaviour towards others; and

     (b) the community responsible medical officer considers that it is appropriate for steps such as are mentioned in that paragraph to be taken.

Section 25H(4)
The patient may request that his/her nearest relative is not consulted about ending their supervised discharge and that request must be complied with unless:

(a)   *the patient has a propensity to violent or dangerous behaviour to others; and*

(b)   *the community RMO considers consultation with the nearest relative to be appropriate.*

(5) A patient subject to after-care under supervision shall cease to be so subject if he-

     (a) is admitted to a hospital in pursuance of an application for admission for treatment; or

     (b) is received into guardianship.

Section 25H(5)
A patient's supervised discharge will end if s/he is either compulsorily admitted to hospital for treatment or received into guardianship.

Note: neither voluntary admission for treatment nor compulsory admission for assessment (under s.2) terminate a supervised discharge. However admission under s.2 does lead to suspension of any supervision requirements (under s25I).

(6) Where a patient (for any reason) ceases to be subject to after-care under supervision the responsible after-care bodies shall-

   (a) inform the patient both orally and in writing;

   (b) inform any person who they believe plays a substantial part in the care of the patient but is not professionally concerned with the after-care services provided for the patient under section 117 below; and

   (c) take such steps as are practicable to inform in writing the person (if any) appearing to be the nearest relative of the patient,

that the patient has ceased to be so subject.

Section 25H(6)
On supervised discharge terminating the responsible health authority and social services authority are required to inform the following people that this has occurred:

(a)   the patient (orally and in writing);

(b)   any non-professional involved in the care of the patient (by any means);

(c)   the patient's nearest relative (if they were consulted about the termination) (in writing).

(7) Where the patient has requested that paragraph (c) of subsection (6) above should not apply, that paragraph shall not apply unless subsection (3)(b) above applied in his case by virtue of subsection (4) above.

Section 25H(7)
If, following the patient's request, the patient's nearest relative was not consulted about potential termination of the supervised discharge they need not be told about the supervised discharge actually ending.

25I. Special provisions as to patients sentenced to imprisonment etc

This section suspends supervised discharge whilst a patient is in custody or admitted to hospital for assessment and allows for renewal of any lapsed supervised discharge be effected up to 28 days after release.

(1) This section applies where a patient who is subject to after-care under supervision-

   (a) is detained in custody in pursuance of any sentence or order passed or made by a court in the United Kingdom (including an order committing or remanding him in custody); or

   (b) is detained in hospital in pursuance of an application for admission for assessment.

Section 25I(1)
Section 25I applies to patients who are detained in custody following a court sentence or order and to those compulsorily admitted to hospital for assessment (under s.2).

(2) At any time when the patient is detained as mentioned in subsection (1)(a) or (b) above he is not required-

   (a) to receive any after-care services provided for him under section 117 below; or

   (b) to comply with any requirements imposed on him under section 25D above.

Section 25I(2)
During the period of detention/admission the patient need not receive after-care services under s.117 nor comply with any requirements associated with his/her supervised discharge.

(3) If the patient is detained as mentioned in paragraph (a) of subsection (1) above for a period of, or successive periods amounting in the aggregate to, six months or less, or is detained as mentioned in paragraph (b) of that subsection, and, apart from this subsection, he-

   (a) would have ceased to be subject to after-care under supervision during the period for which he is so detained; or

   (b) would cease to be so subject during the period of 28 days beginning with the day on which he ceases to be so detained,

he shall be deemed not to have ceased, and shall not cease, to be so subject until the end of that period of 28 days.

(4) Where the period for which the patient is subject to after-care under supervision is extended by subsection (3) above, any examination and report to be made and furnished in respect of the patient under section 25G(3) above may be made and furnished within the period as so extended.

Section 25I(3)

If a patient subject to supervised discharge is detained in custody by a court order (e.g. sentenced, remanded) or in hospital for assessment for six or less months but his/her liability for supervised discharge would have expired on or before their release day, or within 28 days of release, s/he does not cease to be liable for supervised discharge until 28 days after his/her release day.

Section 25I(4)

Where the period of supervised discharge is extended by this section a renewal report (under s.25G above) will be effective if provided within the 28 day extension period.

Note: if a supervised discharge order expires during a sentence of longer than six months it can not be renewed under this section. However it is possible that, where a sentence is between six months and a year, that a supervised discharge application may not yet have expired by the time the patient is released.

(5) Where, by virtue of subsection (4) above, the patient is made subject to after-care under supervision for a further period after the day on which (apart from subsection (3) above) he would have ceased to be so subject, the further period shall be deemed to have commenced with that day.

Section 25I(5)

Any renewal of supervised discharge under this section is deemed to begin on the day the supervised discharge would have originally expired had it not been extended by this section.

25J. Patients moving from Scotland to England and Wales

(1) A supervision application may be made in respect of a patient who is subject to a community care order under the Mental Health (Scotland) Act 1984 and who intends to leave Scotland in order to reside in England and Wales.

Section 25J(1)

Allows patients subject to a community care order under the Scottish legislation to be made subject to supervised discharge should s/he move to England or Wales, despite the fact that s/he was not detained in hospital immediately prior to the supervised discharge application being made.

The application must be made before the patient leaves Scotland.

(2) Sections 25A to 25I above, section 117 below and any other provision of this Act relating to supervision applications or patients subject to after-care under supervision shall apply in relation to a patient in respect of whom a supervision application is or is to be made by virtue of this section subject to such modifications as the Secretary of State may by regulations prescribe.

Section 25J(2)
Those sections of the Act which govern supervision applications and after-care will all apply to patients who move from Scotland to England and Wales, subject to modifications made by regulations.

FUNCTIONS OF RELATIVES OF PATIENTS

26. Definition of 'relative' and 'nearest relative'

(1) In this Part of this Act "relative" means any of the following persons:-

(a) husband or wife;
(b) son or daughter;
(c) father or mother;
(d) brother or sister;
(e) grandparent;
(f) grandchild;
(g) uncle or aunt;
(h) nephew or niece.

(2) In deducing relationships for the purposes of this section, any relationship of the half-blood shall be treated as a relationship of the whole blood, and an illegitimate person shall be treated as the legitimate child of

(a) his mother, and
(b) if his father has parental responsibility for him within the meaning of section 3 of the Children Act 1989, his father.

Section 26(1) & 26(2)
Define who is considered to be a 'relative' and are self explanatory.

(3) In this Part of this Act, subject to the provisions of this section and to the following provisions of this Part of this Act, the "nearest relative" means the person first described in subsection (1) above who is for the time being surviving, relatives of the whole blood being preferred to relatives of the same description of the half-blood and the elder or eldest of two or more relatives described in any paragraph of that subsection being preferred to the other or others of those relatives, regardless of sex.

Section 26(3)
Describes how who is to be the 'nearest relative' is established and is self explanatory.

(4) Subject to the provisions of this section and to the following provisions of this Part of this Act, where the patient ordinarily resides with or is cared for by one or more of his relatives (or, if he is for the time being an in-patient in a hospital, he last ordinarily resided with or was cared for by one or more of his relatives) his nearest relative shall be determined-

(a) by giving preference to that relative or those relatives over the other or others; and

(b) as between two or more such relatives, in accordance with subsection (3) above.

(5) Where the person who, under subsection (3) or (4) above, would be the nearest relative of a patient-

(a) in the case of a patient ordinarily resident in the United Kingdom, the Channel Islands or the Isle of Man, is not so resident; or

(b) is the husband or wife of the patient, but is permanently separated from the patient, either by agreement or under an order of a court, or has deserted or has been deserted by the patient for a period which has come to an end; or

(c) is a person other than the husband, wife, father or mother of the patient, and is for the time being under 18 years of age.

the nearest relative of the patient shall be ascertained as if that person were dead.

(6) In this section "husband" and "wife" include a person who is living with the patient as the patient's husband or wife, as the case may be (or, if the patient is for the time being an in-patient in a hospital, was so living until the patient was admitted), and has been or had been so living for a period of not less than six months; but a person shall not be treated by virtue of this subsection as the nearest relative of a married patient unless the husband or wife of the patient is disregarded by virtue of paragraph (b) of subsection (5) above.

(7) A person, other than a relative, with whom the patient ordinarily resides (or, if the patient is for the time being an in-patient in a hospital, last ordinarily resided before he was admitted), and with whom he has or had been ordinarily residing for a period of not less than five years, shall be treated for the purposes of this Part of this Act as if he were a relative but-

(a) shall be treated for the purposes of subsection (3) above as if mentioned last in subsection (1) above; and

(b) shall not be treated by virtue of this subsection as the nearest relative of a married patient unless the husband or wife of the patient is disregarded by virtue of paragraph (b) of subsection (5) above.

When deciding who is the 'nearest relative':

Section 26(4)
Those relatives with whom the patient usually lives, or who take care of the patient have precedence over others.

Section 26(5)
Those relatives who either (a) live abroad (b) are divorced or separated spouses or (c) are under 18 (unless they are the patient's parent or spouse) are to be ignored.

Section 26(6)
Live in partners of more than six months duration will be treated as if they were the spouse of the patient providing that any existing spouse can be disregarded by virtue of s.26(5).

Section 26(7)
A non-relative with whom the person normally lives (and has lived with for more than five years) may be considered a 'relative'. Such a person will be treated as if at the bottom of the hierarchical list set out in s.26(1) (although, by virtue of s.26(4), they may nevertheless have precedence over others).

If the patient is married their cohabitee may not be the nearest relative unless the spouse can be disregarded by virtue of s.26(5)(b) (i.e. because of separation or desertion).

27. Children and young persons in care of local authority

Where-

   (a) a patient who is a child or young person is in the care of a local authority by virtue of a care order within the meaning of the Children Act 1989; or
   (b) the rights and powers of a parent of a patient who is a child or young person are vested in a local authority by virtue of section 16 of the Social Work (Scotland) Act 1968,

the authority shall be deemed to be the nearest relative of the patient in preference to any person except the patient's husband or wife (if any).

Section 27
If the patient is unmarried, under 18 and in local authority care that local authority will be considered to be the nearest relative.

28. Nearest relative of a minor under Guardianship

(1) Where-

   (a) a guardian has been appointed for a person who has not attained the age of eighteen years; or

(b) a residence order (as defined by section 8 of the Children Act 1989) is in force with respect to such a person,

the guardian (or guardians, where there is more than one) or the person named in the residence order shall, to the exclusion of any other person, be deemed to be his nearest relative.

(2) Subsection (5) of section 26 above shall apply in relation to a person who is, or who is one of the persons, deemed to be the nearest relative of a patient by virtue of this section as it applies in relation to a person who would be the nearest relative under subsection (3) of that section.

(3) In this section "guardian" does not include a guardian under this Part of this Act.

Section 28(1) to (3)
For a patient under 18 years old, where a guardian has been appointed (other than under this Act) or where s/he is subject to a residence order, the guardian or person named in the residence order will be the 'nearest relative', unless s.26(5), above, applies.

(4) In this section "court" includes a court in Scotland or Northern Ireland, and "enactment" includes an enactment of the Parliament of Northern Ireland, a Measure of the Northern Ireland Assembly and an Order in Council under Schedule 1 of the Northern Ireland Act 1974.

Section 28(4)
This sub section is now redundant as amendments made to s.28(1)-(3) by the Children Act 1989 removed the words here defined.

29. Appointment by the court of acting nearest relative

(1) The county court may, upon application made in accordance with the provisions of this section in respect of a patient, by order direct that the functions of the nearest relative of the patient under this Part of this Act and sections 66 and 69 below shall, during the continuance in force of the order, be exercisable by the applicant, or by any other person specified in the application, being a person who, in the opinion of the court, is a proper person to act as the patient's nearest relative and is willing to do so.

(2) An order under this section may be made on the application of-

(a) any relative of the patient;
(b) any other person with whom the patient is residing (or, if the patient is then an in-patient in a hospital, was last residing before he was admitted); or
(c) an approved social worker;

but in relation to an application made by such a social worker, subsection (1) above shall have effect as if for the words "the applicant" there were substituted the words "the local social services authority".

Section 29(1) & 29(2)

A county court may appoint any proper person (or the local social services authority) to act as the nearest relative in response to an application made by any relative of the patient, any person with whom the patient lives or an ASW.

(3) An application for an order under this section may be made upon any of the following grounds, that is to say-

   (a) that the patient has no nearest relative within the meaning of this Act, or that it is not reasonably practicable to ascertain whether he has such a relative, or who that relative is;

   (b) that the nearest relative of the patient is incapable of acting as such by reason of mental disorder or other illness;

   (c) that the nearest relative of the patient unreasonably objects to the making of an application for admission for treatment or a guardianship application in respect of the patient; or

   (d) that the nearest relative of the patient has exercised without due regard to the welfare of the patient or the interests of the public his power to discharge the patient from hospital or guardianship under this Part of this Act, or is likely to do so.

Section 29(3)

An application to the county court may be made if:

(a)   there is no known nearest relative;

(b)   the nearest relative is incapable of acting through mental disorder or illness;

(c)   the nearest relative unreasonably objects to an application for admission for treatment or for guardianship;

(d)   the nearest relative has exercised or is likely to exercise his/her power of discharge contrary to the patient's welfare or the public's interests.

(4) If, immediately before the expiration of the period for which a patient is liable to be detained by virtue of an application for admission for assessment, an application under this section, which is an application made on the ground specified in subsection (3)(c) or (d) above, is pending in respect of the patient, that period shall be extended-

(a) in any case, until the application under this section has been finally disposed of; and

(b) if an order is made in pursuance of the application under this section, for a further period of seven days;

and for the purposes of this subsection an application under this section shall be deemed to have been finally disposed of at the expiration of the time allowed for appealing from the decision of the court or, if notice of appeal has been given within that time, when the appeal has been heard or withdrawn, and "pending" shall be construed accordingly.

Section 29(4)

If a patient has been detained for assessment under s.2, any application to appoint an acting nearest relative under s.29(3)(c) or (d) above will have the effect of extending the 28 day period of detention whilst the application is dealt with by the court.

If the application is successful the detention may then be extended for a further 7 days

Note: this section provides the only authority for more than a 28 day detention under s.2. A further week after appointment/replacement of a nearest relative is allowed for so that, for example, the patient may be kept in hospital whilst the formalities of s.3 are complied with.

(5) An order made on the ground specified in subsection (3)(a) or (b) above may specify a period for which it is to continue in force unless previously discharged under section 30 below.

Section 29(5)

If there is no nearest relative or s/he is incapable of acting through illness an order appointing an acting nearest relative may be made on a time limited basis.

Note: it may appear from this section that a court order replacing a nearest relative who unreasonably objects to an application for admission for treatment or guardianship or is likely to exercise the power of discharge contrary to the patient's welfare or the public's interests can not be made on an interim basis. However the Court of Appeal have recently decided that the county court has a general power to make interim orders under the County Courts Act 1984 (s.38) which is unaffected by this section of the MHA. Therefore, although not the preferable course of action, such interim orders may be made.[24]

[24] R v Central London Court ex parte London [1999] 3 WLR 1.

(6) While an order made under this section is in force, the provisions of this Part of this Act (other than this section and section 30 below) and sections 66, 69, 132(4) and 133 below shall apply in relation to the patient as if for any reference to the nearest relative of the patient there were substituted a reference to the person having the functions of that relative and (without prejudice to section 30 below) shall so apply notwithstanding that the person who was the patient's nearest relative when the order was made is no longer his nearest relative; but this subsection shall not apply to section 66 below in the case mentioned in paragraph (h) of subsection (1) of that section.

Section 29(6)

This gives the power for the acting nearest relative to carry out the functions of the nearest relative. It also provides that any orders already made under Part II of the Act continue despite the change of nearest relative.

The 'removed' nearest relative may still make an application to a MHRT under s.66(1)(h).

30. Discharge and variation of orders under s.29

(1) An order made under section 29 above in respect of a patient may be discharged by the county court upon application made-

  (a) in any case, by the person having the functions of the nearest relative of the patient by virtue of the order;

  (b) where the order was made on the ground specified in paragraph (a) or paragraph (b) of section 29(3) above, or where the person who was the nearest relative of the patient when the order was made has ceased to be his nearest relative, on the application of the nearest relative of the patient.

Section 30(1)

Application for discharge of a s.29 order may be made by the person carrying out the nearest relative functions or by the nearest relative if s/he was supplanted because there was no known nearest relative or because of incapacity through illness. However, if the nearest relative was deposed under s.29(3)(c) or (d) (for unreasonable objection or lack of regard for the patient's welfare or public interest) s/he may not apply to the court.

(2) An order made under section 29 above in respect of a patient may be varied by the county court, on the application of the person having the functions of the nearest relative by virtue of the order or on the application of an approved social worker, by substituting for the first-mentioned person a local social services authority or any other person who in the opinion of the court is a proper person to exercise those functions, being an authority or person who is willing to do so.

Section 30(2)

After a s.29 order has been made either the local social services authority or another proper person may be substituted to carry out the nearest relative's functions providing that the authority or person is willing to accept the role.

Either an ASW or the person who carries out the nearest relative functions can apply to the county court for such a variation of a s.29 order.

(3) If the person having the functions of the nearest relative of a patient by virtue of an order under section 29 above dies-

    (a) subsections (1) and (2) above shall apply as if for any reference to that person there were substituted a reference to any relative of the patient, and

    (b) until the order is discharged or varied under those provisions the functions of the nearest relative under this Part of this Act and sections 66 and 69 below shall not be exercisable by any person.

Section 30(3)

On the death of the person carrying out the nearest relative functions under s.29 the order must be discharged or varied before any other person can carry out those functions. Any relative can make an application for discharge or variation in these circumstances.

(4) An order under section 29 above shall, unless previously discharged under subsection (1) above, cease to have effect at the expiration of the period, if any, specified under subsection (5) of that section or, where no such period is specified-

    (a) if the patient was on the date of the order liable to be detained in pursuance of an application for admission for treatment or by virtue of an order or direction under Part III of this Act (otherwise than under section 35, 36 or 38) or was subject to guardianship under this Part of this Act or by virtue of such an order or direction, or becomes so liable or subject within the period of three months beginning with that date, when he ceases to be so liable or subject (otherwise than on being transferred in pursuance of regulations under section 19 above);

    (b) if the patient was not on the date of the order, and has not within the said period become, so liable or subject, at the expiration of that period.

Section 30(4)

Any order under s.29 lasts either: as long as was specified under s.29(5); or

(a)   if a patient is subject to detention for treatment or guardianship (or becomes so subject within three months of the order being made) until detention/guardianship ceases;

(b)   otherwise for three months.

(5) The discharge or variation under this section of an order made under section 29 above shall not affect the validity of anything previously done in pursuance of the order.

Section 30(5)
Is self explanatory.

31. Procedure on applications to county court

County court rules which relate to applications authorised by this Part of this Act to be made to a county court may make provision-

(a) for the hearing and determination of such applications otherwise than in open court;

(b) for the admission on the hearing of such applications of evidence of such descriptions as may be specified in the rules notwithstanding anything to the contrary in any enactment or rule of law relating to the admissibility of evidence;

(c) for the visiting and interviewing of patients in private by or under the directions of the court.

Section 31
Allows for County Court Rules (CCR) to (a) make provision for applications under Part II of the Act to be heard in private (b) specify the type and nature of admissible evidence (c) make provision for visiting and interviewing of patients in private or otherwise.

Note: the current rules are found in CCR Order 49 rule 12. Any proceedings must now be brought by a claim form complying with the new Civil Procedure Rules (CPR) 1998 (see CPR Schedule 2). CPR do not apply to proceedings under part VII of the Act (see CPR part 2.1(2)).

32. Regulations for purposes of Part II

(1) The Secretary of State may make regulations for prescribing anything which, under this Part of this Act, is required or authorised to be prescribed, and otherwise for carrying this Part of this Act into full effect.

(2) Regulations under this section may in particular make provision-

(a) for prescribing the form of any application, recommendation, report, order, notice or other document to be made or given under this Part of this Act;

(b) for prescribing the manner in which any such application, recommendation, report, order, notice or other document may be proved, and for regulating the service of any such application, report, order or notice;

(c) for requiring such bodies as may be prescribed by the regulations to keep such registers or other records as may be so prescribed in respect of patients liable to be detained or subject to guardianship or to after-care under supervision under this Part of this Act, and to furnish or make available to those patients, and their relatives, such written statements of their rights and powers under this Act as may be so prescribed;

(d) for the determination in accordance with the regulations of the age of any person whose exact age cannot be ascertained by reference to the registers kept under the Births and Deaths Registration Act 1953; and

(e) for enabling the functions under this Part of this Act of the nearest relative of a patient to be performed, in such circumstances and subject to such conditions (if any) as may be prescribed by the regulations, by any person authorised in that behalf by that relative;

and for the purposes of this Part of this Act any application, report or notice the service of which is regulated under paragraph (b) above shall be deemed to have been received by or furnished to the authority or person to whom it is authorised or required to be furnished, addressed or given if it is duly served in accordance with the regulations.

(3) Without prejudice to subsections (1) and (2) above, but subject to section 23(4) above, regulations under this section may determine the manner in which functions under this Part of this Act of the managers of hospitals, local social services authorities,Health Authorities, Special Health Authorities or National Health Service trusts are to be exercised, and such regulations may in particular specify the circumstances in which, and the conditions subject to which, any such functions may be performed by officers of or other persons acting on behalf of those managers authorities and trusts.

Section 32
Empowers the Secretary of State for Health to make regulations as to the manner in which the provisions of Part II of the Mental Health Act are to be carried out, the types of forms to be used, the registers and records to be kept etc. Such regulations are regularly made by means of statutory instruments.

33. Special Provisions as to wards of court

(1) An application for the admission to hospital of a minor who is a ward of court may be made under this Part of this Act with the leave of the court; and section 11(4) above shall not apply in relation to an application so made.

(2) Where a minor who is a ward of court is liable to be detained in a hospital by virtue of an application for admission under this Part of this Act, any power exercisable under this Part of this Act or under section 66 below in relation to the patient by his nearest relative shall be exercisable by or with the leave of the court.

Leave of the court is required before either:

Section 33(1)
an application can be made to admit to hospital a child who is a ward of court (in which case no consultation with the nearest relative is required); or

Section 33(2)
any power of the nearest relative is exercised in respect of a ward of court.

(3) Nothing in this Part of this Act shall be construed as authorising the making of a guardianship application in respect of a minor who is a ward of court, or the transfer into guardianship of any such minor.

Section 33(3)
A ward of court may not be received into guardianship under the Mental Health Act.

(4) Where a supervision application has been made in respect of a minor who is a ward of court, the provisions of this Part of this Act relating to after-care under supervision have effect in relation to the minor subject to any order which the court may make in the exercise of its wardship jurisdiction.

Section 33(4)
Any powers relating to after-care under supervision (s.25A-s.25J) are subject to the court's exercise of its own wardship jurisdiction in respect of a ward of court.

34. Interpretation of terms in Part II

(1) In this Part of this Act-

"the community responsible medical officer", in relation to a patient subject to after-care under supervision, means the person who, in accordance with section 117(2A)(a) below, is in charge of medical treatment provided for him;

"the nominated medical attendant", in relation to a patient who is subject to the guardianship of a person other than a local social services authority, means the person appointed in pursuance of regulations made under section 9(2) above to act as the medical attendant of the patient;

"the responsible medical officer" means (except in the phrase "the community responsible medical officer")-

(a) in relation to a patient who is liable to be detained by virtue of an application for admission for assessment or an application for admission for treatment or who is to be subject to after-care under supervision after leaving hospital, the registered medical practitioner in charge of the treatment of the patient;

(b) in relation to a patient subject to guardianship, the medical officer authorised by the local social services authority to act (either generally or in any particular case or for any particular purpose) as the responsible medical officer.

"the supervisor", in relation to a patient subject to after-care under supervision, means the person who, in accordance with section 117(2A)(b) below, is supervising him.

(1A) Nothing in this Act prevents the same person from acting as more than one of the following in relation to a patient, that is-

(a) the responsible medical officer;

(b) the community responsible medical officer; and

(c) the supervisor.

Section 34(1)
Defines terms used in part II of the Act and is self-explanatory.

Note: the RMO of a detained patient need not be a consultant psychiatrist, nor need s/he be approved under s.12 of the Act.

Section 34(1)A
The patient's RMO, community RMO and community supervisor may be the same person.

(2) Except where otherwise expressly provided, this Part of this Act applies in relation to a mental nursing home, being a home in respect of which the particulars of registration are for the time being entered in the separate part of the register kept for the purposes of section 23(5)(b) of the Registered Homes Act 1984, as it applies in relation to a hospital, and references in this Part of this Act to a hospital, and any reference in this Act to a hospital to which this Part of this Act applies, shall be construed accordingly.

Section 34(2)
Any reference to 'hospital' in Part II of this Act can also be read as ' registered mental nursing home' unless otherwise stated.

(3) In relation to a patient who is subject to guardianship in pursuance of a guardianship application, any reference in this Part of this Act to the responsible local social services authority is a reference-

(a) where the patient is subject to the guardianship of a local social services authority, to that authority;

(b) where the patient is subject to the guardianship of a person other than a local social services authority, to the local social services authority for the area in which that person resides.

Section 34(3)
Is self-explanatory.

PART III

PATIENTS CONCERNED IN CRIMINAL PROCEEDINGS OR UNDER SENTENCE
REMANDS TO HOSPITAL

Note: by virtue of s.55(5), "hospital" in Part III includes a registered mental nursing home.

35. Remand to hospital for report on accused's mental condition

(1) Subject to the provisions of this section, the Crown Court or a magistrates' court may remand an accused person to a hospital specified by the court for a report on his mental condition.

Section 35(1)

An accused person may be sent to hospital by a Crown Court or a magistrates' court for a report on his/her mental condition.

Note: the court must decide on the hospital to which s/he is to be referred and will take into account the level of security that is required.

A person detained under this section has no right to apply to a Mental Health Review Tribunal.

(2) For the purposes of this section an accused person is—

(a) in relation to the Crown Court, any person who is awaiting trial before the court for an offence punishable with imprisonment or who has been arraigned before the court for such an offence and has not yet been sentenced or otherwise dealt with for the offence on which he has been arraigned;

(b) in relation to a magistrates' court, any person who has been convicted by the court of an offence punishable on summary conviction with imprisonment and any person charged with such an offence if the court is satisfied that he did the act or made the omission charged or he has consented to the exercise by the court of the powers conferred by this section.

Section 35(2)

Defines an "accused person" as:

(a)   in the Crown Court, a person who is awaiting trial or sentence for an offence which may be punished by imprisonment, other than a person convicted of murder;

(b)   in the magistrates' court, a person who:

(i)   has been convicted of an offence for which the magistrates have power to imprison; or

(ii)   has been charged with, but not convicted of, an imprisonable offence, but whom the court are satisfied did the act in relation to which s/he has been charged or who consents to be referred by the court under this section.

(3) Subject to subsection (4) below, the powers conferred by this section may be exercised if–

    (a) the court is satisfied, on the written or oral evidence of a registered medical practitioner, that there is reason to suspect that the accused person is suffering from mental illness, psychopathic disorder, severe mental impairment or mental impairment; and

    (b) the court is of the opinion that it would be impracticable for a report on his mental condition to be made if he were remanded on bail;

but those powers shall not be exercised by the Crown Court in respect of a person who has been convicted before the court if the sentence for the offence of which he has been convicted is fixed by law.

Section 35(3)

A person may only be detained if both subsections (a) and (b) apply.

(a)   *There need only be <u>reason to suspect</u> that the accused person is suffering from one of the four forms of mental disorder.*

       A s.12 approved doctor must provide the evidence (see s.54).

(b)   *This is likely to be, for example, because the person will not attend hospital unless compelled to do so.*

The Crown Court may not exercise this power where the person has been convicted of murder, which attracts a mandatory life sentence, though it may do so where the person is awaiting trial.

Note: courts other than magistrates' courts may exercise the power under this section where they are dealing with a person in relation to a contempt of court for which s/he could be committed to prison and there is reason to suspect that s/he is suffering from mental illness or severe mental impairment[25].

Courts, including magistrates' courts, may also exercise this power where there is reason to suspect that a person arrested for breach of an occupation order or a non-molestation order is suffering from mental illness or severe mental impairment[26].

[25] s.14(4A) Contempt of Court Act 1981.
[26] ss47 and 48 Family Law Act 1996.

(4) The court shall not remand an accused person to a hospital under this section unless satisfied, on the written or oral evidence of the registered medical practitioner who would be responsible for making the report or of some other person representing the managers of the hospital, that arrangements have been made for his admission to that hospital and for his admission to it within the period of seven days beginning with the date of the remand; and if the court is so satisfied it may, pending his admission, give directions for his conveyance to and detention in a place of safety.

Section 35(4)
The court must first be satisfied that arrangements have been made for the person's admission to the hospital within seven days and may give directions for him/her to be taken to and detained in a place of safety pending his/her admission.

Note: for an adult, a "place of safety" is a police station, prison, remand centre or any hospital which can temporarily accommodate him/her. For a child or young person, i.e. person under 18, it is a community home provided by a local authority or a controlled community home, a police station or any hospital, surgery or other suitable place whose occupier is willing temporarily to accommodate him/her.

(5) Where a court has remanded an accused person under this section it may further remand him if it appears to the court, on the written or oral evidence of the registered medical practitioner responsible for making the report, that a further remand is necessary for completing the assessment of the accused person's mental condition.

Section 35(5)
The period of detention can be extended by the court where the doctor making the report states that this is <u>necessary</u> for completing the assessment.

Note: the Code of Practice (1999 ed.), at 17.4, gives details of what the report should contain.

(6) The power of further remanding an accused person under this section may be exercised by the court without his being brought before the court if he is represented by counsel or a solicitor and his counsel or solicitor is given an opportunity of being heard.

Section 35(6)
The extension can be made in the person's absence, if s/he has a legal representative present who is given an opportunity to speak on his/her behalf.

(7) An accused person shall not be remanded or further remanded under this section for more than 28 days at a time or for more than 12 weeks in all; and the court may at any time terminate the remand if it appears to the court that it is appropriate to do so.

Section 35(7)

There is a limit of twelve weeks' total detention, with the court being able to remand for no more than 28 days at a time. Where appropriate, the court may terminate the detention at any time: this will require information from the relevant doctor that the object of the remand has been achieved before the expiry of the stipulated time.

Note: the Crime (Sentences) Act 1997 had made provision for the time spent in hospital to count as part of any sentence of imprisonment and for the person to earn time off any sentence of imprisonment for good behaviour. However, the relevant sections of that Act have been repealed without ever coming into force.[27]

[27]s.8 and ss10-27 of the Crime (Sentences) Act 1997 were repealed by the Crime and Disorder Act 1998, ss107(2), 120(2), Sch 10 on 30 September 1998.

(8) An accused person remanded to hospital under this section shall be entitled to obtain at his own expense an independent report on his mental condition from a registered medical practitioner chosen by him and to apply to the court on the basis of it for his remand to be terminated under subsection (7) above.

Section 35(8)

A person detained under this section may obtain his/her own medical report and thereafter apply for his/her detention to be terminated.

Note: the Code of Practice (1999 ed.) makes clear at 17.1 that hospital managers should help people to exercise this right by enabling them to contact a suitably qualified and experienced solicitor or other adviser.

(9) Where an accused person is remanded under this section–
   (a) a constable or any other person directed to do so by the court shall convey the accused person to the hospital specified by the court within the period mentioned in subsection (4) above; and
   (b) the managers of the hospital shall admit him within that period and thereafter detain him in accordance with the provisions of this section.

Section 35(9)

The person must be taken to and admitted to the hospital within seven days, including the day the order is made. Once the order is made the hospital cannot refuse to admit him/her.

Note: a constable is any police officer.

The RMO may not grant him leave of absence under s.17 nor transfer him/her to another hospital: s/he remains under the control of the court that sent him/her to hospital. The hospital is responsible for returning the person to court when required, but may ask for help from the police where necessary (see the Code of Practice (1999 ed.) at 29.6).

(10) If an accused person absconds from a hospital to which he has been remanded under this section, or while being conveyed to or from that hospital, he may be arrested without warrant by any constable and shall, after being arrested, be brought as soon as practicable before the court that remanded him; and the court may thereupon terminate the remand and deal with him in any way in which it could have dealt with him if he had not been remanded under this section.

Section 35(10)

Any police officer has a power to arrest without warrant a person who absconds from detention under this section. The person must then be brought before the court as soon as practicable and the court may proceed as if a remand under this section had not been made.

Note: by virtue of s.56(1)(b) a person remanded under this section is not subject to the provisions of Part IV of the Act (consent to treatment). Strictly speaking, therefore, a person in hospital under this section could be given the serious forms of treatment under s.57 without the safeguards provided for in that section. There is no obvious reason why s/he should not have the protection of s.57 and it is suggested that s/he should be treated as if s.57 did apply.

S/he may be treated with his/her consent or, in an emergency, under common law. Where a person needs treatment for mental disorder the Code of Practice (1999 ed.) suggests at 17.3 that the person should be referred back to court with an appropriate recommendation and that, in the case of delay in obtaining a court hearing, consideration should be given to whether the criteria for detention under s.3 of the Act are met.

36. Remand of accused person to hospital for treatment

(1) Subject to the provisions of this section, the Crown Court may, instead of remanding an accused person in custody, remand him to a hospital specified by the court if satisfied, on the written or oral evidence of two registered medical practitioners, that he is suffering from mental illness or severe mental impairment of a nature or degree which makes it appropriate for him to be detained in a hospital for medical treatment.

Section 36(1)

A person suffering from mental illness or severe mental impairment of a type and severity such that it is appropriate for him/her to be detained for treatment may be sent to hospital by the Crown Court instead of being remanded in custody. (See also the power of the Home Secretary under s.48.) The power may not be exercised in respect of persons with only psychopathic disorder or mental impairment.

One of the two doctors providing evidence must be s.12 approved (see s.54) and both may come from the hospital to which the person is to be admitted.

Note: a person detained under this section has no right to apply to a Mental Health Review Tribunal.

(2) For the purposes of this section an accused person is any person who is in custody awaiting trial before the Crown Court for an offence punishable with imprisonment (other than an offence the sentence for which is fixed by law) or who at any time before sentence is in custody in the course of a trial before that court for such an offence.

Section 36(2)
Defines an "accused person" as a person who is in custody awaiting trial or sentence or being tried for an offence which may be punished by imprisonment. The power under this section <u>may not</u> be exercised in relation to a person who is awaiting <u>either</u> trial or sentence for murder.

(3) The court shall not remand an accused person under this section to a hospital unless it is satisfied, on the written or oral evidence of the registered medical practitioner who would be in charge of his treatment or of some other person representing the managers of the hospital, that arrangements have been made for his admission to that hospital and for his admission to it within the period of seven days beginning with the date of the remand; and if the court is so satisfied it may, pending his admission, give directions for his conveyance to and detention in a place of safety.

Section 36(3)
Before making an order the court must first be satisfied that arrangements have been made for the person's admission to the hospital within seven days and may give directions for him/her to be taken to and detained in a place of safety pending his/her admission.

Note: for an adult, a "place of safety" is a police station, prison, remand centre or any hospital which can temporarily accommodate him/her. For a child or young person, i.e. person under 18, it is a community home provided by a local authority or a controlled community home, a police station or any hospital, surgery or other suitable place whose occupier is willing temporarily to accommodate him/her.

(4) Where a court has remanded an accused person under this section it may further remand him if it appears to the court, on the written or oral evidence of the responsible medical officer, that a further remand is warranted.

Section 36(4)
Is self explanatory.

Note: s/he must still be suffering from mental illness or severe mental impairment of the required nature or degree.

(5) The power of further remanding an accused person under this section may be exercised by the court without his being brought before the court if he is represented by counsel or a solicitor and his counsel or solicitor is given an opportunity of being heard.

Section 36(5)

The extension can be made in the person's absence, if s/he has a legal representative present who is given an opportunity to speak on his/her behalf.

(6) An accused person shall not be remanded or further remanded under this section for more than 28 days at a time or for more than 12 weeks in all; and the court may at any time terminate the remand if it appears to the court that it is appropriate to do so.

Section 36(6)

There is a limit of twelve weeks' total detention, with the court being able to remand for no more than 28 days at a time. Where appropriate, the court may terminate the detention at any time. The court will depend upon being informed by the relevant doctor of a change in circumstances justifying a termination of the detention.

Note: the Crime (Sentences) Act 1997 had made provision for the time spent in hospital to count as part of any sentence of imprisonment and for the person to earn time off any sentence of imprisonment for good behaviour. However, the relevant sections of that Act have been repealed without ever coming into force.[28]

[28] s.8 and ss10-27 of the Crime (Sentences) Act 1997 were repealed by the Crime and Disorder Act 1998, ss107(2), 120(2), Sch 10 on 30 September 1998.

(7) An accused person remanded to hospital under this section shall be entitled to obtain at his own expense an independent report on his mental condition from a registered medical practitioner chosen by him and to apply to the court on the basis of it for his remand to be terminated under subsection (6) above.

Section 36(7)

A person detained under this section may obtain his/her own medical report and thereafter apply for his/her detention to be terminated.

Note: the Code of Practice (1999 ed.) makes clear at 17.1 that hospital managers should help people to exercise this right by enabling them to contact a suitably qualified and experienced solicitor or other adviser.

(8) Subsections (9) and (10) of section 35 above shall have effect in relation to a remand under this section as they have effect in relation to a remand under that section.

Section 36(8)

The person must be taken to and admitted to the hospital within seven days, including the day the order is made. Once the order is made the hospital cannot refuse to admit him/her.

Any police officer has a power to arrest without warrant a person who absconds from detention under this section. The person must then be brought before the court as soon as practicable and the court may proceed as if a remand under this section had not been made.

Note: by virtue of s.56(1) a person remanded under this section is subject to the provisions of Part IV of the Act (consent to treatment).

The RMO may not grant him/her leave of absence under s.17 nor transfer him/her to another hospital: s/he remains under the control of the court that sent him/her to hospital. The hospital is responsible for returning the person to court when required, but may ask for help from the police where necessary (see the Code of Practice (1999 ed.), at 29.6).

HOSPITAL AND GUARDIANSHIP ORDERS

37. Powers of courts to order hospital admission or guardianship

(1) Where a person is convicted before the Crown Court of an offence punishable with imprisonment other than an offence the sentence for which is fixed by law or falls to be imposed under section 2(2) of the Crime (Sentences) Act 1997, or is convicted by a magistrates' court of an offence punishable on summary conviction with imprisonment, and the conditions mentioned in subsection (2) below are satisfied, the court may by order authorise his admission to and detention in such hospital as may be specified in the order or, as the case may be, place him under the guardianship of a local social services authority or of such other person approved by a local social services authority as may be so specified.

Section 37(1)

Hospital and guardianship orders are available as an alternative to imprisonment, except where the person has been convicted of murder or a "second serious offence", e.g. attempted murder, manslaughter, rape, wounding or causing grievous bodily arm with intent, robbery with a firearm.[29]

Note: where a hospital order is made the court's involvement with the person effectively comes to an end and s/he becomes subject only to the hospital regime.

The duration of his/her detention will be determined in accordance with s.20, s/he will have a right to apply to a Mental Health Review Tribunal (see s.69(1)), the consent to treatment provisions in Part IV of the Act will apply to his/her detention, s/he may be given leave of absence by the RMO under s.17, and s/he will be entitled to aftercare services under s.117 when discharged. His/her nearest relative will not, however, have power to discharge him/her under s.23(2).

[29]See s.2 Crime (Sentences) Act 1997 for a full list.

A guardianship order under this section is similar in effect to Part II guardianship, although the nearest relative does not have a power of discharge (see s.40(4)). The person under guardianship has a right to apply to a Mental Health Review Tribunal (see s.69(1)).

(1A) In the case of an offence the sentence for which would otherwise fall to be imposed under subsection (2) of section 3 or 4 of the Crime (Sentences) Act 1997, nothing in that subsection shall prevent a court from making an order under subsection (1) above for the admission of the offender to a hospital.

Section 37(1A)
ss3 and 4 Crime (Sentences) Act 1997 lay down minimum sentences for a person convicted of a third offence of class A drug trafficking (s.3) and a third offence of domestic burglary (s.4). Hospital and guardianship orders under this section are available where one of these prescribed minimum sentences would otherwise be imposed.

Note: s.4 Crime (Sentences) Act 1997 is not in force at the time of publication.

(2) The conditions referred to in subsection (1) above are that–
  (a) the court is satisfied, on the written or oral evidence of two registered medical practitioners, that the offender is suffering from mental illness, psychopathic disorder, severe mental impairment or mental impairment and that either–
    (i) the mental disorder from which the offender is suffering is of a nature or degree which makes it appropriate for him to be detained in a hospital for medical treatment and, in the case of psychopathic disorder or mental impairment, that such treatment is likely to alleviate or prevent a deterioration of his condition; or
    (ii) in the case of an offender who has attained the age of 16 years, the mental disorder is of a nature or degree which warrants his reception into guardianship under this Act; and
  (b) the court is of the opinion, having regard to all the circumstances including the nature of the offence and the character and antecedents of the offender, and to the other available methods of dealing with him, that the most suitable method of disposing of the case is by means of an order under this section.

Section 37(2)

(a)   *One of the doctors must be s.12 approved (see s.54) and both may come from the hospital to which the person is to be admitted. The person must <u>currently be suffering</u> from one of the four forms of mental disorder <u>and either</u> (i) or (ii) must apply.*

(i)   *The disorder must be of the required nature or degree. A further requirement of "treatability" applies in relation to psychopathic disorder and mental impairment.*

(ii)   *Is self explanatory.*

(b)   *A hospital or guardianship order is the most suitable disposal in all circumstances.*

Note: courts other than magistrates' courts may make a hospital or guardianship order under this section where they are dealing with a person in relation to a contempt of court for which s/he could be committed to prison, if s/he is suffering from mental illness or severe mental impairment.[30]

A magistrates' court may make a hospital or guardianship order under this section where a person who is suffering from mental illness or severe mental impairment could otherwise be committed to custody for breach of an occupation order, a non-molestation order, or an exclusion requirement included in an interim care order or an emergency protection order.[31]

---

[30]s.14(4) Contempt of Court Act 1981.
[31]s.51 Family Law Act 1996.

(3) Where a person is charged before a magistrates' court with any act or omission as an offence and the court would have power, on convicting him of that offence, to make an order under subsection (1) above in his case as being a person suffering from mental illness or severe mental impairment, then, if the court is satisfied that the accused did the act or made the omission charged, the court may, if it thinks fit, make such an order without convicting him.

Section 37(3)

A magistrates' court may also exercise the powers under this section without convicting a person of a relevant offence, where s/he is suffering from mental illness or severe mental impairment and they are satisfied that s/he did the act in relation to which s/he has been charged.

Note: the power under this subsection is to be used only in very rare circumstances.

(4) An order for the admission of an offender to a hospital (in this Act referred to as "a hospital order") shall not be made under this section unless the court is satisfied on the written or oral evidence of the registered medical practitioner who would be in charge of his treatment or of some other person representing the managers of the

hospital that arrangements have been made for his admission to that hospital . . ., and for his admission to it within the period of 28 days beginning with the date of the making of such an order; and the court may, pending his admission within that period, give such directions as it thinks fit for his conveyance to and detention in a place of safety.

Section 37(4)

Before making a hospital order the court must first be satisfied that arrangements have been made for the person's admission to the hospital within 28 days and may give directions for him/her to be taken to and detained in a place of safety pending his/her admission.

Note: for an adult, a "place of safety" is a police station, prison, remand centre or any hospital which can temporarily accommodate him/her. For a child or young person, i.e. person under 18, it is a community home provided by a local authority or a controlled community home, a police station or any hospital, surgery or other suitable place whose occupier is willing temporarily to accommodate him/her.

While detained at a place of safety the provisions of Part IV of the Act (consent to treatment) will not apply.

(5) If within the said period of 28 days it appears to the Secretary of State that by reason of an emergency or other special circumstances it is not practicable for the patient to be received into the hospital specified in the order, he may give directions for the admission of the patient to such other hospital as appears to be appropriate instead of the hospital so specified; and where such directions are given–

   (a) the Secretary of State shall cause the person having the custody of the patient to be informed, and

   (b) the hospital order shall have effect as if the hospital specified in the directions were substituted for the hospital specified in the order.

Section 37(5)

If, within the 28 day period, the Home Secretary considers that, because of an emergency or other special circumstance, it is not possible to admit him/her to the specified hospital, s/he can arrange admission to another hospital.

(6) An order placing an offender under the guardianship of a local social services authority or of any other person (in this Act referred to as "a guardianship order") shall not be made under this section unless the court is satisfied that that authority or person is willing to receive the offender into guardianship.

Section 37(6)
Before making a guardianship order the court must be satisfied that the prospective guardian is willing to act as guardian for the person concerned.

(7) A hospital order or guardianship order shall specify the form or forms of mental disorder referred to in subsection (2)(a) above from which, upon the evidence taken into account under that subsection, the offender is found by the court to be suffering; and no such order shall be made unless the offender is described by each of the practitioners whose evidence is taken into account under that subsection as suffering from the same one of those forms of mental disorder, whether or not he is also described by either of them as suffering from another of them.

Section 37(7)
Hospital and guardianship orders must specify the form(s) of mental disorder on which the court has relied in making the order and both doctors on whose evidence the court has relied must agree as to at least one of the forms of disorder from which the person is suffering.

(8) Where an order is made under this section, the court shall not–

    (a) pass a sentence of imprisonment, impose a fine or make a community order (within the meaning of Part I of the Criminal Justice Act 1991) in respect of the offence; or

    (b) make an order under section 58 of that Act (binding over of parent or guardian) in respect of the offender,

but may make any other order which the court has power to make apart from this section; and for the purposes of this subsection "sentence of imprisonment" includes any sentence or order for detention.

Section 37(8)
Where the court makes an order under this section its powers to use additional methods of disposal are restricted, though it may, for example, make a compensation order or an order disqualifying the person from driving.

38. Interim hospital orders

(1) Where a person is convicted before the Crown Court of an offence punishable with imprisonment (other than an offence the sentence for which is fixed by law) or is convicted by a magistrates' court of an offence punishable on summary conviction with imprisonment and the court before or by which he is convicted is satisfied, on the written or oral evidence of two registered medical practitioners–

(a) that the offender is suffering from mental illness, psychopathic disorder, severe mental impairment or mental impairment; and

(b) that there is reason to suppose that the mental disorder from which the offender is suffering is such that it may be appropriate for a hospital order to be made in his case,

the court may, before making a hospital order or dealing with him in some other way, make an order (in this Act referred to as "an interim hospital order") authorising his admission to such hospital as may be specified in the order and his detention there in accordance with this section.

Section 38(1)

Where, after convicting a person, a Crown Court or a magistrates' court is considering making a hospital order it may instead send the person to hospital for a period, for assessment to determine whether a hospital order will be appropriate. One of the doctors giving evidence to the court must be s.12 approved (see s.54).

(a)   The person must currently be suffering from one of the four forms of mental disorder.

(b)   There need only be reason to suppose that a hospital order may be appropriate.

Note: the consent to treatment provisions in Part IV of the Act will apply to his/her detention but s/he will have no right to apply to a Mental Health Review Tribunal (see s.69(1)), s/he may not be given leave of absence by the RMO under s.17 and neither the hospital nor his/her nearest relative will have power to discharge him/her.

Courts other than magistrates' courts may make an interim hospital order under this section where they are dealing with a person in relation to a contempt of court for which s/he could be committed to prison if s/he is suffering from mental illness or severe mental impairment.[32]

A magistrates' court may make an interim hospital order under this section where a person who is suffering from mental illness or severe mental impairment could otherwise be committed to custody for breach of an occupation order, a non-molestation order, or an exclusion requirement included in an interim care order or an emergency protection order.[33]

[32] s.14(4) Contempt of Court Act 1981.
[33] s.51 Family Law Act 1996.

(2) In the case of an offender who is subject to an interim hospital order the court may make a hospital order without his being brought before the court if he is represented by counsel or a solicitor and his counsel or solicitor is given an opportunity of being heard.

> ### Section 38(2)
> *Once an interim hospital order has been made, the court can make a full hospital order in the person's absence provided that s/he has a legal representative present who is given a chance to speak on his/her behalf.*

(3) At least one of the registered medical practitioners whose evidence is taken into account under subsection (1) above shall be employed at the hospital which is to be specified in the order.

> ### Section 38(3)
> *One of the doctors must work at the specified hospital; both of them may do so.*

(4) An interim hospital order shall not be made for the admission of an offender to a hospital unless the court is satisfied, on the written or oral evidence of the registered medical practitioner who would be in charge of his treatment or of some other person representing the managers of the hospital, that arrangements have been made for his admission to that hospital and for his admission to it within the period of 28 days beginning with the date of the order; and if the court is so satisfied the court may, pending his admission, give directions for his conveyance to and detention in a place of safety.

> ### Section 38(4)
> *Before making an interim hospital order the court must first be satisfied that arrangements have been made for the person's admission to the hospital within 28 days and may give directions for him/her to be taken to and detained in a place of safety pending his/her admission.*
>
> Note: for an adult, a "place of safety" is a police station, prison, remand centre or any hospital which can temporarily accommodate him/her. For a child or young person, i.e. person under 18, it is a community home provided by a local authority or a controlled community home, a police station or any hospital, surgery or other suitable place whose occupier is willing temporarily to accommodate him/her.
>
> While detained at a place of safety under this section the provisions of Part IV of the Act (consent to treatment) will apply.

(5) An interim hospital order–

    (a) shall be in force for such period, not exceeding 12 weeks, as the court may specify when making the order; but

(b) may be renewed for further periods of not more than 28 days at a time if it appears to the court, on the written or oral evidence of the responsible medical officer, that the continuation of the order is warranted;

but no such order shall continue in force for more than twelve months in all and the court shall terminate the order if it makes a hospital order in respect of the offender or decides after considering the written or oral evidence of the responsible medical officer to deal with the offender in some other way.

Section 38(5)

(a) The court must specify how long the order is to last, the limit being twelve weeks.

(b) The court may renew the order for up to 28 days at a time where the RMO states that this is warranted. The person must still be suffering from one of the four forms of mental disorder and the court must still be satisfied that there is reason to suppose that a hospital order may be appropriate.

There is a limit of twelve months' total detention under an interim hospital order. The court must terminate the interim hospital order if it subsequently makes a hospital order or decides, after considering the RMO's view, that a hospital order is not appropriate.

Note: the Crime (Sentences) Act 1997 had made provision for the time spent in hospital to count as part of any sentence of imprisonment and for the person to earn time off any sentence of imprisonment for good behaviour. However, the relevant sections of that Act have been repealed without ever coming into force.[34]

The hospital is responsible for returning the person to court when required, but may ask for help from the police where necessary (see the Code of Practice (1999 ed.), at 29.6).

---

[34]s.8 and ss10-27 of the Crime (Sentences) Act 1997 were repealed by the Crime and Disorder Act 1998, ss107(2), 120(2), Sch 10 on 30 September 1998.

---

(6) The power of renewing an interim hospital order may be exercised without the offender being brought before the court if he is represented by counsel or a solicitor and his counsel or solicitor is given an opportunity of being heard.

Section 38(6)

The order can be renewed in the person's absence, if s/he has a legal representative present who is given an opportunity to speak on his/her behalf.

---

(7) If an offender absconds from a hospital in which he is detained in pursuance of an interim hospital order, or while being conveyed to or from such a hospital, he may be arrested without warrant by a constable and shall, after being arrested, be brought as soon as practicable before the court that made the order; and the court may thereupon terminate the order and deal with him in any way in which it could have dealt with him if no such order had been made.

Section 38(7)
Any police officer has a power to arrest without warrant a person who absconds from detention under this section. The person must be brought before the court as soon as practicable and the court may then terminate the interim hospital order and proceed as if it had not been made.

39. Information as to hospitals

(1) Where a court is minded to make a hospital order or interim hospital order in respect of any person it may request–

    (a) the Health Authority for the area in which that person resides or last resided; or

    (b) any other Health Authority that appears to the court to be appropriate,

    to furnish the court with such information as that Health Authority have or can reasonably obtain with respect to the hospital or hospitals (if any) in their area or elsewhere at which arrangements could be made for the admission of that person in pursuance of the order, and that Health Authority shall comply with any such request.

Section 39(1)
Where a court is inclined to make a hospital or an interim hospital order, or a hospital direction and a limitation direction[35], it may request any appropriate Health Authority to provide information as to availability of beds at hospitals within its area or elsewhere. Health Authorities must supply the information and should be in a position to do so promptly.

Note: subsection (2) has been repealed.

[35]See s.45A(8).

39A. Information to facilitate guardianship orders

Where a court is minded to make a guardianship order in respect of any offender, it may request the local social services authority for the area in which the offender resides or last resided, or any other local social services authority that appears to the court to be appropriate–

    (a) to inform the court whether it or any other person approved by it is willing to receive the offender into guardianship; and

    (b) if so, to give such information as it reasonably can about how it or the other person could be expected to exercise in relation to the offender the powers conferred by section 40(2) below;

and that authority shall comply with any such request.

Section 39A

Where a court is inclined to make a guardianship order it may request any appropriate local social services authority to:

(a)   tell the court whether it or some person approved by it is willing to act as guardian for the person concerned; and

(b)   give reasonable information about how it or the other person could be expected to exercise the relevant powers of a guardian i.e. under s.8(1). The authorities are obliged to comply with such a request.

40. Effect of hospital orders, guardianship orders and interim hospital orders

(1) A hospital order shall be sufficient authority–

(a) for a constable, an approved social worker or any other person directed to do so by the court to convey the patient to the hospital specified in the order within a period of 28 days; and

(b) for the managers of the hospital to admit him at any time within that period and thereafter detain him in accordance with the provisions of this Act.

Section 40(1)

A hospital order gives authority:

(a)   to police officers, ASWs or other people specified by the court to take the person to the specified hospital within 28 days; and

(b)   to the hospital managers to admit and detain him/her in accordance with the Act.

(2) A guardianship order shall confer on the authority or person named in the order as guardian the same powers as a guardianship application made and accepted under Part II of this Act.

Section 40(2)

A guardianship order gives the guardian the same powers as are granted under Part II i.e. to require the person to live in a place specified and to attend for treatment, work, education or training at a place specified, and to require access to the person to be given to any doctor, ASW or other person specified by the guardians (see s.8(1)).

(3) Where an interim hospital order is made in respect of an offender–

(a) a constable or any other person directed to do so by the court shall convey the offender to the hospital specified in the order within the period mentioned in section 38(4) above; and

(b) the managers of the hospital shall admit him within that period and thereafter detain him in accordance with the provisions of section 38 above.

Section 40(3)

Where an interim hospital order is made:

(a) *a police officer or any other person instructed by the court must take the person to the specified hospital within 28 days; and*

(b) *the hospital managers must admit him/her within that period and detain him/her in accordance with the provisions of s.38.*

(4) A patient who is admitted to a hospital in pursuance of a hospital order, or placed under guardianship by a guardianship order, shall, subject to the provisions of this subsection, be treated for the purposes of the provisions of this Act mentioned in Part I of Schedule 1 to this Act as if he had been so admitted or placed on the date of the order in pursuance of an application for admission for treatment or a guardianship application, as the case may be, duly made under Part II of this Act, but subject to any modifications of those provisions specified in that Part of that Schedule.

Section 40(4)

Part I of Schedule 1 to the Act applies many of the provisions from Part II of the Act to persons subject to hospital and guardianship orders under s.37, so that they are treated, for the most part, as if they were detained or subject to guardianship under the civil sections of the Act. Some of the provisions are applied with no modification; for the others, the changes are set out in full in Part I of Schedule 1 and are, in the main, simply to give consistency of reference between criminal and civil provisions.

Note: the most significant differences are as follows:

(1) for a person subject to a hospital order, his/her nearest relative cannot order his/her discharge under s.23, and s/he cannot apply to a Mental Health Review Tribunal until the second six months of his/her detention;

(2) for a person subject to a s.37 guardianship order, his/her nearest relative cannot order his/her discharge from guardianship under s.23.

(5) Where a patient is admitted to a hospital in pursuance of a hospital order, or placed under guardianship by a guardianship order, any previous application, hospital order or guardianship order by virtue of which he was liable to be detained in a hospital or subject to guardianship shall cease to have effect; but if the first-mentioned order, or the conviction on which it was made, is quashed on appeal, this subsection shall not apply and section 22 above shall have effect as if during any period for which the patient was liable to be detained or subject to guardianship under the order, he had been detained in custody as mentioned in that section.

> **Section 40(5)**
> *The effect of admitting a person to hospital under a hospital order, or placing him/her under guardianship, is that any earlier application (under Part II of the Act), or earlier hospital or guardianship order ceases to have effect. However, if the later order, or the conviction that led to it, is quashed on appeal, the earlier order comes back into operation; s.22 then applies and the period during which the person was subject to the order that has been quashed is treated as if it had been a period of detention in custody.*

(6) Where–

   (a) a patient admitted to a hospital in pursuance of a hospital order is absent without leave;

   (b) a warrant to arrest him has been issued under section 72 of the Criminal Justice Act 1967; and

   (c) he is held pursuant to the warrant in any country or territory other than the United Kingdom, any of the Channel Islands and the Isle of Man,

he shall be treated as having been taken into custody under section 18 above on first being so held.

> **Section 40(6)**
> *Where a person has absconded from hospital, has been arrested pursuant to a warrant and is held abroad, the provisions in s.18, in relation to return and readmission of patients, apply to him/her. Time runs under s.18 from the time s/he was first held under the warrant.*

RESTRICTION ORDERS

41. Power of higher courts to restrict discharge from hospital

(1) Where a hospital order is made in respect of an offender by the Crown Court, and it appears to the court, having regard to the nature of the offence, the antecedents of the offender and the risk of his committing further offences if set at large, that it is necessary for the protection of the public from serious harm so to do, the court may, subject to the provisions of this section, further order that the offender shall be subject to the special restrictions set out in this section, either without limit of time or during such period as may be specified in the order; and an order under this section shall be known as "a restriction order".

Section 41(1)

A Crown Court which has made a hospital order may impose special restrictions on the person's discharge in accordance with the section, where it considers that this is <u>necessary</u> to protect the public from <u>serious harm</u>. The order can be for an unlimited period of time (which is usual), or for such period as the court specifies.

Note: where a restriction order is made the court may, as well as specifying the hospital at which the person is to be detained, specify a unit within the hospital. The person must then be detained in that unit.[36]

[36]s.47(1) Crime (Sentences) Act 1997.

(2) A restriction order shall not be made in the case of any person unless at least one of the registered medical practitioners whose evidence is taken into account by the court under section 37(2)(a) above has given evidence orally before the court.

Section 41(2)

At least one of the doctors whose evidence the court has considered in making the hospital order under s.37(2)(a) must have given <u>oral</u> evidence to the court.

Note: the court need not follow any advice given by either doctor as to the dangerousness of the person.

(3) The special restrictions applicable to a patient in respect of whom a restriction order is in force are as follows–

  (a) none of the provisions of Part II of this Act relating to the duration, renewal and expiration of authority for the detention of patients shall apply, and the patient shall continue to be liable to be detained by virtue of the relevant hospital order until he is duly discharged under the said Part II or absolutely discharged under section 42, 73, 74 or 75 below;

  (aa) none of the provisions of Part II of this Act relating to after-care under supervision shall apply;

  (b) no application shall be made to a Mental Health Review Tribunal in respect of a patient under section 66 or 69(1) below;

  (c) the following powers shall be exercisable only with the consent of the Secretary of State, namely–

    (i) power to grant leave of absence to the patient under section 17 above;

    (ii) power to transfer the patient in pursuance of regulations under section 19 above or in pursuance of subsection (3) of that section; and

    (iii) power to order the discharge of the patient under section 23 above;

and if leave of absence is granted under the said section 17 power to recall the patient under that section shall vest in the Secretary of State as well as the responsible medical officer; and

(d) the power of the Secretary of State to recall the patient under the said section 17 and power to take the patient into custody and return him under section 18 above may be exercised at any time;

and in relation to any such patient section 40(4) above shall have effect as if it referred to Part II of Schedule 1 to this Act instead of Part I of that Schedule.

Section 41(3)

The special restrictions under a restriction order are as follows:

(a) *his/her detention need not be renewed periodically under s.20. S/he may still be detained, therefore, even after the original criteria for detaining him/her have ceased to apply;*

(aa) *s/he cannot be given a supervised discharge;*

(b) *s/he may only make an application to a Mental Health Review Tribunal under s.70 (below);*

(c) *s/he cannot be granted leave of absence, transferred or discharged without permission from the Home Secretary. Where leave of absence is granted, the Home Secretary and the RMO will have a power of recall;*

(d) *the Home Secretary can recall him/her under s.17 or have him/her taken into custody and returned to hospital under s.18 at any time. The RMO may recall him/her under s.17 up until twelve months from the first day of his/her absence on leave.*

Part II of Schedule 1 applies many of the provisions from Part II of the Act to persons subject to restriction orders. Some of the provisions are applied with no modification; for the others, the changes are set out in full in Part II of Schedule 1.

(4) A hospital order shall not cease to have effect under section 40(5) above if a restriction order in respect of the patient is in force at the material time.

Section 41(4)

Where a hospital order with a restriction order is in force at the relevant time, making a new hospital or guardianship order will not cause the earlier hospital order to cease to have effect.

(5) Where a restriction order in respect of a patient ceases to have effect while the relevant hospital order continues in force, the provisions of section 40 above and Part I of Schedule 1 to this Act shall apply to the patient as if he had been admitted to the hospital in pursuance of a hospital order (without a restriction order) made on the date on which the restriction order ceased to have effect.

Section 41(5)
If a hospital order continues after the restriction order has been lifted, the person will be treated as if s/he were subject to a hospital order beginning on the date on which the restriction order was lifted.

(6) While a person is subject to a restriction order the responsible medical officer shall at such intervals (not exceeding one year) as the Secretary of State may direct examine and report to the Secretary of State on that person; and every report shall contain such particulars as the Secretary of State may require.

Section 41(6)
The RMO must examine the person subject to a restriction order and report to the Home Secretary at least once every twelve months.

42. Powers of Secretary of State in respect of patients subject to restriction orders

(1) If the Secretary of State is satisfied that in the case of any patient a restriction order is no longer required for the protection of the public from serious harm, he may direct that the patient cease to be subject to the special restrictions set out in section 41(3) above; and where the Secretary of State so directs, the restriction order shall cease to have effect, and section 41(5) above shall apply accordingly.

Section 42(1)
The Home Secretary can remove the special restrictions at any time if s/he is satisfied that they are no longer necessary to protect the public from serious harm. The person will then be treated as if s/he were subject to a hospital order beginning on the date on which the restriction order was lifted (under s.41(5)).

(2) At any time while a restriction order is in force in respect of a patient, the Secretary of State may, if he thinks fit, by warrant discharge the patient from hospital, either absolutely or subject to conditions; and where a person is absolutely discharged under this subsection, he shall thereupon cease to be liable to be detained by virtue of the relevant hospital order, and the restriction order shall cease to have effect accordingly.

Section 42(2)

While a restriction order is in force, the Home Secretary can discharge the person from hospital, either absolutely or subject to conditions. An absolute discharge means that the person ceases to be liable to detention under the hospital order: the restriction order then also ceases to have effect.

Note: a person who has been conditionally discharged may make an application to a Mental Health Review Tribunal (see s.75(2)). The consent to treatment provisions in Part IV of the Act will not apply to him/her (unless s/he is recalled), but one of the conditions of his/her discharge may be that s/he take medication.

(3) The Secretary of State may at any time during the continuance in force of a restriction order in respect of a patient who has been conditionally discharged under subsection (2) above by warrant recall the patient to such hospital as may be specified in the warrant.

Section 42(3)

If the person is conditionally discharged, and so long as the restriction order continues in force, the Home Secretary can at any time recall the person to hospital (which need not be the hospital from which s/he was discharged.) There is no need for the person to have breached the conditions of his/her discharge; there should, however, be medical evidence to show that at the time of recall the person is suffering from mental disorder.[37]

Note: one of the conditions imposed on discharge will usually be that the person have a social and/or medical supervisor, who should report to the Home Secretary where something occurs which would be likely to necessitate recall under this section. Chapter 29 of the Code of Practice (1999 ed.) gives guidance on supervised discharge.

[37]Kay v United Kingdom (1998) 40 BMLR 20.

(4) Where a patient is recalled as mentioned in subsection (3) above-

(a) if the hospital specified in the warrant is not the hospital from which the patient was conditionally discharged, the hospital order and the restriction order shall have effect as if the hospital specified in the warrant were substituted for the hospital specified in the hospital order;

(b) in any case, the patient shall be treated for the purposes of section 18 above as if he had absented himself without leave from the hospital specified in the warrant, and, if the restriction order was made for a specified period, that period shall not in any event expire until the patient returns to the hospital or is returned to the hospital under that section.

Section 42(4)(a)
If the person is recalled to a different hospital, the new hospital is effectively substituted into the original hospital order and restriction order.

Section 42(4)(b)
Where a person has been recalled, s/he will be treated as if s/he had been absent without leave and may be taken into custody and taken to a hospital in accordance with, and subject to the time limits contained in, s.18. His/her liability to be detained will not cease at any time between the issuing of the recall and his/her return to hospital.

(5) If a restriction order in respect of a patient ceases to have effect after the patient has been conditionally discharged under this section, the patient shall, unless previously recalled under subsection (3) above, be deemed to be absolutely discharged on the date when the order ceases to have effect, and shall cease to be liable to be detained by virtue of the relevant hospital order accordingly.

Section 42(5)
If after being conditionally discharged a restriction order expires, and the person has not been recalled under subsection (3), s/he will be deemed to have been absolutely discharged, and will therefore no longer be liable to detention under the hospital order.

(6) The Secretary of State may, if satisfied that the attendance at any place in Great Britain of a patient who is subject to a restriction order is desirable in the interests of justice or for the purposes of any public inquiry, direct him to be taken to that place; and where a patient is directed under this subsection to be taken to any place he shall, unless the Secretary of State otherwise directs, be kept in custody while being so taken, while at that place and while being taken back to the hospital in which he is liable to be detained.

Section 42(6)
The Home Secretary can have the person taken to any place in Great Britain in the interests of justice or for the purpose of any public inquiry. S/he will remain in custody at all times.

43. Power of magistrates' courts to commit for restriction order

(1) If in the case of a person of or over the age of 14 years who is convicted by a magistrates' court of an offence punishable on summary conviction with imprisonment-

(a) the conditions which under section 37(1) above are required to be satisfied for the making of a hospital order are satisfied in respect of the offender; but

(b) it appears to the court, having regard to the nature of the offence, the antecedents of the offender and the risk of his committing further offences if set at large, that if a hospital order is made a restriction order should also be made,

the court may, instead of making a hospital order or dealing with him in any other manner, commit him in custody to the Crown Court to be dealt with in respect of the offence.

Section 43(1)

The magistrates' court has no power to make a restriction order. Thus, where a magistrates' court convicts someone of at least 14 years of age of an imprisonable offence and could make a hospital order, but considers that a restriction order should also be made, it can send the person to the Crown Court to be dealt with for the offence.

(2) Where an offender is committed to the Crown Court under this section, the Crown Court shall inquire into the circumstances of the case and may-

(a) if that court would have power so to do under the foregoing provisions of this Part of this Act upon the conviction of the offender before that court of such an offence as is described in section 37(1) above, make a hospital order in his case, with or without a restriction order;

(b) if the court does not make such an order, deal with the offender in any other manner in which the magistrates' court might have dealt with him.

Section 43(2)

The Crown Court can then either make a hospital order, with or without restrictions, or take any other action that the magistrates' court would have had power to take.

(3) The Crown Court shall have the same power to make orders under sections 35, 36 and 38 above in the case of a person committed to the court under this section as the Crown Court has under those sections in the case of an accused person within the meaning of section 35 or 36 above or of a person convicted before that court as mentioned in section 38 above.

Section 43(3)

Where a person is sent to the Crown Court under this section, the Court also has power to send him/her to hospital for a report on his/her mental condition (s.35) or for treatment (s.36) or to make an interim hospital order (s.38).

(4) The power of a magistrates' court under section 38 of the Magistrates' Courts Act 1980 (which enables such a court to commit an offender to the Crown Court where the court is of the opinion that greater punishment should be inflicted for the offence than the court has power to inflict) shall also be exercisable by a magistrates' court where it is of the opinion that greater punishment should be inflicted as aforesaid on the offender unless a hospital order is made in his case with a restriction order.

Section 43(4)

The magistrates' court has a general power to send offenders to the Crown Court where it considers that greater punishment should be given than its own powers of sentencing permit; the Crown Court can then sentence as it sees fit. The magistrates' court can also exercise this power where it considers that, unless the person is made the subject of a hospital order and a restriction order, greater punishment should be given than its powers permit.

(5) The power of the Crown Court to make a hospital order, with or without a restriction order, in the case of a person convicted before that court of an offence may, in the same circumstances and subject to the same conditions, be exercised by such a court in the case of a person committed to the court under section 5 of the Vagrancy Act 1824 (which provides for the committal to the Crown Court of persons who are incorrigible rogues within the meaning of that section).

Section 43(5)

Where someone is committed to the Crown Court as being an "incorrigible rogue" under the Vagrancy Act 1824 the Crown Court has power to make a hospital order, with or without restrictions, in the same way as under ss37 and 41.

Note: an "incorrigible rogue" is someone convicted for the second time of, amongst other offences, flashing, displaying injuries or physical deformities to assist begging or collecting charitable contributions under false pretences.

44. Committal to hospital under s 43

(1) Where an offender is committed under section 43(1) above and the magistrates' court by which he is committed is satisfied on written or oral evidence that arrangements have been made for the admission of the offender to a hospital in the event of an order being made under this section, the court may, instead of committing him in custody, by order direct him to be admitted to that hospital, specifying it, and to be detained there until the case is disposed of by the Crown Court, and may give such directions as it thinks fit for his production from the hospital to attend the Crown Court by which his case is to be dealt with.

Section 44(1)
The magistrates have a power, instead of committing a person to custody when sending him/her to the Crown Court for sentencing, to have him/her admitted to hospital instead, until such time as the Crown Court can deal with him/her. They must first be satisfied, on written or oral evidence, that arrangements have been made for his/her admission.

(2) The evidence required by subsection (1) above shall be given by the registered medical practitioner who would be in charge of the offender's treatment or by some other person representing the managers of the hospital in question.

Section 44(2)
The evidence must be given by the doctor who is to be in charge of the person's treatment or by a person representing the hospital managers.

(3) The power to give directions under section 37(4) above, section 37(5) above and section 40(1) above shall apply in relation to an order under this section as they apply in relation to a hospital order, but as if references to the period of 28 days mentioned in section 40(1) above were omitted; and subject as aforesaid an order under this section shall, until the offender's case is disposed of by the Crown Court, have the same effect as a hospital order together with a restriction order, made without limitation of time.

Section 44(3)
When making an order under this section the magistrates' court can give directions for conveying the person to and detaining him/her in a place of safety (see s.37(4)), sending him/her in an emergency to a hospital other than that specified in the order (see s.37(5)) and conveying him/her to the specified hospital at any time (see s.40(1)). Until the person comes before the Crown Court, the order has the same effect as a hospital order together with a restriction order with no time limit.

Note: the court should send to the hospital any information it has that is likely to assist in the person's treatment until s/he is dealt with by the Crown Court. After admission to hospital a person with mental illness or severe mental impairment can be made the subject of a hospital order, with or without restrictions, without being brought before the court (see s.51(5) and (6) below).

The hospital is responsible for returning the person to court when required, but may ask for help from the police where necessary (see the Code of Practice (1999 ed.), at 29.6).

45. Appeals from magistrates' courts

(1) Where on the trial of an information charging a person with an offence a magistrates' court makes a hospital order or guardianship order in respect of him without convicting him, he shall have the same right of appeal against the order as if it had been made on his conviction; and on any such appeal the Crown Court shall have the same powers as if the appeal had been against both conviction and sentence.

Section 45(1)

If a person has been made the subject of a hospital or guardianship order by the magistrates' court without being convicted of any offence, s/he has the usual right of appeal to the Crown Court as if the order had been made after his/her being convicted. The Crown Court will then proceed as if the appeal was against conviction and sentence, and will therefore completely rehear the case.

(2) An appeal by a child or young person with respect to whom any such order has been made, whether the appeal is against the order or against the finding upon which the order was made, may be brought by him or by his parent or guardian on his behalf.

Section 45(2)

An appeal against a hospital order, a guardianship order or a finding upon which such an order has been made, in respect of a person under the age of 18, may be brought by that person or on his/her behalf by a parent or guardian (within the ordinary meaning of the word, not a Mental Health Act guardian).

HOSPITAL AND LIMITATION DIRECTIONS

45A. Power of higher courts to direct hospital admission

This section creates a power to make a "hybrid order", enabling the Crown Court to order that a person for whom imprisonment is appropriate receive a prison sentence but also be taken to hospital at once for medical treatment.

(1) This section applies where, in the case of a person convicted before the Crown Court of an offence the sentence for which is not fixed by law-

  (a) the conditions mentioned in subsection (2) below are fulfilled; and
  (b) except where the offence is one the sentence for which falls to be imposed under section 2 of the Crime (Sentences) Act 1997, the court considers making a hospital order in respect of him before deciding to impose a sentence of imprisonment ("the relevant sentence") in respect of the offence.

Section 45A(1)
The power to make a hybrid order applies in the case of a person convicted of an offence other than murder, where

(a)   s/he is suffering from "treatable" psychopathic disorder (see subsection (2)); and

(b)   either:

    (i)   the court has decided to impose a sentence of imprisonment but, before doing so, has considered making a hospital order; or

    (ii)   the sentence is a mandatory life sentence for a "second serious offence", such as attempted murder, manslaughter, rape, wounding or causing grievous bodily arm with intent, robbery with a firearm.[38]

[38]See s.2 Crime (Sentences) Act 1997 for a full list.

(2) The conditions referred to in subsection (1) above are that the court is satisfied, on the written or oral evidence of two registered medical practitioners-

    (a) that the offender is suffering from psychopathic disorder;

    (b) that the mental disorder from which the offender is suffering is of a nature or degree which makes it appropriate for him to be detained in a hospital for medical treatment; and

    (c) that such treatment is likely to alleviate or prevent a deterioration of his condition.

Section 45A(2)
One of the doctors must be s.12 approved (see s.54) and both may be on the staff of the hospital to which the person is to be admitted. Hybrid orders can be used <u>only</u> in cases of <u>psychopathic disorder</u>, although the person may also be suffering from other forms of mental disorder. The "treatability" test applies (see s.3).

Note: the RMO may seek the person's transfer to prison at any time before his/her release date if further treatment is not likely to be beneficial (see the Code of Practice (1999 ed.), at 3.16).

(3) The court may give both of the following directions, namely-

    (a) a direction that, instead of being removed to and detained in a prison, the offender be removed to and detained in such hospital as may be specified in the direction (in this Act referred to as a "hospital direction"); and

    (b) a direction that the offender be subject to the special restrictions set out in section 41 above (in this Act referred to as a "limitation direction").

Section 45A(3)

A person may be given a sentence of imprisonment but be taken to hospital at once for medical treatment. Although the subsection appears to create two separate directions, in fact, a hospital direction can only be used in combination with a limitation direction.

Note: Where a hybrid order is made the court may, as well as specifying the hospital at which the person is to be detained, specify a unit within the hospital. The person must then be detained in that unit.[39]

The consent to treatment provisions in Part IV of the Act will apply to his/her detention following a hospital direction and a limitation direction. The Crime (Sentences) Act 1997 had made provision for the time spent in hospital to count as part of any sentence of imprisonment and for the person to earn time off any sentence of imprisonment for good behaviour. However, the relevant sections of that Act have been repealed without ever coming into force.[40]

[39] s.47(1) Crime (Sentences) Act 1997.
[40] s.8 and ss10-27 of the Crime (Sentences) Act 1997 were repealed by the Crime and Disorder Act 1998, ss107(2), 120(2), Sch 10 on 30 September 1998.

(4) A hospital direction and a limitation direction shall not be given in relation to an offender unless at least one of the medical practitioners whose evidence is taken into account by the court under subsection (2) above has given evidence orally before the court.

Section 45A(4)

Before making a hybrid order the court must hear oral medical evidence.

(5) A hospital direction and a limitation direction shall not be given in relation to an offender unless the court is satisfied on the written or oral evidence of the registered medical practitioner who would be in charge of his treatment, or of some other person representing the managers of the hospital that arrangements have been made-

(a) for his admission to that hospital; and
(b) for his admission to it within the period of 28 days beginning with the day of the giving of such directions;

and the court may, pending his admission within that period, give such directions as it thinks fit for his conveyance to and detention in a place of safety.

Section 45A(5)
Before making a hybrid order the court must be satisfied that arrangements have been made for the person's admission to the hospital within 28 days and may give directions for him/her to be taken to and detained in a place of safety pending his/her admission.

Note: for an adult, a "place of safety" is a police station, prison, remand centre or any hospital which can temporarily accommodate him/her. For a child or young person, i.e. person under 18, it is a community home provided by a local authority or a controlled community home, a police station or any hospital, surgery or other suitable place whose occupier is willing temporarily to accommodate him/her.

(6) If within the said period of 28 days it appears to the Secretary of State that by reason of an emergency or other special circumstances it is not practicable for the patient to be received into the hospital specified in the hospital direction, he may give instructions for the admission of the patient to such other hospital as appears to be appropriate instead of the hospital so specified.

Section 45A(6)
If within 28 days of the hybrid order being made the Home Secretary considers that, because of an emergency or other special circumstance, it is not possible to admit the person to the specified hospital, s/he can arrange admission to another hospital.

(7) Where such instructions are given-
  (a) the Secretary of State shall cause the person having the custody of the patient to be informed, and
  (b) the hospital direction shall have effect as if the hospital specified in the instructions were substituted for the hospital specified in the hospital direction.

Section 45A(7)
Is self explanatory.

(8) Section 38(1) and (5) and section 39 above shall have effect as if any reference to the making of a hospital order included a reference to the giving of a hospital direction and a limitation direction.

> **Section 45A(8)**
> *Where a Crown Court is considering making a hybrid order it may instead send the person to hospital for a period, for assessment to determine whether the directions will be appropriate i.e. the court can make an interim hospital order.*
>
> *The person must currently be suffering from one of the four forms of mental disorder and there must be reason to suppose that a hybrid order may be appropriate. The court must specify how long the order is to last, the limit being twelve weeks, and may renew the order for up to 28 days at a time where the RMO states that this is warranted, with a maximum limit of twelve months' total detention (see s.38(1) and (5)).*
>
> *The court may request any appropriate Health Authority to provide information as to hospitals within its area or elsewhere at which the person could be admitted. Health Authorities must supply the information (see s.39).*

(9) A hospital direction and a limitation direction given in relation to an offender shall have effect not only as regards the relevant sentence but also (so far as applicable) as regards any other sentence of imprisonment imposed on the same or a previous occasion.

> **Section 45A(9)**
> *Hospital and limitation directions will apply to all the prison sentences that have already been imposed on the person.*

(10) The Secretary of State may by order provide that this section shall have effect as if the reference in subsection (2) above to psychopathic disorder included a reference to a mental disorder of such other description as may be specified in the order.

> **Section 45A(10)**
> *Gives the Home Secretary a very wide power to extend hybrid orders beyond people with psychopathic disorders, not only to those with mental illness, mental impairment or severe mental impairment, but also to those with any other disorder or disability of mind.*

(11) An order made under this section may-
- (a) apply generally, or in relation to such classes of offenders or offences as may be specified in the order;
- (b) provide that any reference in this section to a sentence of imprisonment, or to a prison, shall include a reference to a custodial sentence, or to an institution, of such description as may be so specified; and
- (c) include such supplementary, incidental or consequential provisions as appear to the Secretary of State to be necessary or expedient.

Section 45A(11)
Refers to orders made by the Home Secretary under subsection 10 and is self explanatory.

45B. Effect of hospital and limitation directions

(1) A hospital direction and a limitation direction shall be sufficient authority-

   (a) for a constable or any other person directed to do so by the court to convey the patient to the hospital specified in the hospital direction within a period of 28 days; and

   (b) for the managers of the hospital to admit him at any time within that period and thereafter detain him in accordance with the provisions of this Act.

Section 45B(1)
A hybrid order gives authority:

(a)   to police officers or other people specified by the court to take the person to the specified hospital within 28 days; and

(b)   to the hospital managers to admit and detain him/her in accordance with the Act.

(2) With respect to any person-

   (a) a hospital direction shall have effect as a transfer direction; and

   (b) a limitation direction shall have effect as a restriction direction.

Section 45B(2)
For the purpose of his/her detention in hospital, a person subject to a hybrid order will be treated as if s/he had been sentenced to imprisonment and then transferred to hospital by the Home Secretary under s.47 (below) and placed under a restriction direction under s.49 (below).

Thus, if the person's need for treatment ceases before his/her sentence has expired s/he can be returned to prison under s.50 and if s/he is still in hospital when the sentence expires s/he will be entitled to be released under s.49.

(3) While a person is subject to a hospital direction and a limitation direction the responsible medical officer shall at such intervals (not exceeding one year) as the Secretary of State may direct examine and report to the Secretary of State on that person; and every report shall contain such particulars as the Secretary of State may require.

Section 45B(3)
The RMO must examine the person subject to a hybrid order and provide a report to the Home Secretary at least once every twelve months.

DETENTION DURING HER MAJESTY'S PLEASURE

46. Persons ordered to be kept in custody during Her Majesty's pleasure

(1) The Secretary of State may by warrant direct that any person who, by virtue of any enactment to which this subsection applies, is required to be kept in custody during Her Majesty's pleasure or until the directions of Her Majesty are known shall be detained in such hospital (not being a mental nursing home) as may be specified in the warrant and, where that person is not already detained in the hospital, give directions for his removal there.

Section 46(1)
Applies to service personnel who have been ordered to be detained indefinitely. The Home Secretary may direct that s/he be detained in a hospital, which may not be a mental nursing home.

(2) The enactments to which subsection (1) above applies are section 16 of the Courts-Martial (Appeals) Act 1968, section 116 of the Army Act 1955, section 116 of the Air Force Act 1955 and section 63 of the Naval Discipline Act 1957.

Section 46(2)
This section will apply where a serviceman/woman has been found by a naval, army or air force court-martial, or by the Courts-Martial Appeal Court, to be not guilty by reason of insanity or to be unfit to stand trial.

(3) A direction under this section in respect of any person shall have the same effect as a hospital order together with a restriction order, made without limitation of time; and where such a direction is given in respect of a person while he is in the hospital, he shall be deemed to be admitted in pursuance of, and on the date of, the direction.

Section 46(3)

A direction under this section has the same effect as a hospital order, with a restriction order, with no time limit. However, s.69(2)(b) gives servicemen/women detained under this section a right to make an application to a Mental Health Review Tribunal within six months of the order being made.

Note: s.46 is to be repealed, but the relevant provision (in the Armed Forces Act 1996 Schedule 7 Part III) has not at the time of publishing been brought into force.

TRANSFER TO HOSPITAL OF PRISONERS, ETC

47. Removal to hospital of persons serving sentences of imprisonment, etc

(1) If in the case of a person serving a sentence of imprisonment the Secretary of State is satisfied, by reports from at least two registered medical practitioners-

 (a) that the said person is suffering from mental illness, psychopathic disorder, severe mental impairment or mental impairment; and

 (b) that the mental disorder from which that person is suffering is of a nature or degree which makes it appropriate for him to be detained in a hospital for medical treatment and, in the case of psychopathic disorder or mental impairment, that such treatment is likely to alleviate or prevent a deterioration of his condition;

the Secretary of State may, if he is of the opinion having regard to the public interest and all the circumstances that it is expedient so to do, by warrant direct that that person be removed to and detained in such hospital . . . as may be specified in the direction; and a direction under this section shall be known as "a transfer direction".

Section 47(1)

The Home Secretary may, where s/he considers it appropriate to do so, give a "transfer direction" to have a person serving a sentence of imprisonment transferred to hospital.

Note: where a transfer direction is given with a restriction direction (under s.49) the Home Secretary may, as well as specifying the hospital at which the person is to be detained, specify a unit within the hospital. The person must then be detained in that unit.[41]

One of the doctors making the report must be s.12 approved (see s.54) and both may be on the staff of the hospital to which the person is to be admitted.

---

[41]s.47(1) Crime (Sentences) Act 1997.

(a)   *The person must be suffering from at least one of the four forms of mental disorder.*

(b)   *The disorder must be of a nature or degree warranting detention in hospital for treatment and, if s/he is suffering from psychopathic disorder or mental impairment, s/he must be likely to benefit from that treatment.*

Note: the consent to treatment provisions in Part IV of the Act will apply to his/her detention, the RMO or hospital managers may discharge him/her at any time and s/he will be entitled to aftercare services under s.117 when discharged. S/he may make an application to a Mental Health Review Tribunal (see s.69(2)(b)).

The Crime (Sentences) Act 1997 had made provision for the time spent in hospital to count as part of any sentence of imprisonment, for the person to earn time off any sentence of imprisonment for good behaviour and for a "release supervision order" to come into effect if the person was detained in hospital on the date his/her sentence would otherwise expire. However, the relevant sections of that Act have been repealed without ever coming into force.[42]

---

[42] s.8 and ss.10-27 of the Crime (Sentences) Act 1997 were repealed by the Crime and Disorder Act 1998, ss107(2), 120(2), Sch 10 on 30 September 1998.

(2) A transfer direction shall cease to have effect at the expiration of the period of 14 days beginning with the date on which it is given unless within that period the person with respect to whom it was given has been received into the hospital specified in the direction.

Section 47(2)
The person must be transferred from prison to the specified hospital within 14 days, otherwise the direction will lapse.

(3) A transfer direction with respect to any person shall have the same effect as a hospital order made in his case.

Section 47(3)
A transfer direction has the same effect as a hospital order thus ss37 and 40 apply in full.

Note: the Home Secretary can also impose restrictions under s.49 on the person's transfer, leave and discharge; in some cases s/he must do so. The Code of Practice outlines at 7.2 the responsibilities of the hospital managers and RMO to give the person specified information where restrictions are imposed.

(4) A transfer direction shall specify the form or forms of mental disorder referred to in paragraph (a) of subsection (1) above from which, upon the reports taken into account under that subsection, the patient is found by the Secretary of State to be suffering; and no such direction shall be given unless the patient is described in each of those reports as suffering from the same form of disorder, whether or not he is also described in either of them as suffering from another form.

Section 47(4)

A transfer direction must specify the form(s) of mental disorder on which the Home Secretary has relied in making the direction and both doctors on whose evidence s/he has relied must agree as to at least one of the forms of disorder from which the person is suffering.

(5) References in this Part of this Act to a person serving a sentence of imprisonment include references-

(a) to a person detained in pursuance of any sentence or order for detention made by a court in criminal proceedings (other than an order under any enactment to which section 46 above applies);

(b) to a person committed to custody under section 115(3) of the Magistrates' Courts Act 1980 (which relates to persons who fail to comply with an order to enter into recognisances to keep the peace or be of good behaviour); and

(c) to a person committed by a court to a prison or other institution to which the Prison Act 1952 applies in default of payment of any sum adjudged to be paid on his conviction.

Section 47(5)

In this Part of the Act, a "person serving a sentence of imprisonment" includes:

(a)   a person detained by order of a criminal court (except a court-martial);

(b)   a person detained for not keeping the peace or being of good behaviour after being ordered by the magistrates' court to do so;

(c)   a person detained for failure to pay fines, compensation, costs etc after being convicted.

48. Removal to hospital of other prisoners

(1) If in the case of a person to whom this section applies the Secretary of State is satisfied by the same reports as are required for the purposes of section 47 above that that person is suffering from mental illness or severe mental impairment of a nature or degree which makes it appropriate for him to be detained in a hospital for

medical treatment and that he is in urgent need of such treatment, the Secretary of State shall have the same power of giving a transfer direction in respect of him under that section as if he were serving a sentence of imprisonment.

Section 48(1)

The Home Secretary can make a transfer direction under this section, only in cases of mental illness or severe mental impairment, where the person is <u>in urgent need</u> of medical treatment for his/her mental disorder. One of the doctors reporting on the person's condition must be s.12 approved (see s.54) and both may be on the staff of the hospital to which the person is to be admitted.

Note: the Crime (Sentences) Act 1997 had made provision for the time spent in hospital to count as part of any sentence of imprisonment and for the person to earn time off any sentence of imprisonment for good behaviour. However, the relevant sections of that Act have been repealed without ever coming into force.[43]

[43] s.8 and ss10-27 of the Crime (Sentences) Act 1997 were repealed by the Crime and Disorder Act 1998, ss107(2), 120(2), Sch 10 on 30 September 1998.

(2) This section applies to the following persons, that is to say-

(a) persons detained in a prison or remand centre, not being persons serving a sentence of imprisonment or persons falling within the following paragraphs of this subsection;

(b) persons remanded in custody by a magistrates' court;

(c) civil prisoners, that is to say, persons committed by a court to prison for a limited term (including persons committed to prison in pursuance of a writ of attachment), who are not persons falling to be dealt with under section 47 above;

(d) persons detained under the Immigration Act 1971.

Section 48(2)

A transfer direction under this section can be made for certain forms of unsentenced prisoner.

(a) A person detained in a prison or remand centre who has not been sentenced and does not fall into categories (b), (c) or (d).

Note: where such a person has been transferred, the special restrictions set out in s.41 and the further provisions in s.51 will also apply. The Code of Practice (1999 ed.) outlines at 7.2 the responsibilities of the hospital managers and RMO to give the person specified information where restrictions are imposed.

(b) Is self explanatory.

Note: where such a person has been transferred, the special restrictions set out in s.41 and the further provisions in s.52 will also apply. The Code of Practice outlines at 7.2 the responsibilities of the hospital managers and RMO to give the person specified information where restrictions are imposed.

(c)   A person, other than one mentioned in s.47(5), detained in prison for a civil rather than a criminal matter.

Note: s.53 will also apply to such a person. The special restrictions set out in s.41 may be applied by the Home Secretary.

(d)   Is self explanatory.

Note: s.53 will also apply to such a person. The special restrictions set out in s.41 may be applied by the Home Secretary.

(3) Subsections (2) to (4) of section 47 above shall apply for the purposes of this section and of any transfer direction given by virtue of this section as they apply for the purposes of that section and of any transfer direction under that section.

Section 48(3)
The person must be transferred from prison to the specified hospital within 14 days, otherwise the direction will lapse. The direction must specify the form(s) of mental disorder on which the Home Secretary has relied in making the direction and both doctors on whose evidence s/he has relied must agree as to at least one of the forms of disorder from which the person is suffering.

S/he will be treated as if subject to a hospital order (see s.37 and s.40).

49. Restriction on discharge of prisoners removed to hospital

(1) Where a transfer direction is given in respect of any person, the Secretary of State, if he thinks fit, may by warrant further direct that that person shall be subject to the special restrictions set out in section 41 above; and where the Secretary of State gives a transfer direction in respect of any such person as is described in paragraph (a) or (b) of section 48(2) above, he shall also give a direction under this section applying those restrictions to him.

> **Section 49(1)**
> *Where the Home Secretary has made a transfer direction s/he can also make what is, in effect, a s.41 restriction order; for persons in the categories under s.48(2)(a) and (b), i.e. unsentenced remand prisoners, s/he __must__ do so.*
>
> Note: the Code of Practice (1999 ed.) outlines at 7.2 the responsibilities of the hospital managers and RMO to give the person specified information where restrictions are imposed.

(2) A direction under this section shall have the same effect as a restriction order made under section 41 above and shall be known as "a restriction direction".

> **Section 49(2)**
> *Is self explanatory.*
>
> Note: a transfer direction made with a restriction direction has a similar effect to a hospital order with s.41 restrictions. The main differences are created by s.50(1) and (2) below.

(3) While a person is subject to a restriction direction the responsible medical officer shall at such intervals (not exceeding one year) as the Secretary of State may direct examine and report to the Secretary of State on that person; and every report shall contain such particulars as the Secretary of State may require.

> **Section 49(3)**
> *The RMO must examine the person subject to a restriction direction and provide a report to the Home Secretary at least once every twelve months.*

50. Further provisions as to prisoners under sentence

(1) Where a transfer direction and a restriction direction have been given in respect of a person serving a sentence of imprisonment and before the expiration of that person's sentence the Secretary of State is notified by the responsible medical officer, any other registered medical practitioner or a Mental Health Review Tribunal that that person no longer requires treatment in hospital for mental disorder or that no effective treatment for his disorder can be given in the hospital to which he has been removed, the Secretary of State may-

   (a) by warrant direct that he be remitted to any prison or other institution in which he might have been detained if he had not been removed to hospital, there to be dealt with as if he had not been so removed; or

(b) exercise any power of releasing him on licence or discharging him under supervision which could have been exercisable if he had been remitted to such a prison or institution as aforesaid,

and on his arrival in the prison or other institution or, as the case may be, his release or discharge as aforesaid, the transfer direction and the restriction direction shall cease to have effect.

Section 50(1)
If the Home Secretary is informed by a doctor or a Mental Health Review Tribunal that a person who has been placed on a restriction direction either does not require treatment any more or that the hospital s/he is in cannot effectively treat him/her s/he can either:

(a) direct that the person be returned to prison to serve the rest of his/her sentence; or

(b) release him/her from hospital (on the same terms on which s/he could have been released from prison).

(2) A restriction direction in the case of a person serving a sentence of imprisonment shall cease to have effect on the expiration of the sentence.

Section 50(2)
Is self explanatory.

Note: the person will continue to be detained in hospital as under a hospital order made without restriction under s.37.

(3) Subject to subsection (4) below, references in this section to the expiration of a person's sentence are references to the expiration of the period during which he would have been liable to be detained in a prison or other institution if the transfer direction had not been given.

Section 50(3)
When calculating the time a prisoner has served towards his/her sentence, time spent in hospital following a transfer direction is treated as if it were time spent in prison.

Note: the Crime (Sentences) Act 1997 had made provision for the insertion of a subsection (3A) to this section, relating to the calculation of early release for good behaviour, but the relevant provision was repealed without ever having come into force.[44]

---

[44] Schedule 4 para 12(4) of the Crime (Sentences) Act 1997 was repealed by the Crime and Disorder Act 1998, ss119, 120(2), Sch 8 para 137, Sch 10 on 30 September 1998.

(4) For the purposes of section 49(2) of the Prison Act 1952 (which provides for discounting from the sentences of certain prisoners periods while they are unlawfully at large) a patient who, having been transferred in pursuance of a transfer direction from any such institution as is referred to in that section, is at large in circumstances in which he is liable to be taken into custody under any provision of this Act, shall be treated as unlawfully at large and absent from that institution.

> **Section 50(4)**
> *If a person is absent from hospital without leave or escapes from other lawful detention under this Act the time s/he spends at large will not count towards his/her sentence.*

(5) The preceding provisions of this section shall have effect as if-

(a) the reference in subsection (1) to a transfer direction and a restriction direction having been given in respect of a person serving a sentence of imprisonment included a reference to a hospital direction and a limitation direction having been given in respect of a person sentenced to imprisonment;

(b) the reference in subsection (2) to a restriction direction included a reference to a limitation direction; and

(c) references in subsections (3) and (4) to a transfer direction included references to a hospital direction.

> **Section 50(5)**
> *The Home Secretary's powers and the provisions of this section also apply in the same way to a person subject to a hybrid order under s.45A.*

51. Further provisions as to detained persons

(1) This section has effect where a transfer direction has been given in respect of any such person as is described in paragraph (a) of section 48(2) above and that person is in this section referred to as "the detainee".

> **Section 51(1)**
> *Applies where an unsentenced person detained in a prison or remand centre by the Crown Court and who does not fall into the categories set out in section 48(2)(b), (c) or (d) has been transferred to hospital under s.48.*

(2) The transfer direction shall cease to have effect when the detainee's case is disposed of by the court having jurisdiction to try or otherwise deal with him, but without prejudice to any power of that court to make a hospital order or other order under this Part of this Act in his case.

(3) If the Secretary of State is notified by the responsible medical officer, any other registered medical practitioner or a Mental Health Review Tribunal at any time before the detainee's case is disposed of by that court-

(a) that the detainee no longer requires treatment in hospital for mental disorder; or

(b) that no effective treatment for his disorder can be given at the hospital to which he has been removed,

the Secretary of State may by warrant direct that he be remitted to any place where he might have been detained if he had not been removed to hospital, there to be dealt with as if he had not been so removed, and on his arrival at the place to which he is so remitted the transfer direction shall cease to have effect.

(4) If (no direction having been given under subsection (3) above) the court having jurisdiction to try or otherwise deal with the detainee is satisfied on the written or oral evidence of the responsible medical officer-

(a) that the detainee no longer requires treatment in hospital for mental disorder; or

(b) that no effective treatment for his disorder can be given at the hospital to which he has been removed,

the court may order him to be remitted to any such place as is mentioned in subsection (3) above or, subject to section 25 of the Criminal Justice and Public Order Act 1994, released on bail and on his arrival at that place or, as the case may be, his release on bail the transfer direction shall cease to have effect.

Section 51(4)
If the Home Secretary does not return the person to prison under subsection (3), and the relevant court is satisfied by the RMO that the person either does not require treatment any more or that the hospital s/he is in cannot effectively treat him/her, the court can direct that the person be returned to prison or released on bail.

(5) If (no direction or order having been given or made under subsection (3) or (4) above) it appears to the court having jurisdiction to try or otherwise deal with the detainee-

(a) that it is impracticable or inappropriate to bring the detainee before the court; and

(b) that the conditions set out in subsection (6) below are satisfied,

the court may make a hospital order (with or without a restriction order) in his case in his absence and, in the case of a person awaiting trial, without convicting him.

Section 51(5)
If the person has not been returned to prison or released on bail the court may, in certain circumstances, make a hospital order in the person's absence and, if s/he has been awaiting trial, without convicting him/her. However, it must be <u>impracticable or inappropriate</u> to bring the person to court.

(6) A hospital order may be made in respect of a person under subsection (5) above if the court-

(a) is satisfied, on the written or oral evidence of at least two registered medical practitioners, that the detainee is suffering from mental illness or severe mental impairment of a nature or degree which makes it appropriate for the patient to be detained in a hospital for medical treatment; and

(b) is of the opinion, after considering any depositions or other documents required to be sent to the proper officer of the court, that it is proper to make such an order.

Section 51(6)
The court may make a hospital order in a person's absence only in the case of a person suffering from mental illness or severe mental impairment of the required nature or degree. One of the doctors giving evidence must be s.12 approved (see s.54) and both may work at the hospital.

(7) Where a person committed to the Crown Court to be dealt with under section 43 above is admitted to a hospital in pursuance of an order under section 44 above, subsections (5) and (6) above shall apply as if he were a person subject to a transfer direction.

Section 51(7)
Where a magistrates' court has sent a person's case to be dealt with by the Crown Court (because it considers a restriction order should be made) and has had the person admitted to hospital in the meantime, the Crown Court can make a hospital order under subsections (5) and (6) above as if the person were the subject of a transfer direction.

52. Further provisions as to persons remanded by magistrates' courts

(1) This section has effect where a transfer direction has been given in respect of any such person as is described in paragraph (b) of section 48(2) above; and that person is in this section referred to as "the accused".

Section 52(1)
Applies to a person who has been remanded in custody by a magistrates' court and transferred to hospital under s.48.

(2) Subject to subsection (5) below, the transfer direction shall cease to have effect on the expiration of the period of remand unless the accused is committed in custody to the Crown Court for trial or to be otherwise dealt with.

Section 52(2)
When the period for which the person was remanded comes to an end the transfer direction also ceases, unless at that time the person is committed to the Crown Court.

(3) Subject to subsection (4) below, the power of further remanding the accused under section 128 of the Magistrates' Courts Act 1980 may be exercised by the court without his being brought before the court; and if the court further remands the accused in custody (whether or not he is brought before the court) the period of remand shall, for the purposes of this section, be deemed not to have expired.

Section 52(3)
If the magistrates' court extends the remand, (which can be done in his/her absence), the transfer direction will continue in force.

(4) The court shall not under subsection (3) above further remand the accused in his/her absence unless s/he has appeared before the court within the previous six months.

> **Section 52(4)**
> *Is self explanatory.*

(5) If the magistrates' court is satisfied, on the written or oral evidence of the responsible medical officer-

  (a) that the accused no longer requires treatment in hospital for mental disorder; or
  (b) that no effective treatment for his disorder can be given in the hospital to which he has been removed,

the court may direct that the transfer direction shall cease to have effect notwithstanding that the period of remand has not expired or that the accused is committed to the Crown Court as mentioned in subsection (2) above.

> **Section 52(5)**
> *If the magistrates' court is satisfied by the RMO that the person either does not require treatment any more or that the hospital s/he is in cannot effectively treat him/her, the court can at any time bring the transfer direction to an end.*

(6) If the accused is committed to the Crown Court as mentioned in subsection (2) above and the transfer direction has not ceased to have effect under subsection (5) above, section 51 above shall apply as if the transfer direction given in his case were a direction given in respect of a person falling within that section.

> **Section 52(6)**
> *When the person is committed to the Crown Court without the transfer direction being brought to an end by the magistrates, s.51 comes into operation.*

(7) The magistrates' court may, in the absence of the accused, inquire as examining justices into an offence alleged to have been committed by him and commit him for trial in accordance with section 6 of the Magistrates' Courts Act 1980 if-

  (a) the court is satisfied, on the written or oral evidence of the responsible medical officer, that the accused is unfit to take part in the proceedings; and
  (b) where the court proceeds under subsection (1) of that section, the accused is represented by counsel or a solicitor.

> ### Section 52(7)
> *Where satisfied on the basis of the RMO's evidence that a person is unfit to take part in a court hearing, the magistrates's court can conduct committal proceedings (to send him/her to the Crown Court for trial) in his/her absence, provided that s/he has legal representation.*

53. Further provisions as to civil prisoners and persons detained under the Immigration Act 1971

(1) Subject to subsection (2) below, a transfer direction given in respect of any such person as is described in paragraph (c) or (d) of section 48(2) above shall cease to have effect on the expiration of the period during which he would, but for his removal to hospital, be liable to be detained in the place from which he was removed.

> ### Section 53(1)
> *When a civil prisoner or person detained under the Immigration Act is in hospital by virtue of a transfer direction (with no restriction direction), the direction ceases to have effect when the period for which the person was to be detained comes to an end.*

(2) Where a transfer direction and a restriction direction have been given in respect of any such person as is mentioned in subsection (1) above, then, if the Secretary of State is notified by the responsible medical officer, any other registered medical practitioner or a Mental Health Review Tribunal at any time before the expiration of the period there mentioned-

  (a) that that person no longer requires treatment in hospital for mental disorder; or
  (b) that no effective treatment for his disorder can be given in the hospital to which he has been removed,

the Secretary of State may by warrant direct that he be remitted to any place where he might have been detained if he had not been removed to hospital, and on his arrival at the place to which he is so remitted the transfer direction and the restriction direction shall cease to have effect.

> ### Section 53(2)
> *Where a transfer direction <u>and</u> a restriction direction have been given, if the Home Secretary is informed that the person either does not require treatment any more or that the hospital s/he is in cannot effectively treat him/her, s/he can direct that the person be returned to prison. When s/he arrives back in prison the transfer direction and restriction direction will then come to an end.*

SUPPLEMENTAL

54. Requirements as to medical evidence

(1) The registered medical practitioner whose evidence is taken into account under section 35(3)(a) above and at least one of the registered medical practitioners whose evidence is taken into account under sections 36(1), 37(2)(a), 38(1), 45A(2) and 51(6)(a) above and whose reports are taken into account under sections 47(1) and 48(1) above shall be a practitioner approved for the purposes of section 12 above by the Secretary of State as having special experience in the diagnosis or treatment of mental disorder.

Section 54(1)
Is self explanatory.

(2) For the purposes of any provision of this Part of this Act under which a court may act on the written evidence of-

   (a) a registered medical practitioner or a registered medical practitioner of any description; or
   (b) a person representing the managers of a hospital,

a report in writing purporting to be signed by a registered medical practitioner or a registered medical practitioner of such a description or by a person representing the managers of a hospital may, subject to the provisions of this section, be received in evidence without proof of the signature of the practitioner or that person and without proof that he has the requisite qualifications or authority or is of the requisite description; but the court may require the signatory of any such report to be called to give oral evidence.

Section 54(2)
Written evidence to a court should be by signed report: the court can accept the signed report without further proof of the identity or qualifications of the doctor. The court can require the doctor or representative of the hospital managers to attend court and give oral evidence as well.

(3) Where, in pursuance of a direction of the court, any such report is tendered in evidence otherwise than by or on behalf of the person who is the subject of the report, then-

   (a) if that person is represented by counsel or a solicitor, a copy of the report shall be given to his counsel or solicitor;

(b) if that person is not so represented, the substance of the report shall be disclosed to him or, where he is a child or young person, to his parent or guardian if present in court; and

(c) except where the report relates only to arrangements for his admission to a hospital, that person may require the signatory of the report to be called to give oral evidence, and evidence to rebut the evidence contained in the report may be called by or on behalf of that person.

> **Section 54(3)**
>
> *Applies when someone other than the (prospective) patient submits the report to the court.*
>
> *(a)   Requires a report to be given to the person's legal representative.*
>
> *(b)   Where the person has no legal representative, requires only the substance of the report to be given to the person or, where the person is under 18, to his/her parent or guardian (within the ordinary meaning of the word, not a Mental Health Act guardian).*
>
> *(c)   Unless the report is only about arrangements for admission, the (prospective) patient may insist that the maker of the report be called to give oral evidence and may also call evidence to contradict what is in the report.*

54A.   Reduction of period for making hospital orders

(1) The Secretary of State may by order reduce the length of the periods mentioned in sections 37(4) and (5) and 38(4) above.

> **Section 54A(1)**
>
> *Allows the Home Secretary to reduce the 28 day periods within which it must be possible for the person to be admitted to hospital if either a hospital order or an interim hospital order is to be made.*

(2) An order under subsection (1) above may make such consequential amendments of sections 40(1) and 44(3) above as appear to the Secretary of State to be necessary or expedient.

> **Section 54A(2)**
>
> *Is self explanatory.*

55. Interpretation of Part III

(1) In this Part of this Act-

"child" and "young person" have the same meaning as in the Children and Young Persons Act 1933;

"civil prisoner" has the meaning given to it by section 48(2)(c) above;

"guardian", in relation to a child or young person, has the same meaning as in the Children and Young Persons Act 1933;

"place of safety", in relation to a person who is not a child or young person, means any police station, prison or remand centre, or any hospital the managers of which are willing temporarily to receive him, and in relation to a child or young person has the same meaning as in the Children and Young Persons Act 1933;

"responsible medical officer", in relation to a person liable to be detained in a hospital within the meaning of Part II of this Act, means the registered medical practitioner in charge of the treatment of the patient.

Section 55(1)

"Child" — *a person under the age of 14.*

"Young person" — *a person who has attained the age of 14 years and is under the age of 18.*[45]

"Civil prisoner" — *a person detained in prison for a civil rather than a criminal matter, other than:*

   (i) a person detained for not keeping the peace or being of good behaviour after being ordered by the magistrates' court to do so;

   (ii) a person detained for failure to pay fines, compensation, costs etc after being convicted.

"Guardian" — *includes any person who, in the opinion of the relevant court, currently has the care of the child or young person.*

"Place of safety" — *for a child or young person it is a community home provided by a local authority or a controlled community home, a police station or any hospital, surgery or other suitable place whose occupier is willing temporarily to accommodate him/her.*

---

[45] The definition in s.107(1) Children and Young Persons Act 1933 used to be a person who has attained the age of 14 years and is under the age of 17 years". This was amended by the Criminal Justice Act 1991 s.68 and Sch 8 para 1(3), which came into effect on 1st October 1992.

---

(2) Any reference in this Part of this Act to an offence punishable on summary conviction with imprisonment shall be construed without regard to any prohibition or restriction imposed by or under any enactment relating to the imprisonment of young offenders.

Section 55(2)

There are special rules in relation to the sentencing of young offenders (persons under the age of 21). Where reference in Part III is made to an offence for which the magistrates' court can impose a sentence of imprisonment, it means an offence for which the court would be able to send an adult offender to prison.

(3) Where a patient who is liable to be detained in a hospital in pursuance of an order or direction under this Part of this Act is treated by virtue of any provision of this Part of this Act as if he had been admitted to the hospital in pursuance of a subsequent order or direction under this Part of this Act or a subsequent application for admission for treatment under Part II of this Act, he shall be treated as if the subsequent order, direction or application had described him as suffering from the form or forms of mental disorder specified in the earlier order or direction or, where he is treated as if he had been so admitted by virtue of a direction under section 42(1) above, such form of mental disorder as may be specified in the direction under that section.

Section 55(3)
Where a provision of Part III provides that a patient's detention is to be treated as if a subsequent order under Part III or Part II has been made, the patient will nevertheless be deemed to be suffering from the form(s) of mental disorder specified in the original order or direction.

(4) Any reference to a hospital order, a guardianship order or a restriction order in section 40(2),(4) or (5), section 41(3) to (5), or section 42 above or section 69(1) below shall be construed as including a reference to any order or direction under this Part of this Act having the same effect as the first-mentioned order; and the exceptions and modifications set out in Schedule 1 to this Act in respect of the provisions of this Act described in that Schedule accordingly include those which are consequential on the provisions of this subsection.

(5) Section 34(2) above shall apply for the purposes of this Part of this Act as it applies for the purposes of Part II of this Act.

Section 55(5)
For the purposes of Part III "hospital" includes a registered mental nursing home.

(6) References in this Part of this Act to persons serving a sentence of imprisonment shall be construed in accordance with section 47(5) above.

Section 55(6)
In this Part of the Act, a "person serving a sentence of imprisonment" includes:

(a)   a person detained by order of a criminal court (except a court-martial);

(b)   a person detained for not keeping the peace or being of good behaviour after being ordered by the magistrates' court to do so;

(c)   a person detained for failure to pay fines, compensation, costs etc after being convicted.

(7) Section 99 of the Children and Young Persons Act 1933 (which relates to the presumption and determination of age) shall apply for the purposes of this Part of this Act as it applies for the purposes of that Act.

Section 55(7)

If a child or young person's exact age is unknown, the court may make a finding as to the person's age, on the evidence available, and he will then be presumed, for the purposes of the Act, to be of that age. No order of the court will be invalidated if this is subsequently proved to have been incorrect.

PART IV CONSENT TO TREATMENT

Note: Guidance on medical treatment, consent and second opinions is given in chapters 15 and 16 of the Code of Practice (1999 ed.)

---

56. Patients to whom Part IV applies

(1) This Part of this Act applies to any patient liable to be detained under this Act except-

   (a) a patient who is liable to be detained by virtue of an emergency application and in respect of whom the second medical recommendation referred to in section 4(4)(a) above has not been given and received;

   (b) a patient who is liable to be detained by virtue of section 5(2) or (4) or 35 above or section 135 or 136 below or by virtue of a direction under section 37(4) above; and

   (c) a patient who has been conditionally discharged under section 42(2) above or section 73 or 74 below and has not been recalled to hospital.

Section 56(1)

This Part applies to all detained patients (including those on leave of absence under s.17) except:

(a)   those admitted as an emergency under s.4 where no second opinion has yet been obtained;

(b)   those detained under the short term provisions of s.5, prisoners remanded in hospital for a report (under s.35); those taken to a place of safety by the police (under s.135 or s.136) or those subject to hospital orders (under s.37);

(c)   conditionally discharged patients not recalled to hospital.

---

(2) Section 57 and, so far as relevant to that section, sections 59, 60 and 62 below, apply also to any patient who is not liable to be detained under this Act.

Section 56(2)
The safeguards (in s.57) in respect of surgical destruction of brain tissue and surgical implantation of hormones also apply to all informal patients.

57. Treatment requiring consent and a second opinion

(1) This section applies to the following forms of medical treatment for mental disorder-

(a) any surgical operation for destroying brain tissue or for destroying the functioning of brain tissue; and

(b) such other forms of treatment as may be specified for the purposes of this section by regulations made by the Secretary of State.

(2) Subject to section 62 below, a patient shall not be given any form of treatment to which this section applies unless he has consented to it and-

(a) a registered medical practitioner appointed for the purposes of this Part of this Act by the Secretary of State (not being the responsible medical officer) and two other persons appointed for the purposes of this paragraph by the Secretary of State (not being registered medical practitioners) have certified in writing that the patient is capable of understanding the nature, purpose and likely effects of the treatment in question and has consented to it; and

(b) the registered medical practitioner referred to in paragraph (a) above has certified in writing that, having regard to the likelihood of the treatment alleviating or preventing a deterioration of the patient's condition, the treatment should be given.

Section 57(1) & Section 57(2)
Neither (a) surgical destruction of brain tissue nor (b) surgical implantation of hormones reducing male sex drive [46] *may be performed unless the patient consents and a 'second opinion doctor' (who is not the RMO) and two other people who are not doctors certify in writing that the patient properly consents to that treatment and a 'second opinion doctor' certifies that the treatment would be beneficial and should be given.*

Note: this section does not apply to the administration of hormones to reduce sex drive if given either orally or by injection. However if administered over more than a three month period such treatment would come under s.58(b) below.

The 'second opinion doctor' who gives the certification and the other two non-medical persons must be appointed by the Mental Health Act commission (see s.121(2)).

[46]Mental Health (Hospital, Guardianship and Consent to Treatment) Regulations 1983 (S.I. 1983/893), reg. 16(1)(a).

(3) Before giving a certificate under subsection (2)(b) above the registered medical practitioner concerned shall consult two other persons who have been professionally concerned with the patient's medical treatment, and of those persons one shall be a nurse and the other shall be neither a nurse nor a registered medical practitioner.

> ### Section 57(3)
> *Before making this/her decision the second opinion doctor must consult two persons concerned with the patient's treatment; one must be a nurse and one must be neither a nurse nor a doctor.*

(4) Before making any regulations for the purpose of this section the Secretary of State shall consult such bodies as appear to him to be concerned.

> ### Section 57(4)
> *Requires the Secretary of State for Health to engage in consultation before making regulations in respect of treatment under this section.*

58. Treatment requiring consent or a second opinion

(1) This section applies to the following forms of medical treatment for mental disorder-

 (a) such forms of treatment as may be specified for the purposes of this section by regulations made by the Secretary of State;

 (b) the administration of medicine to a patient by any means (not being a form of treatment specified under paragraph (a) above or section 57 above) at any time during a period for which he is liable to be detained as a patient to whom this Part of this Act applies if three months or more have elapsed since the first occasion in that period when medicine was administered to him by any means for his mental disorder.

(2) The Secretary of State may by order vary the length of the period mentioned in subsection (1)(b) above.

(3) Subject to section 62 below, a patient shall not be given any form of treatment to which this section applies unless-

 (a) he has consented to that treatment and either the responsible medical officer or a registered medical practitioner appointed for the purposes of this Part of this Act by the Secretary of State has certified in writing that the patient is capable of understanding its nature, purpose and likely effects and has consented to it; or

(b) a registered medical practitioner appointed as aforesaid (not being the responsible medical officer) has certified in writing that the patient is not capable of understanding the nature, purpose and likely effects of that treatment or has not consented to it but that, having regard to the likelihood of its alleviating or preventing a deterioration of his condition, the treatment should be given.

(4) Before giving a certificate under subsection (3)(b) above the registered medical practitioner concerned shall consult two other persons who have been professionally concerned with the patient's medical treatment, and of those persons one shall be a nurse and the other shall be neither a nurse nor a registered medical practitioner.

Section 58(1)
Neither:

(a)   electroconvulsive therapy[47]*; nor*

(b)   medication, where the patient was first given medication for his/her mental disorder 3 months or more earlier in this same period of detention;

may be given unless either:

Section 58(3)
(a)   a patient with capacity consents to that treatment and the RMO or a second opinion doctor certifies this in writing; or

(b)   a second opinion doctor certifies that although the patient does not consent or lacks the capacity to consent, the treatment would be beneficial and should be given.

Section 58(4)
Before so certifying the second opinion doctor must consult two persons concerned with the patient's treatment, one must be a nurse and one must be neither a nurse nor a doctor.

Section 58(2)
Is self explanatory.

[47]Mental Health (Hospital, Guardianship and Consent to Treatment) Regulations 1983 (S.I. 1983/893), reg. 16(2)(a).

(5) Before making any regulations for the purposes of this section the Secretary of State shall consult such bodies as appear to him to be concerned.

Section 58(5)
Requires the Secretary of State for Health to engage in consultation before making regulations in respect of treatment under this section.

59. Plans of Treatment

Any consent or certificate under section 57 or 58 above may relate to a plan of treatment under which the patient is to be given (whether within a specified period or otherwise) one or more of the forms of treatment to which that section applies.

> ### Section 59
>
> *Any consent or second opinion given in respect of treatment under sections 57 and 58 above can relate to a plan of treatment involving different types of treatment which fall within that same section.*

60. Withdrawal of consent to treatment

(1) Where the consent of a patient to any treatment has been given for the purposes of section 57 or 58 above, the patient may, subject to section 62 below, at any time before the completion of the treatment withdraw his consent, and those sections shall then apply as if the remainder of the treatment were a separate form of treatment.

(2) Without prejudice to the application of subsection (1) above to any treatment given under the plan of treatment to which a patient has consented, a patient who has consented to such a plan may, subject to section 62 below, at any time withdraw his consent to further treatment, or to further treatment of any description, under the plan.

> ### Section 60(1) & 60(2)
> *A patient may withdraw his/her consent to a specific treatment or treatment plan at any time before its completion.*
> *Is s/he does so s.57 and s.58 will then apply to the remainder of the treatment or treatment plan as if the treatment were beginning afresh.*

61. Review of Treatment

(1) Where a patient is given treatment in accordance with section 57(2) or 58(3)(b) above a report on the treatment and the patient's condition shall be given by the responsible medical officer to the Secretary of State-

    (a) on the next occasion on which the responsible medical officer furnishes a report under section 20(3) or 21B(2) above renewing the authority for the detention of the patient; and

    (b) at any other time if so required by the Secretary of State.

Section 61(1)

Where any treatment is given under s.57 (psychosurgery or surgical implantation of hormones) or treatment is given without the patient's consent under s.58 (ECT or drug treatment for more than 3 months) the RMO must provide a report on the treatment and the patient's condition for the Secretary of State for Health.

A report must be provided:

(a) when detention is renewed under s.20 or s.21B (on return of a patient absent without leave); and

(b) whenever required by the Secretary of State for Health.

Note: such reports are to be provided to the Mental Health Act Commission by virtue of s.121(2)(b).

(2) In relation to a patient who is subject to a restriction order, limitation direction or restriction direction subsection (1) above shall have effect as if paragraph (a) required the report to be made-

(a) in the case of treatment in the period of six months beginning with the date of the order or direction, at the end of that period;

(b) in the case of treatment at any subsequent time, on the next occasion on which the responsible medical officer makes a report in respect of the patient under section 41(6), 45B(3) or 49(3) above.

Section 61(2)

For restricted patients, or those on restriction or limitation directions, the treatment review report must be provided:

(b) after the first six months of the restriction or limitation order/direction;

(c) annually thereafter with the yearly restricted patient report which is required in any event under s.41, s.45B and s.49.

(3) The Secretary of State may at any time give notice to the responsible medical officer directing that, subject to section 62 below, a certificate given in respect of a patient under section 57(2) or 58(3)(b) above shall not apply to treatment given to him after a date specified in the notice and sections 57 and 58 above shall then apply to any such treatment as if that certificate had not been given.

Section 61(3)

The Mental Health Act Commission (on behalf of the Secretary of State for Health) can, at any time, withdraw the second opinion doctor's certificate for the s.57 or s.58 treatment. The RMO must then stop giving the treatment.

Before treatment can reccommence the RMO must ensure that the full s.57 or s.58 requirements are met anew.

62. Urgent Treatment

(1) Sections 57 and 58 above shall not apply to any treatment-

(a) which is immediately necessary to save the patient's life; or

(b) which (not being irreversible) is immediately necessary to prevent a serious deterioration of his condition; or

(c) which (not being irreversible or hazardous) is immediately necessary to alleviate serious suffering by the patient; or

(d) which (not being irreversible or hazardous) is immediately necessary and represents the minimum interference necessary to prevent the patient from behaving violently or being a danger to himself or to others.

Section 62(1)

Treatment which usually would come under s.57 or s.58 may be given without either a second opinion or the patient's consent if the treatment is <u>immediately necessary</u> to:

(a)   save the patient's life; <u>or</u>

(b)   prevent serious deterioration of her/his condition and is not irreversible; <u>or</u>

(c)   alleviate serious suffering of the patient and is neither irreversible nor hazardous; <u>or</u>

(d)   prevent the patient acting violently or endangering him/herself or others and is neither irreversible nor hazardous.

(2) Sections 60 and 61(3) above shall not preclude the continuation of any treatment or of treatment under any plan pending compliance with section 57 or 58 above if the responsible medical officer considers that the discontinuance of the treatment or of treatment under the plan would cause serious suffering to the patient.

Section 62(2)

Withdrawal of the patient's consent or withdrawal of the second opinion doctor's approval by the Mental Health Act Commission need not prevent the RMO continuing a s.57 or s.58 treatment if to do so would cause the patient <u>serious</u> suffering.

Note: once serious suffering will no longer be caused the treatment should however cease unless and until the requirements of either s.57 or s.58 are subsequently complied with.

(3) For the purposes of this section treatment is irreversible if it has unfavourable irreversible physical or psychological consequences and hazardous if it entails significant physical hazard.

Section 62(3)

An "irreversible" treatment must also have an unfavourable physical or psychological effect. "Hazardous" refers to significant physical danger only.

63. Treatment not requiring consent

The consent of a patient shall not be required for any medical treatment given to him for the mental disorder from which he is suffering, not being treatment falling within section 57 or 58 above, if the treatment is given by or under the direction of the responsible medical officer.

Section 63

If the treatment does not fall within s.57 or s.58 and is for mental disorder it may be given without the patient's consent or any second opinion.

Note: medical treatment is defined in s.145 as including "nursing, care, habilitation and rehabilitation under medical supervision"

This includes any necessary prerequisites to the core treatment, those treatments ancillary to the core treatment, and treatment which alleviates the symptoms of mental disorder but not the underlying cause (such as the refeeding of anorexics by nasogastric tube).

Treatment for physical symptoms or a physical disorder may not be given under this section unless it is ancillary to the core treatment of the mental disorder. However the common law power to treat patients who lack capacity to consent (on the basis of necessity) remains[48].

[48]B v Croydon Health Authority [1995] 1 All ER 683.

64. Supplementary Provisions for Part IV

(1) In this Part of this Act "the responsible medical officer" means the registered medical practitioner in charge of the treatment of the patient in question and "hospital" includes a mental nursing home.

(2) Any certificate for the purposes of this Part of this Act shall be in such form as may be prescribed by regulations made by the Secretary of State.

Section 64

Is self explanatory.

PART V MENTAL HEALTH REVIEW TRIBUNALS

CONSTITUTION ETC.

65. Mental Health Review Tribunals

This section creates Mental Health Review Tribunals (MHRTs) to review decisions in relation to detained patients, patients subject to guardianship and those subject to after-care under supervision.

(1) There shall be tribunals, known as Mental Health Review Tribunals, for the purpose of dealing with applications and references by and in respect of patients under the provisions of this Act.

(1A) There shall be-

(a) one tribunal for each region of England, and

(b) one tribunal for Wales.

(1B) The Secretary of State-

(a) shall by order determine regions for the purpose of subsection (1A)(a) above; and

(b) may by order vary a region determined for that purpose;

and the Secretary of State shall act under this subsection so as to secure that the regions together comprise the whole of England.

(1C) Any order made under subsection (1B) above may make such transitional, consequential, incidental or supplemental provision as the Secretary of State considers appropriate.

Sections 65(1)& 65(1A-C)
Are self explanatory.

(2) The provisions of Schedule 2 to this Act shall have effect with respect to the constitution of Mental Health Review Tribunals.

Section 65(2)
Schedule 2 of the Act sets out provisions for the constitution of MHRTs.

(3) Subject to the provisions of Schedule 2 to this Act, and to rules made by the Lord Chancellor under this Act, the jurisdiction of a Mental Health Review Tribunal may be exercised by any three or more of its members, and references in this Act to a Mental Health Review Tribunal shall be construed accordingly.

Section 65(3)
MHRT's must comprise at least three members.

(4) The Secretary of State may pay to the members of Mental Health Review Tribunals such remuneration and allowances as he may with the consent of the Treasury determine, and defray the expenses of such tribunals to such amount as he may with the consent of the Treasury determine, and may provide for each such tribunal such officers and servants, and such accommodation, as the tribunal may require.

> **Section 65(4)**
> *Permits MHRT members to be paid for their work and have their expenses met as determined by the Secretary of State for Health with permission of the Treasury.*

APPLICATIONS AND REFERENCES CONCERNING PART II PATIENTS

66. Applications to Tribunals

(1) Where-

  (a)   a patient is admitted to a hospital in pursuance of an application for admission for assessment; or

  (b)   a patient is admitted to a hospital in pursuance of an application for admission for treatment; or

  (c)   a patient is received into guardianship in pursuance of a guardianship application; or

  (d)   a report is furnished under section 16 above in respect of a patient; or

  (e)   a patient is transferred from guardianship to a hospital in pursuance of regulations made under section 19 above; or

  (f)   a report is furnished under section 20 above in respect of a patient and the patient is not discharged; or

  (fa) a report is furnished under subsection (2) of section 21B above in respect of a patient and subsection (5) of that section applies (or subsections (5) and (6)(b) of that section apply) in the case of the report; or

  (fb) a report is furnished under subsection (2) of section 21B above in respect of a patient and subsection (8) of that section applies in the case of the report; or

  (g)   a report is furnished under section 25 above in respect of a patient who is detained in pursuance of an application for admission for treatment; or

  (ga) a supervision application is accepted in respect of a patient; or

  (gb) a report is furnished under section 25F above in respect of a patient; or

  (gc) a report is furnished under section 25G above in respect of a patient; or

  (h)   an order is made under section 29 above in respect of a patient who is or subsequently becomes liable to be detained or subject to guardianship under Part II of this Act, an application may be made to a Mental Health Review Tribunal within the relevant period-

(i) by the patient (except in the cases mentioned in paragraphs (g) and (h) above) or, in the cases mentioned in paragraphs (d),(ga),(gb) and (gc), by his nearest relative if he has been (or was entitled to be) informed under this Act of the report or acceptance, and

(ii) in the cases mentioned in paragraphs (g) and (h) above, by his nearest relative.

Section 66(1)

An application may be made to a MHRT when:

(a)   *a patient is admitted for assessment;*

(b)   *a patient is admitted for treatment;*

(c)   *a patient is received into guardianship;*

(d)   *a patient's mental disorder is re-classified (under s.16);*

(e)   *a patient subject to guardianship is transferred to hospital (under s.19);*

(f)   *a renewal of detention or guardianship is effected (under s.20);*

(fa)   *authority for detention of a patient is renewed where the patient has been taken into custody after more than 28 days absence without leave and the previous detention period would have expired during his/her absence save for the provisions of s.21B(5);*

(fb)   *authority for detention of a patient is renewed where the patient has been taken into custody after more than 28 days absence without leave and the patient's mental disorder has been reclassified by this renewal (under s.21B(8));*

(g)   *a RMO's report is made barring the discharge of a patient by his/her nearest relative (under s.25);*

(ga)   *a supervised discharge application is accepted;*

(gb)   *a patient subject to after-care under supervision has had his/her mental disorder reclassified (under s.25F);*

(gc)   *a patient's period of after-care under supervision is renewed (under s.25G);*

(h)   *a county court order is made appointing an acting 'nearest relative' of a patient subsequently subject to detention or guardianship (under s.29).*

An application to the MHRT may be made:

(i)   *by the patient save for cases (g) and (h) above;*

(ii)   *by the patient's nearest relative in cases of (d),(g),(ga),(gb),(gc) & (h) above.*

Note: s.69 also governs applications by patients subject to guardianship and hospital orders; s. 70 & s.79 govern applications by restricted patients.

---

(2) In subsection (1) above "the relevant period" means-

(a) in the case mentioned in paragraph (a) of that subsection, 14 days beginning with the day on which the patient is admitted as so mentioned;

(b) in the case mentioned in paragraph (b) of that subsection, six months beginning with the day on which the patient is admitted as so mentioned;

(c) in the cases mentioned in paragraphs (c) and (ga) of that subsection, six months beginning with the day on which the application is accepted;

(d) in the cases mentioned in paragraphs (d),(fb),(g) and (gb) of that subsection, 28 days beginning with the day on which the applicant is informed that the report has been furnished;

(e) in the case mentioned in paragraph (e) of that subsection, six months beginning with the day on which the patient is transferred;

(f) in the case mentioned in paragraph (f)or (fa) of that subsection, the period or periods for which authority for the patient's detention or guardianship is renewed by virtue of the report;

(fa) in the case mentioned in paragraph (gc) of that subsection, the further period for which the patient is made subject to after-care under supervision by virtue of the report;

(g) in the case mentioned in paragraph (h) of that subsection, 12 months beginning with the date of the order, and in any subsequent period of 12 months during which the order continues in force.

Section 66(2)
Details the periods within applications to the MHRT must be made in respect of each case under s.66(1) and is self explanatory.

(3) Section 32 above shall apply for the purposes of this section as it applies for the purposes of Part II of this Act.

Section 66(3)
Empowers the Secretary of State for Health to make regulations as to the manner in which the provisions of this section are to be carried out, the types of forms to be used, the registers and records to be kept etc.[49]

[49]MHRT Rules 1983 (S.I. 1983/942 as amended by S.I. 1996/314 and S.I. 1998/1189).

67. References to Mental Health Review Tribunals by the Secretary of State concerning Part II patients.

(1) The Secretary of State may, if he thinks fit, at any time refer to a Mental Health Review Tribunal the case of any patient who is liable to be detained or subject to guardianship or to after-care under supervision under Part II of this Act.

Section 67(1)

A patient subject to detention, guardianship or after-care under supervision under Part II of the Act (the civil sections) or under s.37 can have his/her case referred to a MHRT by the Secretary of State for Health at any time regardless of eligibility under s.66(2).

Note: this section applies to s.37 patients by virtue of Schedule 1, Part 1. Section 71 allows for referral of restricted patients.

(2) For the purpose of furnishing information for the purposes of a reference under subsection (1) above any registered medical practitioner authorised by or on behalf of the patient may, at any reasonable time, visit the patient and examine him in private and require the production of and inspect any records relating to the detention or treatment of the patient in any hospital or to any after-care services provided for the patient under section 117 below.

Section 67(2)

Allows a patient whose case has been referred to a tribunal by the Secretary of State for Health to obtain an independent medical opinion. The authorised doctor may examine the patient and any records of his/her treatment and after-care.

(3) Section 32 above shall apply for the purposes of this section as it applies for the purposes of Part II of this Act.

Section 67(3)

Empowers the Secretary of State for Health to make regulations as to the manner in which the provisions of this section are to be carried out.

68. Duty of Hospital Managers to refer cases to a Mental Health Review Tribunal

(1) Where a patient who is admitted to a hospital in pursuance of an application for admission for treatment or a patient who is transferred from guardianship to hospital does not exercise his right to apply to a Mental Health Review Tribunal under section 66(1) above by virtue of his case falling within paragraph (b) or, as the case may be, paragraph (e) of that section, the managers of the hospital shall at the expiration of the period for making such an application refer the patient's case to such a tribunal unless an application or reference in respect of the patient has then been made under section 66(1) above by virtue of his case falling within paragraph (d),(g) or (h) of that section or under section 67(1) above.

Section 68(1)

If a patient does not apply to a MHRT within the first six months of his/her detention for treatment (or his/her admission to hospital if transferred under guardianship) the hospital managers are under a duty to refer his/her case to the tribunal unless the nearest relative has made an application in respect of the patient's case or the case has been referred by the Secretary of State for Health.

(2) If the authority for the detention of a patient in a hospital is renewed under section 20 or 21B above and a period of three years (or, if the patient has not attained the age of sixteen years, one year) has elapsed since his case was last considered by a Mental Health Review Tribunal, whether on his own application or otherwise, the managers of the hospital shall refer his case to such a tribunal.

Section 68(2)

If a patient's detention has been renewed and his case has not been before a MHRT within the past three years (or one year if aged under sixteen) the hospital managers are under a duty to refer his case to a MHRT.

(3) For the purpose of furnishing information for the purposes of any reference under this section, any registered medical practitioner authorised by or on behalf of the patient may at any reasonable time visit and examine the patient in private and require the production of and inspect any records relating to the detention or treatment of the patient in any hospital or to any after-care services provided for the patient under section 117 below.

Section 68(3)

Allows a patient whose case is referred by the hospital managers under this section to obtain an independent medical opinion. The authorised doctor may examine the patient and his/her records.

(4) The Secretary of State may by order vary the length of the periods mentioned in subsection (2) above.

Section 68(4)

Is self explanatory.

(5) For the purposes of subsection (1) above a person who applies to a tribunal but subsequently withdraws his application shall be treated as not having exercised his right to apply, and where a person withdraws his application on a date after the expiration of the period mentioned in that subsection, the managers shall refer the patient's case as soon as possible after that date.

Section 68(5)

For the purposes of deciding whether the hospital managers' duty to refer a case to a MHRT has arisen under section 68(1) above, if an application to a MHRT has been made but withdrawn the duty will arise as if that application had never been made.

If an application made in respect of the initial six month period of detention is withdrawn after that first six months has ended the hospital managers must refer the case to a MHRT as soon as possible.

APPLICATIONS AND REFERENCES CONCERNING PART III PATIENTS

69. Applications to Tribunals concerning patients subject to hospital and guardianship orders

(1) Without prejudice to any provision of section 66(1) above as applied by section 40(4) above, an application to a Mental Health Review Tribunal may also be made-

    (a) in respect of a patient admitted to a hospital in pursuance of a hospital order, by the nearest relative of the patient in the period between the expiration of six months and the expiration of 12 months beginning with the date of the order and in any subsequent period of 12 months; and

    (b) in respect of a patient placed under guardianship by a guardianship order-

        (i) by the patient, within the period of six months beginning with the date of the order;

        (ii) by the nearest relative of the patient, within the period of 12 months beginning with the date of the order and in any subsequent period of 12 months.

Section 69(1)

In addition to those occasions on which MHRT applications are permitted under section 66(1) above an application to a MHRT may also be made:

(a)   for a patient admitted under a hospital order:

      by the nearest relative in the second six months of detention and in any subsequent 12 month period;

Note: unlike patients detained under Part II of the Act unrestricted patients detained under s.37 have no right to a tribunal hearing in the first six months of their detention.

(b)   for a patient subject to guardianship:

      (i) by the patient in the first six months of the order;

      (ii) by the nearest relative in the first year of the order and any subsequent 12 month period.

Note: patients under guardianship can also apply on their own behalf on any occasion when their guardianship is renewed (by virtue of s.66(2)(f) above).

(2) Where a person detained in a hospital-

  (a) is treated as subject to a hospital order or transfer direction by virtue of section 41(5) above, 82(2) or 85(2) below, section 77(2) of the Mental Health (Scotland) Act 1984 or section 5(1) of the Criminal Procedure (Insanity) Act 1964; or

  (b) is subject to a direction having the same effect as a hospital order by virtue of section 45B(2), 46(3), 47(3) or 48(3) above,

then, without prejudice to any provision of Part II of this Act as applied by section 40 above, that person may make an application to a Mental Health Review Tribunal in the period of six months beginning with the date of the order or direction mentioned in paragraph (a) above or, as the case may be, the date of the direction mentioned in paragraph (b) above.

> **Section 69(2)**
> *Outlines the other categories of detained patients who may make an application to a tribunal in the first six months of their detention.*
>
> *This section removes an otherwise six month gap in the right to apply to a MHRT for a group of patients whose restriction orders have expired or who have been transferred from prison or between hospital systems.*

70. Applications to tribunals concerning restricted patients

A patient who is a restricted patient within the meaning of section 79 below and is detained in a hospital may apply to a Mental Health Review Tribunal-

  (a) in the period between the expiration of six months and the expiration of 12 months beginning with the date of the relevant hospital order, hospital direction or transfer direction; and

  (b) in any subsequent period of 12 months.

> **Section 70**
> *Applications to MHRTs by restricted patients may be made by the patient:*
>
> *(a) in the second six month period after the order or direction was made;*
>
> *(b) in any subsequent 12 month period.*

71. References to Mental Health Review Tribunals by the Secretary of State on behalf of restricted patients

(1) The Secretary of State may at any time refer the case of a restricted patient to a Mental Health Review Tribunal.

(2) The Secretary of State shall refer to a Mental Health Review Tribunal the case of any restricted patient detained in a hospital whose case has not been considered by such a tribunal, whether on his own application or otherwise, within the last three years.

> **Section 71(1) & (2)**
> *The Home Secretary has a discretion to refer a restricted patient's case to a MHRT at any time. He/she must refer a restricted patient's case to a tribunal if his/her case has not been considered in the past three years.*

(3) The Secretary of State may by order vary the length of the period mentioned in subsection (2) above.

> **Section 71(3)**
> *Is self explanatory.*

(4) Any reference under subsection (1) above in respect of a patient who has been conditionally discharged and not recalled to hospital shall be made to the tribunal for the area in which the patient resides.

> **Section 71(4)**
> *The case of a conditionally discharged patient who has not been recalled will be referred to the MHRT for the region in which s/he lives.*

(5) Where a person who is treated as subject to a hospital order and a restriction order by virtue of an order under section 5(1) of the Criminal Procedure (Insanity) Act 1964 does not exercise his right to apply to a Mental Health Review Tribunal in the period of six months beginning with the date of that order, the Secretary of State shall at the expiration of that period refer his case to a tribunal.

> **Section 71(5)**
> *Where a patient found not guilty by reason of insanity or unfit to plead has been made subject to hospital order and restriction order the Home Secretary <u>must</u> refer his/her case to a tribunal if his/her case has not been considered in the first six months following the order.*

(6) For the purposes of subsection (5) above a person who applies to a tribunal but subsequently withdraws his application shall be treated as not having exercised his right to apply, and where a patient withdraws his application on a date after the expiration of the period there mentioned the Secretary of State shall refer his case as soon as possible after that date.

> **Section 71(6)**
>
> *For the purposes of subsection (5) above, if an application to a MHRT has been made but withdrawn the duty will arise as if that application had never been made.*
>
> *If an application made in respect of the initial six month period of detention is withdrawn after that first six months has ended the Home Secretary must refer the case to a MHRT as soon as possible.*

DISCHARGE OF PATIENTS

72. Power of tribunals

> *Gives MHRTs discretion to discharge unrestricted patients from hospital and guardianship. It also sets out criteria which, if met, make discharge mandatory and allows for deferred discharge.*

(1) Where application is made to a Mental Health Review Tribunal by or in respect of a patient who is liable to be detained under this Act, the tribunal may in any case direct that the patient be discharged, and-

(a) the tribunal shall direct the discharge of a patient liable to be detained under section 2 above if they are satisfied-
   (i) that he is not then suffering from mental disorder or from mental disorder of a nature or degree which warrants his detention in a hospital for assessment (or for assessment followed by medical treatment) for at least a limited period; or
   (ii) that his detention as aforesaid is not justified in the interests of his own health or safety or with a view to the protection of other persons;
(b) the tribunal shall direct the discharge of a patient liable to be detained otherwise than under section 2 above if they are satisfied-
   (i) that he is not then suffering from mental illness, psychopathic disorder, severe mental impairment or mental impairment or from any of those forms of disorder of a nature or degree which makes it appropriate for him to be liable to be detained in a hospital for medical treatment; or
   (ii) that it is not necessary for the health or safety of the patient or for the protection of other persons that he should receive such treatment; or
   (iii) in the case of an application by virtue of paragraph (g) of section 66(1) above, that the patient, if released, would not be likely to act in a manner dangerous to other persons or to himself.

Section 72(1)

A tribunal __may__ direct discharge of a patient in any case.

(a) *A tribunal __must__ direct discharge of a patient detained for assessment under s.2 if satisfied that:*

   (i)   *s/he is not suffering from mental disorder of a type or current severity which justifies detention in hospital for assessment;*

or

   (ii) *his/her detention is not justified for his/her own health or safety or for protection of others.*

(b) *A tribunal __must__ direct discharge of a detained patient (except those under s.2) if satisfied that:*

   (i)   *s/he is not suffering from a form of mental disorder of a type or current severity which requires detention in hospital for treatment ('appropriateness test');*

or

   (ii) *it is not necessary for his/her own health or safety or for protection of others that s/he should receive medical treatment ('safety test');*

or

   (iii) *where the application for discharge is made after the RMO has barred a nearest relative's order for discharge (under s.25), the patient would not be likely to be a danger to himself or others if released.*

Note: the grounds under paragraph (b) are similar to those for admission for treatment under s.3 save for the 'treatability' criterion not being repeated here.

The Court of Appeal[50] have said that a MHRT need not have regard to the 'treatability' test when considering the mandatory discharge of a patient with psychopathic disorder or mental impairment. Thus a patient can remain detained in hospital even if deemed untreatable providing the other conditions (of 'appropriateness' and 'safety') are met. However, note that the House of Lords have taken a different view in respect of discharge of restricted patients under the similarly worded Scottish legislation[51] (see notes to s.73(1) below).

[50] R v Cannons Park MHRT ex parte A [1995] QB 60.
[51] Reid v Secretary of State for Scotland [1999] 2 WLR 28.

(2) In determining whether to direct the discharge of a patient detained otherwise than under section 2 above in a case not falling within paragraph (b) of subsection (1) above, the tribunal shall have regard-

(a) to the likelihood of medical treatment alleviating or preventing a deterioration of the patient's condition; and

(b) in the case of a patient suffering from mental illness or severe mental impairment, to the likelihood of the patient, if discharged, being able to care for himself, to obtain the care he needs or to guard himself against serious exploitation.

> **Section 72(2)**
> *In deciding whether to exercise its discretion to discharge a patient who does not meet criteria within sub-section (1)(b) above a MHRT must consider:*
> *(a)   the likelihood of treatment helping the patient or preventing him/her deteriorating (the 'treatability test'); and*
> *(b)   the likelihood that a patient with mental illness or severe mental impairment would be able to look after himself, get the help he needed and avoid serious exploitation by others.*

(3) A tribunal may under subsection (1) above direct the discharge of a patient on a future date specified in the direction; and where a tribunal do not direct the discharge of a patient under that subsection the tribunal may-

   (a) with a view to facilitating his discharge on a future date, recommend that he be granted leave of absence or transferred to another hospital or into guardianship; and
   (b) further consider his case in the event of any such recommendation not being complied with.

> **Section 72(3)**
> *A MHRT may defer the discharge of a patient.*
> *A MHRT may, as an alternative to directing discharge, recommend leave of absence, transfer to another hospital or guardianship to facilitate future discharge and may reconsider the case if that recommendation is not acted upon.*

(3A) Where, in the case of an application to a tribunal by or in respect of a patient who is liable to be detained in pursuance of an application for admission for treatment or by virtue of an order or direction for his admission or removal to hospital under Part III of this Act, the tribunal do not direct the discharge of the patient under subsection (1) above, the tribunal may-

   (a) recommend that the responsible medical officer consider whether to make a supervision application in respect of the patient; and
   (b) further consider his case in the event of no such application being made.

> **Section 72(3A)**
> *As an alternative to discharge of a patient detained under s.3 or a hospital order the MHRT may:*
> *(a)   recommend that the RMO consider applying for after-care under supervision; and*
> *(b)   reconsider the case if that recommendation is not acted upon.*

(4) Where application is made to a Mental Health Review Tribunal by or in respect of a patient who is subject to guardianship under this Act, the tribunal may in any case direct that the patient be discharged, and shall so direct if they are satisfied-

- (a) that he is not then suffering from mental illness, psychopathic disorder, severe mental impairment or mental impairment; or
- (b) that it is not necessary in the interests of the welfare of the patient, or for the protection of other persons, that the patient should remain under such guardianship.

Section 72(4)

A MHRT __may__ direct that a patient be discharged from guardianship in any case.

A MHRT __must__ direct discharge of a patient from guardianship if satisfied that either:

(a)   s/he is not suffering from one of the four forms of mental disorder; or

(b)   it is not necessary for his/her health or safety or for the protection of others that s/he remain under guardianship.

(4A)   Where application is made to a Mental Health Review Tribunal by or in respect of a patient who is subject to after-care under supervision (or, if he has not yet left hospital, is to be so subject after he leaves hospital), the tribunal may in any case direct that the patient shall cease to be so subject (or not become so subject), and shall so direct if they are satisfied-

- (a) in a case where the patient has not yet left hospital, that the conditions set out in section 25A(4) above are not complied with; or
- (b) in any other case, that the conditions set out in section 25G(4) above are not complied with.

Section 72(4A)

A MHRT __may__ direct that a patient be discharged from supervised discharge in any case.

A MHRT __must__ direct discharge of a patient from supervised discharge if satisfied that either:

(a)   the application criteria for supervised discharge (set out in s.25A(4)) are not met by a patient still in hospital;

or

(b)   the renewal criteria for supervised discharge (set out in s.25G(4)) are not met.

(5) Where application is made to a Mental Health Review Tribunal under any provision of this Act by or in respect of a patient and the tribunal do not direct that the patient be discharged or, if he is (or is to be) subject to after-care under supervision, that he cease to be so subject (or not become so subject), the tribunal may, if satisfied that the patient is suffering from a form of mental disorder other than the form specified in the application, order or direction relating to him, direct that that application, order or direction be amended by substituting for the form of mental disorder specified in it such other form of mental disorder as appears to the tribunal to be appropriate.

Section 72(5)
A tribunal may reclassify the form of mental disorder of a patient whom they do not discharge.

(6) Subsections (1) to (5) above apply in relation to references to a Mental Health Review Tribunal as they apply in relation to applications made to such a tribunal by or in respect of a patient.

Section 72(6)
Ss.72(1) to (5) above apply to all cases before to a MHRT whether by reference by the Secretary of State or by application.

(7) Subsection (1) above shall not apply in the case of a restricted patient except as provided in sections 73 and 74 below.

Section 72(7)
s.72(1) does not apply to restricted patients.

73. Power of MHRTs to discharge restricted patients

Sets out criteria which if met must result in the absolute or conditional discharge of a restricted patient by a MHRT.

(1) Where an application to a Mental Health Review Tribunal is made by a restricted patient who is subject to a restriction order, or where the case of such a patient is referred to such a tribunal, the tribunal shall direct the absolute discharge of the patient if satisfied-
(a) as to the matters mentioned in paragraph (b)(i) or (ii) of section 72(1) above; and
(b) that it is not appropriate for the patient to remain liable to be recalled to hospital treatment.

Section 73(1)

A tribunal must direct absolute discharge of a restricted patient if satisfied that:

(a)   (i)   *s/he is not suffering from mental disorder of a type or severity which requires detention in hospital for treatment ('appropriateness test'); or*

     (ii)   *it is not necessary for his/her own or others' health or safety or the protection of others that s/he should receive medical treatment ('safety test'); and*

(b)   *it is not appropriate for the patient to remain liable to be recalled to hospital for treatment in the future.*

Note: there is no general discretion to discharge restricted patients as there is with unrestricted patients in s.72.

As with s.72(1) there is no explicit requirement that a restricted patient who does not meet the 'treatability' test be mandatorily discharged. However in a recent case considering interpretation of the similarly worded Scottish Mental Health legislation the House of Lords has said that to justify continuing detention all the criteria for initial detention should be met including the 'treatability' test. Indeed it was said that the 'treatability' test was the first aspect to consider and should be met before a tribunal even go on to consider the 'appropriateness' and 'safety' tests.[52]

Their Lordships specifically considered and declined to follow the earlier English Court of Appeal decision in R v Cannons Park MHRT ex parte A [1995] QB 60 (see note to s.72(1) above). That earlier case was however distinguished on the basis that it concerned an un-restricted patient and the English and Scottish provisions are not identical. Although a Scottish House of Lords decision is not binding on English courts it is nevertheless highly persuasive and it remains to be seen whether English lower courts will follow the decision in Reid. Should the matter come before an English court it is likely to go to the House of Lords for resolution.

[52] Reid v Secretary of State for Scotland [1999] 2 WLR 28, at 42E.

(2) Where in the case of any such patient as is mentioned in subsection (1) above the tribunal are satisfied as to the matters referred to in paragraph (a) of that subsection but not as to the matter referred to in paragraph (b) of that subsection the tribunal shall direct the conditional discharge of the patient.

Section 73(2)

If the MHRT are satisfied that a patient meets either the 'appropriateness test' or the 'safety test' but are of the view that it remains appropriate for him/her to be liable to be recalled to hospital they must order conditional discharge.

(3) Where a patient is absolutely discharged under this section he shall thereupon cease to be liable to be detained by virtue of the relevant hospital order, and the restriction order shall cease to have effect accordingly.

Section 73(3)

Absolute discharge of a restricted patient may not be deferred.

(4) Where a patient is conditionally discharged under this section-

(a) he may be recalled by the Secretary of State under subsection (3) of section 42 above as if he had been conditionally discharged under subsection (2) of that section; and

(b) the patient shall comply with such conditions (if any) as may be imposed at the time of discharge by the tribunal or at any subsequent time by the Secretary of State.

Section 73(4)

A conditionally discharged restricted patient:

(a)   may be recalled by the Home Secretary at any time (under s.42(3) above);

(b)   must comply with the conditions set by the MHRT and any conditions subsequently imposed by the Home Secretary.

(5) The Secretary of State may from time to time vary any condition imposed (whether by the tribunal or by him) under subsection (4) above.

Section 73(5)

The Home Secretary may vary or remove any conditions on discharge set by the MHRT or by himself.

(6) Where a restriction order in respect of a patient ceases to have effect after he has been conditionally discharged under this section the patient shall, unless previously recalled, be deemed to be absolutely discharged on the date when the order ceases to have effect and shall cease to be liable to be detained by virtue of the relevant hospital order.

Section 73(6)

When a restriction order in respect of a conditionally discharged patient expires the patient is treated as if absolutely discharged.

(7) A tribunal may defer a direction for the conditional discharge of a patient until such arrangements as appear to the tribunal to be necessary for that purpose have been made to their satisfaction; and where by virtue of any such deferment no direction has been given on an application or reference before the time when the patient's case comes before the tribunal on a subsequent application or reference, the previous application or reference shall be treated as one on which no direction under this section can be given.

Section 73(7)

Conditional discharge of a restricted patient may be deferred until the discharge arrangements or conditions required by the MHRT are made.

If a patient's case comes before a MHRT again, prior to a previously deferred conditional discharge being effected, the hearing of that further application for discharge nullifies any previous direction for deferred conditional discharge.

Note: although it is desirable that a MHRT only orders conditions which are capable of implementation within a reasonable time it may nevertheless order conditions which are likely to be difficult to meet. Once conditions are specified by a tribunal the burden of implementing them passes to the local social services authority and health authority and a MHRT has no power to police the work of those authorities[53].

The ECHR has found that, where a health authority could not fulfill the conditions attached by a MHRT, although the deferral of release and the setting of conditions by a MHRT was valid it led to the patient's discharge being unreasonably delayed for over three years which constituted a breach of his human rights under Article 5.1.[54]

[53] See: R v MHRT and others ex parte Russell Hall [1999] Lloyd's Rep Med 274 and the subsequent Court of Appeal decision of 30th July 1999 (unreported).
[54] Johnson v United Kingdom (1998) 40 BMLR 1, [1998] HRCD 41.

(8) This section is without prejudice to section 42 above.

Section 73(8)

This section does not affect any of the Home Secretary's powers in respect of restricted patients, which are set out in s.42 above.

74. Restricted patients subject to restriction directions

Sets out procedures when a MHRT considers the cases of discharge of transferred prisoners i.e. patients subject to restriction directions (under s.49) or limitation directions (under s.45A). The MHRT has no power to discharge such patients without the consent of the Home Secretary.

(1) Where an application to a Mental Health Review Tribunal is made by a restricted patient who is subject to a limitation direction or restriction direction, or where the case of such a patient is referred to such a tribunal the tribunal-

(a) shall notify the Secretary of State whether, in their opinion, the patient would, if subject to a restriction order, be entitled to be absolutely or conditionally discharged under section 73 above; and

(b) if they notify him that the patient would be entitled to be conditionally discharged, may recommend that in the event of his not being discharged under this section he should continue to be detained in hospital.

Section 74(1)

When a restricted patient subject to restriction or a limitation direction (a transferred prisoner) applies or is referred to a MHRT:

(a)   the Home Secretary must be informed if the MHRT's view is that the patient would be entitled to absolute or conditional discharge (based on the same criteria as apply to restricted patients); and

(b)   if the MHRT's view is that the patient would be entitled to conditional discharge they may recommend that the patient remains in hospital if not discharged, rather than transferred back to prison.

(2) If in the case of a patient not falling within subsection (4) below-

(a) the tribunal notify the Secretary of State that the patient would be entitled to be absolutely or conditionally discharged; and

(b) within the period of 90 days beginning with the date of that notification the Secretary of State gives notice to the tribunal that the patient may be so discharged,

the tribunal shall direct the absolute or, as the case may be, the conditional discharge of the patient.

Section 74(2)

Once so informed if, within 90 days, the Home Secretary consents to the discharge of a patient who was a sentenced prisoner his/her absolute or conditional discharge must be directed by the MHRT (i.e. a sentenced prisoner in these circumstances will not be returned to prison to complete his/her sentence).

(3) Where a patient continues to be liable to be detained in a hospital at the end of the period referred to in subsection (2)(b) above because the Secretary of State has not given the notice there mentioned, the managers of the hospital shall, unless the tribunal have made a recommendation under subsection (1)(b) above, transfer the patient to a prison or other institution in which he might have been detained if he had not been removed to hospital, there to be dealt with as if he had not been so removed.

Section 74(3)
If the Home Secretary does not give consent within 90 days the patient must be transferred to prison unless the MHRT have recommended his continued detention in hospital under s.74(1)(b) above (i.e. if returned to prison s/he will complete his/her sentence as if s/he had never been removed to hospital).

(4) If, in the case of a patient who is subject to a transfer direction under section 48 above, the tribunal notify the Secretary of State that the patient would be entitled to be absolutely or conditionally discharged, the Secretary of State shall, unless the tribunal have made a recommendation under subsection (1)(b) above, by warrant direct that the patient be remitted to a prison or other institution in which he might have been detained if he had not been removed to hospital, there to be dealt with as if he had not been so removed.

Section 74(4)
If a MHRT notifies the Home Secretary of its view that a remand or civil prisoner would be entitled to absolute or conditional discharge (and does not recommend that the patient stays in hospital if not discharged) the Home Secretary must direct that the person be returned to prison and dealt with as if the transfer to hospital had not occurred (i.e. transferred remand prisoners must either be returned to prison or remain in hospital; they can not be simply released).

(5) Where a patient is transferred or remitted under subsection (3) or (4) above the relevant hospital direction and the limitation direction or, as the case may be, the relevant transfer direction and the restriction direction shall cease to have effect on his arrival in the prison or other institution.

Section 74(5)
On return of a transferred prisoner to prison any previous direction ends.

(6) Subsections (3) to (8) of section 73 above shall have effect in relation to this section as they have effect in relation to that section, taking references to the relevant hospital order and the restriction order as references to the hospital direction and the limitation direction or, as the case may be, to the transfer direction and the restriction direction.

Section 74(6)
The provisions of s.73(3)-(8) above will also apply to transferred remand prisoners.

(7) This section is without prejudice to sections 50 to 53 above in their application to patients who are not discharged under this section.

> **Section 74(7)**
> *This section does not affect any of provisions of s.50 or s.53 in respect of sentenced and civil prisoners.*

75. Applications and references in respect of conditionally discharged restricted patients.

(1) Where a restricted patient has been conditionally discharged under section 42(2), 73 or 74 above and is subsequently recalled to hospital-

    (a) the Secretary of State shall, within one month of the day on which the patient returns or is returned to hospital, refer his case to a Mental Health Review Tribunal; and

    (b) section 70 above shall apply to the patient as if the relevant hospital order, hospital direction or transfer direction had been made on that day.

> **Section 75(1)**
> *If a conditionally discharged restricted patient is recalled to hospital:*
> *(a)   the Home Secretary must refer his case to a MHRT within a month.*
> *(b)   further applications to MHRTs by the restricted patient may be made by the patient in the second six month period after his recall and in any subsequent 12 month period.*

(2) Where a restricted patient has been conditionally discharged as aforesaid but has not been recalled to hospital he may apply to a Mental Health Review Tribunal-

    (a) in the period between the expiration of 12 months and the expiration of two years beginning with the date on which he was conditionally discharged; and

    (b) in any subsequent period of two years.

> **Section 75(2)**
> *A conditionally discharged restricted patient not recalled to hospital may apply to his local MHRT:*
> *(a)   after a year but within two years of his conditional discharge being effected;*
> *(b)   in any subsequent two year period.*

(3) Sections 73 and 74 above shall not apply to an application under subsection (2) above but on any such application the tribunal may-

    (a) vary any condition to which the patient is subject in connection with his discharge or impose any condition which might have been imposed in connection therewith; or

(b) direct that the restriction order or restriction direction to which he is subject shall cease to have effect;

and if the tribunal give a direction under paragraph (b) above the patient shall cease to be liable to be detained by virtue of the relevant hospital order or transfer direction.

Section 75(3)

The provisions in relation to discharge of restricted patients in s.73 and s.74 do not apply to applications by a conditionally discharged patient who has not been recalled, but a MHRT may:

(a)   vary or impose new conditions on discharge;

(b)   end the restriction order/direction such that the patient is no longer liable to be detained.

GENERAL

76. Visiting and examining patients

(1) For the purpose of advising whether an application to a Mental Health Review Tribunal should be made by or in respect of a patient who is liable to be detained or subject to guardianship or to after-care under supervision (or, if he has not yet left hospital, is to be subject to after-care under supervision after he leaves hospital) under Part II of this Act or of furnishing information as to the condition of a patient for the purposes of such an application, any registered medical practitioner authorised by or on behalf of the patient or other person who is entitled to make or has made the application-

(a) may at any reasonable time visit the patient and examine him in private, and

(b) may require the production of and inspect any records relating to the detention or treatment of the patient in any hospital or to any after-care services provided for the patient under section 117 below.

Section 76(1)

Any doctor advising or providing information for a MHRT application on behalf of the person making the application may:

(a)   visit and examine the patient in private at any reasonable time;

(b)   ask to see any records relating to the patient's detention and treatment in hospital or his/her aftercare.

(2) Section 32 above shall apply for the purposes of this section as it applies for the purposes of Part II of this Act.

Section 76(2)
The Secretary of State for Health may make regulations as to how this section is to be applied.

77. General provisions concerning tribunal applications

(1) No application shall be made to a Mental Health Review Tribunal by or in respect of a patient except in such cases and at such times as are expressly provided by this Act.

Section 77(1)
MHRT applications can only be made at the times and in the circumstances expressly allowed by this Act.

(2) Where under this Act any person is authorised to make an application to a Mental Health Review Tribunal within a specified period, not more than one such application shall be made by that person within that period but for that purpose there shall be disregarded any application which is withdrawn in accordance with rules made under section 78 below.

Section 77(2)
An authorised person can only make one application to a MHRT in each of the specified periods in the Act, although withdrawn applications will be discounted.

(3) Subject to subsection (4) below an application to a Mental Health Review Tribunal authorised to be made by or in respect of a patient under this Act shall be made by notice in writing addressed to the tribunal for the area in which the hospital in which the patient is detained is situated or in which the patient is residing under guardianship or when subject to after-care under supervision (or in which he is to reside on becoming so subject after leaving ospital) as the case may be.

Section 77(3)
MHRT applications must be made in writing to the MHRT for the area local to the hospital or in the case of a person subject to guardianship or supervised discharged the MHRT for the area where he lives or is going to live on leaving hospital.

(4) Any application under section 75(2) above shall be made to the tribunal for the area in which the patient resides.

> ### Section 77(4)
> *Applications by a conditionally discharged restricted patient must be made to the MHRT for the area in which he lives.*

78. Procedure of tribunals

(1) The Lord Chancellor may make rules with respect to the making of applications to Mental Health Review Tribunals and with respect to the proceedings of such tribunals and matters incidental to or consequential on such proceedings.

> ### Section 78(1)
> *Is self explanatory.*
>
> Note: rules made under this section are the Mental Health Review Tribunal Rules 1983 (S.I. 1983 No. 942) and the Mental Health Review Tribunal (Amendment) Rules 1996 (S.I. 1996 No. 314) (S.I. 1998 No. 1189).

(2) Rules made under this section may in particular make provision-

   (a) for enabling a tribunal, or the chairman of a tribunal, to postpone the consideration of any application by or in respect of a patient, or of any such application of any specified class, until the expiration of such period (not exceeding 12 months) as may be specified in the rules from the date on which an application by or in respect of the same patient was last considered and determined by that or any other tribunal under this Act;

   (b) for the transfer of proceedings from one tribunal to another in any case where, after the making of the application, the patient is removed out of the area of the tribunal to which it was made;

   (c) for restricting the persons qualified to serve as members of a tribunal for the consideration of any application, or of an application of any specified class;

   (d) for enabling a tribunal to dispose of an application without a formal hearing where such a hearing is not requested by the applicant or it appears to the tribunal that such a hearing would be detrimental to the health of the patient;

   (e) for enabling a tribunal to exclude members of the public, or any specified class of members of the public, from any proceedings of the tribunal, or to prohibit the publication of reports of any such proceedings or the names of any persons concerned in such proceedings;

   (f) for regulating the circumstances in which, and the persons by whom, applicants and patients in respect of whom applications are made to a tribunal may, if not desiring to conduct their own case, be represented for the purposes of those applications;

   (g) for regulating the methods by which information relevant to an application may be obtained by or furnished to the tribunal, and in particular for authorising the members of a tribunal, or any one or more of them, to visit and interview in private any patient by or in respect of whom an application has been made;

(h) for making available to any applicant, and to any patient in respect of whom an application is made to a tribunal, copies of any documents obtained by or furnished to the tribunal in connection with the application, and a statement of the substance of any oral information so obtained or furnished except where the tribunal considers it undesirable in the interests of the patient or for other special reasons;

(i) for requiring a tribunal, if so requested in accordance with the rules, to furnish such statements of the reasons for any decision given by the tribunal as may be prescribed by the rules, subject to any provision made by the rules for withholding such a statement rom a patient or any other person in cases where the tribunal considers that furnishing it would be undesirable in the interests of the patient or for other special reasons;

(j) for conferring on the tribunals such ancillary powers as the Lord Chancellor thinks necessary for the purposes of the exercise of their functions under this Act;

(k) for enabling any functions of a tribunal which relate to matters preliminary or incidental to an application to be performed by the chairman of the tribunal.

Section 78(2)
Sets out the matters about which rules may be made and includes:

(a)   the postponement of tribunal hearings;

(b)   the transfer of tribunal proceedings to another area;

(c)   the membership of tribunal panels;

(d)   situations in which formal hearings may be dispensed with;

(e)   the privacy of hearings and confidentiality of reports;

(f)   representation at tribunal hearings;

(g)   methods of information gathering by tribunal panels;

(h)   provision of information received by a tribunal panel to the applicant/patient;

(i)   the giving of reasons for decisions reached by the tribunal;

(j)   creating additional powers of tribunals;

(k)   allowing 'chairmans action' on matters preliminary and incidental to tribunal applications.

(3) Subsections (1) and (2) above apply in relation to references to Mental Health Review Tribunals as they apply in relation to applications to such tribunals by or in respect of patients.

Section 78(3)
Subsections (1) and (2) above apply not only to applications to MHRTs but also to references made by the Secretary of State and hospital managers.

(4) Rules under this section may make provision as to the procedure to be dopted in cases concerning restricted patients and, in particular-

(a) for restricting the persons qualified to serve as president of a tribunal for the consideration of an application or reference relating to a restricted patient;

(b) for the transfer of proceedings from one tribunal to another in any case where, after the making of a reference or application in accordance with section 71(4) or 77(4) above, the patient ceases to reside in the area of the tribunal to which the reference or application was made.

Section 78(4)
Sets out the matters about which rules may be made in respect of restricted patients and includes:
(a) who may act as a president of MHRT panel;
(b) the transfer of tribunal proceedings to another area.

(5) Rules under this section may be so framed as to apply to all applications or references or to applications or references of any specified class and may make different provision in relation to different cases.

Section 78(5)
Is self explanatory.

(6) Any functions conferred on the chairman of a Mental Health Review Tribunal by rules under this section may, if for any reason he is unable to act, be exercised by another member of that tribunal appointed by him for the purpose.

Section 78(6)
Another tribunal panel member may carry out any of the Chairman's functions conferred by the MHRT rules if so authorised by him.

(7) A Mental Health Review Tribunal may pay allowances in respect of travelling expenses, subsistence and loss of earnings to any person attending the tribunal as an applicant or witness, to the patient who is the subject of the proceedings if he attends otherwise than as the applicant or a witness and to any person (other than counsel or a solicitor) who attends as the representative of an applicant.

Section 78(7)
A MHRT may reimburse expenses incurred by applicants, witnesses or a patient's lay representative through attendance (but not barristers' or solicitors' expenses).

(8) A Mental Health Review Tribunal may, and if so required by the High Court shall, state in the form of a special case for determination by the High Court ny question of law which may arise before them.

Section 78(8)
A MHRT may make a referral to the High Court for clarification of a question of law which has arisen in a MHRT hearing. It must do so if ordered to by the High Court.

(9) Part I of the Arbitration Act 1996 shall not apply to any proceedings before a Mental Health Review Tribunal except so far as any provisions of that Act may be applied, with or without modifications, by rules made under this section.

Section 78(9)
Is self explanatory.

79. Interpretation of Part V

(1) In this Part of this Act "restricted patient" means a patient who is subject to a restriction order, limitation direction or restriction direction and this Part of this Act shall, subject to the provisions of this section, have effect in relation to any person who-

  (a) is subject to a direction which by virtue of section 46(3) above has the same effect as a hospital order and a restriction order; or
  (b) is treated as subject to a hospital order and a restriction order by virtue of an order under section 5(1) of the Criminal Procedure (Insanity) Act 1964 or section 6 or 14(1) of the Criminal Appeal Act 1968; or

(c) is treated as subject to a hospital order and a restriction order or to a transfer direction and a restriction direction by virtue of section 82(2) or 85(2) below or section 77(2) of the Mental Health (Scotland) Act 1984,

as it has effect in relation to a restricted patient.

Section 79(1)
The provisions of Part V of the Act in relation to restricted patients similarly apply to those who are to be considered as if under a hospital order and restriction order or transfer direction and restriction direction by virtue either of other sections of this Act, or by the other Acts listed.

(2) Subject to the following provisions of this section, in this Part of this Act "the relevant hospital order", "the relevant hospital direction" and "the relevant transfer direction", in relation to a restricted patient, mean the hospital order, the hospital direction or transfer direction by virtue of which he is liable to be detained in a hospital.

(3) In the case of a person within paragraph (a) of subsection (1) above, references in this Part of this Act to the relevant hospital order or restriction order shall be construed as references to the direction referred to in that paragraph.

(4) In the case of a person within paragraph (b) of subsection (1) above, references in this Part of this Act to the relevant hospital order or restriction order shall be construed as references to the order under the provisions mentioned in that paragraph.

(5) In the case of a person within paragraph (c) of subsection (1) above, references in this Part of this Act to the relevant hospital order, the relevant transfer direction, the restriction order or the restriction direction or to a transfer direction under section 48 above shall be construed as references to the hospital order, transfer direction, restriction order, restriction direction or transfer direction under that section to which that person is treated as subject by virtue of the provisions mentioned in that paragraph.

(6) In this Part of this Act, unless the context otherwise requires, "hospital" means a hospital, and "the responsible medical officer" means the responsible medical officer, within the meaning of Part II of this Act.

(7) In this Part of this Act any reference to the area of a tribunal is-

(a) in relation to a tribunal for a region of England, a reference to that region; and
(b) in relation to the tribunal for Wales, a reference to Wales.

Sections 79(2)-(7)
Are self explanatory.

PART VI

REMOVAL AND RETURN OF PATIENTS WITHIN UNITED KINGDOM, ETC

REMOVAL TO SCOTLAND

80. Removal of patients to Scotland

(1) If it appears to the Secretary of State, in the case of a patient who is for the time being liable to be detained or subject to guardianship under this Act (otherwise than by virtue of section 35, 36 or 38 above), that it is in the interests of the patient to remove him to Scotland, and that arrangements have been made for admitting him to a hospital or, as the case may be, for receiving him into guardianship there, the Secretary of State may authorise his removal to Scotland and may give any necessary directions for his conveyance to his destination.

Section 80(1)

If it is in a patient's best interests to be moved to Scotland and arrangements have been made for this to be done the Secretary of State for Health may authorise this, unless the patient was admitted to hospital for reports or treatment while awaiting trial or sentencing (s.35 and s.36) or was subject to an interim hospital order (s.38).

If the patient is subject to a restriction order or a restriction direction, only the Home Secretary can authorise such a move.

(2) Subject to the provisions of subsection (4) below, where a patient liable to be detained under this Act by virtue of an application, order or direction under any enactment in force in England and Wales is removed under this section and admitted to a hospital in Scotland, he shall be treated as if on the date of his admission he had been so admitted in pursuance of an application forwarded to the Health Board responsible for the administration of the hospital, or an order or direction made or given, on that date under the corresponding enactment in Scotland, and, where he is subject to a restriction order or restriction direction under any enactment in this Act, as if he were subject to a restriction order or restriction direction under the corresponding enactment in force in Scotland.

Section 80(2)

Once in Scotland the detained patient will be dealt with as if s/he had been admitted under the corresponding Scottish legislation (the Health Board is a Scottish body) on the date of admission to the Scottish hospital. If s/he was subject to a restriction order or direction in England or Wales s/he will be subject to the corresponding Scottish order or direction.

(3) Where a patient subject to guardianship under this Act by virtue of an application, order or direction under any enactment in force in England and Wales is removed under this section and received into guardianship in Scotland, he shall be treated as if on the date on which he arrives at the place where he is to reside he had been so received in pursuance of an application, order or direction under the corresponding enactment in force in Scotland, and as if the application had been forwarded or, as the case may be, the order or direction had been made or given on that date.

Section 80(3)
Once in Scotland the patient under guardianship will be dealt with as if s/he had been received into guardianship under the corresponding Scottish legislation on the date of arrival at his/her new place of residence.

(4) Where a person removed under this section was immediately before his removal liable to be detained by virtue of an application for admission for assessment under this Act, he shall, on his admission to a hospital in Scotland, be treated as if he had been admitted to the hospital in pursuance of an emergency recommendation under the Mental Health (Scotland) Act 1984 made on the date of his admission.

Section 80(4)
There is no Scottish equivalent to an admission for assessment under s.2. Thus, once in Scotland, a patient admitted for assessment will be dealt with as if s/he had been admitted following an "emergency recommendation".

(5) Where a patient removed under this section was immediately before his removal liable to be detained under this Act by virtue of a transfer direction given while he was serving a sentence of imprisonment (within the meaning of section 47(5) above) imposed by a court in England and Wales, he shall be treated as if the sentence had been imposed by a court in Scotland.

Section 80(5)
Under s.47(5) a person serving a sentence of imprisonment includes:

    (i)   a person detained by order of a criminal court (except a court-martial);

    (ii) a person detained for not keeping the peace or being of good behaviour after being ordered by the magistrates' court to do so;

    (iii) a person detained for failure to pay fines, compensation, costs etc after being convicted.

Where such a person was in hospital in England and Wales by virtue of a transfer direction s/he will be dealt with in Scotland as if s/he had been sentenced to imprisonment in Scotland.

(6) Where a person removed under this section was immediately before his removal subject to a restriction order or restriction direction of limited duration, the restriction order or restriction direction to which he is subject by virtue of subsection (2) of this section shall expire on the date on which the first-mentioned order or direction would have expired if he had not been so removed.

Section 80(6)
The Scottish restriction order or direction will expire on the same date that the original English or Welsh order or direction would have done.

(7) In this section "hospital" has the same meaning as in the Mental Health (Scotland) Act 1984.

Section 80(7)
Is self explanatory.

80A. Transfer of responsibility for patients to Scotland

(1) If it appears to the Secretary of State, in the case of a patient who-

(a) is subject to a restriction order under section 41 above; and
(b) has been conditionally discharged under section 42 or 73 above,

that a transfer under this section would be in the interests of the patient, the Secretary of State may, with the consent of the Minister exercising corresponding functions in Scotland, transfer responsibility for the patient to that Minister.

Section 80A(1)
Where a patient subject to a restriction order has been conditionally discharged by the Home Secretary (under s.42) or by a Mental Health Review Tribunal (under s.73) the Home Secretary may, if it is in the patient's best interests, transfer responsibility for him/her to the appropriate Scottish minister (who must first agree).

(2) Where responsibility for such a patient is transferred under this section, the patient shall be treated-

(a) as if on the date of the transfer he had been conditionally discharged under the corresponding enactment in force in Scotland; and
(b) as if he were subject to a restriction order under the corresponding enactment in force in Scotland.

Section 80A(2)
The patient will be dealt with as if his/her conditional discharge had been under the corresponding Scottish provision on the date of the transfer, and as if s/he was subject to a Scottish restriction order.

(3) Where a patient responsibility for whom is transferred under this section was immediately before the transfer subject to a restriction order of limited duration, the restriction order to which he is subject by virtue of subsection (2) above shall expire on the date on which the first-mentioned order would have expired if the transfer had not been made.

Section 80A(3)
A time limited restriction order will last no longer than it would have done in England and Wales.

REMOVAL TO AND FROM NORTHERN IRELAND

81. Removal of patients to Northern Ireland

(1) If it appears to the Secretary of State, in the case of a patient who is for the time being liable to be detained or subject to guardianship under this Act (otherwise than by virtue of section 35, 36 or 38 above), that it is in the interests of the patient to remove him to Northern Ireland, and that arrangements have been made for admitting him to a hospital or, as the case may be, for receiving him into guardianship there, the Secretary of State may authorise his removal to Northern Ireland and may give any necessary directions for his conveyance to his destination.

Section 81(1)
If it is in a patient's best interests to be moved to Northern Ireland and arrangements have been made for this to be done the Secretary of State for Health may authorise this, unless the patient was admitted to hospital for reports or treatment while awaiting trial or sentencing (s.35 and s.36) or was subject to an interim hospital order (s.38).

If the patient is subject to a restriction order or a restriction direction, only the Home Secretary can authorise such a move.

(2) Subject to the provisions of subsections (4) and (5) below, where a patient liable to be detained under this Act by virtue of an application, order or direction under any enactment in force in England and Wales is removed under this section and admitted to a hospital in Northern Ireland, he shall be treated as if on the date of his admission he had been so admitted in pursuance of an application made, or an order or direction made or given, on that date under the corresponding enactment in force in Northern Ireland, and, where he is subject to a restriction order or restriction direction under any enactment in this Act, as if he were subject to a restriction order or a restriction direction under the corresponding enactment in force in Northern Ireland.

> ### Section 81(2)
> *Once in Northern Ireland the detained patient will be dealt with as if s/he had been admitted under the corresponding Northern Irish legislation on the date of admission to the Northern Irish hospital. If s/he was subject to a restriction order or direction in England or Wales s/he will be subject to the corresponding Northern Irish order or direction.*

(3) Where a patient subject to guardianship under this Act by virtue of an application, order or direction under any enactment in force in England and Wales is removed under this section and received into guardianship in Northern Ireland, he shall be treated as if on the date on which he arrives at the place where he is to reside he had been so received in pursuance of an application, order or direction under the corresponding enactment in force in Northern Ireland, and as if the application had been accepted or, as the case may be, the order or direction had been made or given on that date.

> ### Section 81(3)
> *Once in Northern Ireland the patient under guardianship will be dealt with as if s/he had been received into guardianship under the corresponding Northern Irish legislation on the date of arrival at his/her new place of residence.*

(4) Where a person removed under this section was immediately before his removal liable to be detained by virtue of an application for admission for assessment under this Act, he shall, on his admission to a hospital in Northern Ireland, be treated as if he had been admitted to the hospital in pursuance of an application for assessment under Article 4 of the Mental Health (Northern Ireland) Order 1986 made on the date of his admission.

> ### Section 81(4)
> *Once in Northern Ireland the patient admitted for assessment will be dealt with as if s/he had been admitted for assessment under the corresponding Northern Irish legislation on the date of admission to the Northern Irish hospital.*

(5) Where a person removed under this section was immediately before his removal liable to be detained by virtue of an application for admission for treatment under this Act, he shall, on his admission to a hospital in Northern Ireland, be treated as if he were detained for treatment under Part II of the Mental Health (Northern Ireland) Order 1986 by virtue of a report under Article 12(1) of that Order made on the date of his admission.

Section 81(5)
Once in Northern Ireland the patient admitted for treatment will be dealt with as if s/he had been admitted for treatment under the corresponding Northern Irish legislation on the date of admission to the Northern Irish hospital.

(6) Where a patient removed under this section was immediately before his removal liable to be detained under this Act by virtue of a transfer direction given while he was serving a sentence of imprisonment (within the meaning of section 47(5) above) imposed by a court in England and Wales, he shall be treated as if the sentence had been imposed by a court in Northern Ireland.

Section 81(6)
Under s.47(5) a person serving a sentence of imprisonment includes:

    (i)   *a person detained by order of a criminal court (except a court-martial);*

    (ii)   *a person detained for not keeping the peace or being of good behaviour after being ordered by the magistrates' court to do so;*

    (iii)   *a person detained for failure to pay fines, compensation, costs etc after being convicted.*

Where such a person was in hospital in England and Wales by virtue of a transfer direction s/he will be dealt with in Northern Ireland as if s/he had been sentenced to imprisonment in Northern Ireland.

(7) Where a person removed under this section was immediately before his removal subject to a restriction order or restriction direction of limited duration, the restriction order or restriction direction to which he is subject by virtue of subsection (2) above shall expire on the date on which the first-mentioned restriction order would have expired if he had not been so removed.

Section 81(7)
The Northern Irish restriction order or direction will expire on the same date that the original English or Welsh order or direction would have done.

(8) In this section "hospital" has the same meaning as in the (Northern Ireland) Order 1986.

Section 81(8)
Is self explanatory.

81A. Transfer of responsibility for patients to Northern Ireland

(1) If it appears to the Secretary of State, in the case of a patient who-

  (a) is subject to a restriction order or restriction direction under section 41 or 49 above; and

  (b) has been conditionally discharged under section 42 or 73 above,

  that a transfer under this section would be in the interests of the patient, the Secretary of State may, with the consent of the Minister exercising corresponding functions in Northern Ireland, transfer responsibility for the patient to that Minister.

Section 81A(1)
Where a patient subject to a restriction order or direction has been conditionally discharged by the Home Secretary (under s.42) or by a Mental Health Review Tribunal (under s.73) the Home Secretary may, if it is in the patient's best interests, transfer responsibility for the patient to the appropriate Northern Irish minister (who must first agree).

(2) Where responsibility for such a patient is transferred under this section, the patient shall be treated-

  (a) as if on the date of the transfer he had been conditionally discharged under the corresponding enactment in force in Northern Ireland; and

  (b) as if he were subject to a restriction order or restriction direction under the corresponding enactment in force in Northern Ireland.

Section 81A(2)
The patient will be dealt with as if his/her conditional discharge had been under the corresponding Northern Irish provision on the date of the transfer, and as if s/he was subject to a Northern Irish restriction order.

(3) Where a patient responsibility for whom is transferred under this section was immediately before the transfer subject to a restriction order or restriction direction of limited duration, the restriction order or restriction direction to which he is subject by virtue of subsection (2) above shall expire on the date on which the first-mentioned order or direction would have expired if the transfer had not been made.

Section 81A(3)
A time limited restriction order or direction will last no longer than it would have done in England and Wales.

82. Removal to England and Wales of patients from Northern Ireland

(1) If it appears to the responsible authority, in the case of a patient who is for the time being liable to be detained or subject to guardianship under the (Northern Ireland) Order 1986 (otherwise than by virtue of Article 42, 43 or 45 of that Order), that it is in the interests of the patient to remove him to England and Wales, and that arrangements have been made for admitting him to a hospital or, as the case may be, for receiving him into guardianship there, the responsible authority may authorise his removal to England and Wales and may give any necessary directions for his conveyance to his destination.

> **Section 82(1)**
> *The transfer of a patient from Northern Ireland to England and Wales may be authorised by the Department of Health and Social Security for Northern Ireland or by the Secretary of State for Northern Ireland (see s.82(7)) if it is considered to be in his/her best interests and arrangements for the transfer have been made.*

(2) Subject to the provisions of subsections (4) and (4A) below, where a patient who is liable to be detained under the Mental Health (Northern Ireland) Order 1986 by virtue of an application, order or direction under any enactment in force in Northern Ireland is removed under this section and admitted to a hospital in England and Wales, he shall be treated as if on the date of his admission he had been so admitted in pursuance of an application made, or an order or direction made or given, on that date under the corresponding enactment in force in England and Wales and, where he is subject to a restriction order or restriction direction under any enactment in that Order, as if he were subject to a restriction order or restriction direction under the corresponding enactment in force in England and Wales.

> **Section 82(2)**
> *Once in England or Wales the detained patient will be dealt with as if s/he had been admitted under this Act on the date of admission to the English or Welsh hospital. If s/he was subject to a restriction order or direction in Northern Ireland, s/he will be subject to the same order or direction under this Act.*
>
> Note: s/he will have a right to apply to a Mental Health Review Tribunal within six months of his/her transfer (see s.66(1) and s.69(2)(a)).

(3) Where a patient subject to guardianship under the Mental Health (Northern Ireland) Order 1986 by virtue of an application, order or direction under any enactment in force in Northern Ireland is removed under this section and received into guardianship in England and Wales, he shall be treated as if on the date on which he arrives at the place where he is to reside he had been so received in pursuance of an application, order or direction under the corresponding enactment in force in England and Wales and as if the application had been accepted or, as the case may be, the order or direction had been made or given on that date.

Section 82(3)
Once in England or Wales the patient under guardianship will be dealt with as if s/he had been received into guardianship under this Act on the date of arrival at his/her new place of residence.

(4) Where a person removed under this section was immediately before his removal liable to be detained for treatment by virtue of a report under Article 12(1) or 13 of the Mental Health (Northern Ireland) Order 1986, he shall be treated, on his admission to a hospital in England and Wales, as if he had been admitted to the hospital in pursuance of an application for admission for treatment made on the date of his admission.

Section 82(4)
Once in England or Wales the patient who had been previously detained for treatment in Northern Ireland will be dealt with as if s/he had been admitted for treatment under this Act on the date of his/her admission to the English or Welsh hospital.

(4A) Where a person removed under this section was immediately before his removal liable to be detained by virtue of an application for assessment under Article 4 of the Mental Health (Northern Ireland) Order 1986, he shall be treated, on his admission to a hospital in England and Wales, as if he had been admitted to the hospital in pursuance of an application for admission for assessment made on the date of his admission.

Section 82(4A)
Once in England or Wales the patient who had been previously detained for assessment in Northern Ireland will be dealt with as if s/he had been admitted for assessment under this Act on the date of his/her admission to the English or Welsh hospital.

(5) Where a patient removed under this section was immediately before his removal liable to be detained under the Mental Health (Northern Ireland) Order 1986 by virtue of a transfer direction given while he was serving a sentence of imprisonment (within the meaning of Article 53(5) of that Order) imposed by a court in Northern Ireland, he shall be treated as if the sentence had been imposed by a court in England and Wales.

Section 82(5)
Where such a person was in hospital in Northern Ireland by virtue of a transfer direction s/he will be dealt with in England or Wales as if s/he had been sentenced to imprisonment in England or Wales.

(6) Where a person removed under this section was immediately before his removal subject to a restriction order or restriction direction of limited duration, the restriction order or restriction direction to which he is subject by virtue of subsection (2) above shall expire on the date on which the first-mentioned restriction order or restriction direction would have expired if he had not been so removed.

Section 82(6)

The English or Welsh restriction order or direction will expire on the same date that the original Northern Irish order or direction would have done.

(7) In this section "the responsible authority" means the Department of Health and Social Services for Northern Ireland or, in relation to a patient who is subject to a restriction order or restriction direction, the Secretary of State.

Section 82(7)

The decision to move a patient under this section is made by the Department of Health and Social Services for Northern Ireland or, where a restriction order or direction is in force, by the Secretary of State for Northern Ireland.

82A. Transfer of responsibility for patients to England and Wales from Northern Ireland

(1) If it appears to the relevant Minister, in the case of a patient who-

    (a) is subject to a restriction order or restriction direction under Article 47(1) or 55(1) of the Mental Health (Northern Ireland) Order 1986; and

    (b) has been conditionally discharged under Article 48(2) or 78(2) of that Order,

that a transfer under this section would be in the interests of the patient, that Minister may, with the consent of the Secretary of State, transfer responsibility for the patient to the Secretary of State.

Section 82A(1)

Where a patient subject to a restriction order or direction in Northern Ireland has been conditionally discharged, and it is in his/her best interests, responsibility for him/her can be transferred from the Secretary of State for Northern Ireland to the Home Secretary (who must first agree).

(2) Where responsibility for such a patient is transferred under this section, the patient shall be treated-

    (a) as if on the date of the transfer he had been conditionally discharged under section 42 or 73 above; and

    (b) as if he were subject to a restriction order or restriction direction under section 41 or 49 above.

Section 82A(2)
The patient will be dealt with as if his/her conditional discharge had been under this Act on the date of the transfer, and as if s/he was subject to a restriction order or direction under this Act.

(3) Where a patient responsibility for whom is transferred under this section was immediately before the transfer subject to a restriction order or restriction direction of limited duration, the restriction order or restriction direction to which he is subject by virtue of subsection (2) above shall expire on the date on which the first-mentioned order or direction would have expired if the transfer had not been made.

Section 82A(3)
The English or Welsh restriction order or direction will expire on the same date that the original Northern Irish order or direction would have done.

(4) In this section "the relevant Minister" means the Minister exercising in Northern Ireland functions corresponding to those of the Secretary of State.

Section 82A(4)
The decision to transfer responsibility for a patient under this section is made by the Secretary of State for Northern Ireland.

REMOVAL TO AND FROM CHANNEL ISLANDS AND ISLE OF MAN

83. Removal of patients to Channel Islands or Isle of Man

If it appears to the Secretary of State, in the case of a patient who is for the time being liable to be detained or subject to guardianship under this Act (otherwise than by virtue of section 35, 36 or 38 above), that it is in the interests of the patient to remove him to any of the Channel Islands or to the Isle of Man, and that arrangements have been made for admitting him to a hospital or, as the case may be, for receiving him into guardianship there, the Secretary of State may authorise his removal to the island in question and may give any necessary directions for his conveyance to his destination.

> **Section 83**
>
> *If it is in a patient's best interests to be moved to the Channel Islands or Isle of Man and arrangements have been made for this to be done the Secretary of State for Health may authorise this, unless the patient was admitted to hospital for reports or treatment while awaiting trial or sentencing (s.35 and s.36) or was subject to an interim hospital order (s.38).*
>
> *If the patient is subject to a restriction order or a restriction direction, only the Home Secretary can authorise such a move.*

83A. Transfer of responsibility for patients to Channel Islands or Isle of Man

If it appears to the Secretary of State, in the case of a patient who-

(a) is subject to a restriction order or restriction direction under section 41 or 49 above; and

(b) has been conditionally discharged under section 42 or 73 above,

that a transfer under this section would be in the interests of the patient, the Secretary of State may, with the consent of the authority exercising corresponding functions in any of the Channel Islands or in the Isle of Man, transfer responsibility for the patient to that authority.

> **Section 83A**
>
> *Where a patient subject to a restriction order or direction has been conditionally discharged by the Home Secretary (under s.42) or by a Mental Health Review Tribunal (under s.73) the Home Secretary may, if it is in the patient's best interests, transfer responsibility for the patient to the appropriate authority in the Channel Islands or the Isle of Man (who must first agree).*

84. Removal to England and Wales of offenders found insane in Channel Islands and Isle of Man

(1) The Secretary of State may by warrant direct that any offender found by a court in any of the Channel Islands or in the Isle of Man to be insane or to have been insane at the time of the alleged offence, and ordered to be detained during Her Majesty's pleasure, be removed to a hospital in England and Wales.

> **Section 84(1)**
>
> *Is self explanatory. The Secretary of State mentioned here is the Home Secretary.*

(2) A patient removed under subsection (1) above shall, on his reception into the hospital in England and Wales, be treated as if he had been removed to that hospital in pursuance of a direction under section 46 above.

> ### Section 84(2)
> *An offender found to be insane by a court in the Channel Islands or the Isle of Man and transferred to a hospital in England and Wales is dealt with as if s/he were a serviceman who had been transferred to hospital by a court-martial.*
>
> Note: s/he will have a right to apply to a Mental Health Review Tribunal in the second six months after his/her transfer (see s.70).

(3) The Secretary of State may by warrant direct that any patient removed under this section from any of the Channel Islands or from the Isle of Man be returned to the island from which he was so removed, there to be dealt with according to law in all respects as if he had not been removed under this section.

> ### Section 84(3)
> *The Home Secretary can send a patient back to the island from which s/he had come, to be dealt with for the offence as if s/he had never been transferred to hospital in England and Wales.*

85. Patients removed from Channel Islands or Isle of Man

(1) This section applies to any patient who is removed to England and Wales from any of the Channel Islands or the Isle of Man under a provision corresponding to section 83 above and who immediately before his removal was liable to be detained or subject to guardianship in the island in question under a provision corresponding to an enactment contained in this Act (other than section 35, 36 or 38 above).

> ### Section 85(1)
> *Applies to a patient who has been transferred to England and Wales because it is in his/her interests and who was detained or subject to guardianship in the Channel Islands or the Isle of Man, other than a patient who was admitted to hospital for reports or treatment while awaiting trial or sentencing or was subject to an interim hospital order.*

(2) Where the patient is admitted to a hospital in England and Wales he shall be treated as if on the date of his admission he had been so admitted in pursuance of an application made, or an order or direction made or given, on that date under the corresponding enactment contained in this Act and, where he is subject to an order

or direction restricting his discharge, as if he were subject to a restriction order or restriction direction.

> **Section 85(2)**
> *Once in England and Wales the detained patient will be dealt with as if s/he had been admitted under this Act on the date of admission to the English or Welsh hospital. If his/her discharge was subject to restrictions s/he will be dealt with as if s/he were subject to a restriction order or direction.*

(3) Where the patient is received into guardianship in England and Wales, he shall be treated as if on the date on which he arrives at the place where he is to reside he had been so received in pursuance of an application, order or direction under the corresponding enactment contained in this Act and as if the application had been accepted or, as the case may be, the order or direction had been made or given on that date.

> **Section 85(3)**
> *Once in England and Wales the patient under guardianship will be dealt with as if s/he had been received into guardianship under this Act on the date of arrival at his/her new place of residence.*

(4) Where the patient was immediately before his removal liable to be detained by virtue of a transfer direction given while he was serving a sentence of imprisonment imposed by a court in the island in question, he shall be treated as if the sentence had been imposed by a court in England and Wales.

> **Section 85(4)**
> *Where the patient was in hospital in the Channel Islands or Isle of Man by virtue of a transfer direction s/he will be dealt with in England and Wales as if s/he had been sentenced to imprisonment in England and Wales.*

(5) Where the patient was immediately before his removal subject to an order or direction restricting his discharge, being an order or direction of limited duration, the restriction order or restriction direction to which he is subject by virtue of subsection (2) above shall expire on the date on which the first-mentioned order or direction would have expired if he had not been removed.

> **Section 85(5)**
> *The English or Welsh restriction order or direction will expire on the same date that the original would have done.*

(6) While being conveyed to the hospital referred to in subsection (2) or, as the case may be, the place referred to in subsection (3) above, the patient shall be deemed to be in legal custody, and section 138 below shall apply to him as if he were in legal custody by virtue of section 137 below.

> **Section 85(6)**
> *While a detained patient is being taken to the specified hospital or a patient under guardianship to the place at which s/he is to live, s/he is deemed to be in legal custody. This gives anyone with the responsibility for his/her custody the ordinary powers of a police constable in respect of him/her, including the power to use reasonable force in his/her arrest and detention and the power to arrest a person who obstructs him/her. S/he will also be subject to recapture under s.138 if s/he escapes.*

(7) In the case of a patient removed from the Isle of Man the reference in subsection (4) above to a person serving a sentence of imprisonment includes a reference to a person detained as mentioned in section 60(6)(a) of the Mental Health Act 1974 (an Act of Tynwald).

> **Section 85(7)**
> *Is self explanatory.*

85A. Responsibility for patients transferred from Channel Islands or Isle of Man

(1) This section applies to any patient responsibility for whom is transferred to the Secretary of State by the authority exercising corresponding functions in any of the Channel Islands or the Isle of Man under a provision corresponding to section 83A above.

> **Section 85A(1)**
> *The section applies to a patient from the Channel Islands or the Isle of Man who has been conditionally discharged and responsibility for whom has been transferred to the Home Secretary because that is in the patient's interests.*

(2) The patient shall be treated-

(a) as if on the date of the transfer he had been conditionally discharged under section 42 or 73 above; and

(b) as if he were subject to a restriction order or restriction direction under section 41 or 49 above.

Section 85A(2)
The patient will be dealt with as if his/her conditional discharge had been under this Act on the date of the transfer and as if s/he was subject to a restriction order or direction under this Act.

(3) Where the patient was immediately before the transfer subject to an order or direction restricting his discharge, being an order or direction of limited duration, the restriction order or restriction direction to which he is subject by virtue of subsection (2) above shall expire on the date on which the first-mentioned order or direction would have expired if the transfer had not been made.

Section 85A(3)
The English or Welsh restriction order or direction will expire on the same date that the original would have done.

REMOVAL OF ALIENS

86. Removal of alien patients

(1) This section applies to any patient who is neither a British citizen nor a Commonwealth citizen having the right of abode in the United Kingdom by virtue of section 2(1)(b) of the Immigration Act 1971, being a patient who is receiving treatment for mental illness as an in-patient in a hospital in England and Wales or a hospital within the meaning of the Mental Health (Northern Ireland) Order 1986 and is detained pursuant to-

(a) an application for admission for treatment or a report under Article 12(1) or 13 of that Order;

(b) a hospital order under section 37 above or Article 44 of that Order; or

(c) an order or direction under this Act (other than under section 35, 36 or 38 above) or under that Order (other than under Article 42, 43 or 45 of that Order) having the same effect as such a hospital order.

> **Section 86(1)**
> *This section applies to people who do not have the right to live in the United Kingdom and who are detained in hospital in England and Wales or Northern Ireland receiving treatment for mental illness.*

(2) If it appears to the Secretary of State that proper arrangements have been made for the removal of a patient to whom this section applies to a country or territory outside the United Kingdom, the Isle of Man and the Channel Islands and for his care or treatment there and that it is in the interests of the patient to remove him, the Secretary of State may, subject to subsection (3) below–

  (a) by warrant authorise the removal of the patient from the place where he is receiving treatment as mentioned in subsection (1) above, and

  (b) give such directions as the Secretary of State thinks fit for the conveyance of the patient to his destination in that country or territory and for his detention in any place or on board any ship or aircraft until his arrival at any specified port or place in any such country or territory.

> **Section 86(2)**
> *If it is in the patient's interests and proper arrangements have been made for his/her treatment and care the Home Secretary can authorise his/her move to another country and direct how this is to happen.*

(3) The Secretary of State shall not exercise his powers under subsection (2) above in the case of any patient except with the approval of a Mental Health Review Tribunal or, as the case may be, of the Mental Health Review Tribunal for Northern Ireland.

> **Section 86(3)**
> *A Mental Health Review Tribunal must first give its approval to the move and the transfer arrangements.*

RETURN OF PATIENTS ABSENT WITHOUT LEAVE

87. Patients absent from hospitals in Northern Ireland

(1) Any person who–

  (a) under Article 29 or 132 of the Mental Health (Northern Ireland) Order 1986(which provide, respectively, for the retaking of patients absent without leave and for the retaking of patients escaping from custody); or

(b) under the said Article 29 as applied by Article 31 of the said Order(which makes special provision as to persons sentenced to imprisonment);

may be taken into custody in Northern Ireland, may be taken into custody in, and returned to Northern Ireland from, England and Wales by an approved social worker, by any constable or by any person authorised by or by virtue of the said Order to take him into custody.

Section 87(1)

A patient who has escaped from custody or is absent without leave from a hospital in Northern Ireland can be taken into custody in England and Wales and returned to Northern Ireland.

(2) This section does not apply to any person who is subject to guardianship.

Section 87(2)

Is self explanatory.

88. Patients absent from hospitals in England and Wales

(1) Subject to the provisions of this section, any person who, under section 18 above or section 138 below or under the said section 18 as applied by section 22 above, may be taken into custody in England and Wales may be taken into custody in, and returned to England and Wales from, any other part of the United Kingdom or the Channel Islands or the Isle of Man.

Section 88(1)

A patient who has escaped from custody or is absent without leave from a hospital in England and Wales can be taken into custody in Scotland, Northern Ireland, the Channel Islands or the Isle or Man and returned to England and Wales.

This section does not apply to patients under guardianship.

(2) For the purposes of the enactments referred to in subsection (1) above, in their application by virtue of this section to Scotland, Northern Ireland, the Channel Islands or the Isle of Man, the expression "constable" includes a Scottish constable, an officer or constable of the Royal Ulster Constabulary, a member of the police in Jersey, an officer of police within the meaning of section 43 of the Larceny (Guernsey) Law 1958 or any corresponding law for the time being in force, or a constable in the Isle of Man, as the case may be.

> **Section 88(2)**
> *For the purpose of taking people into custody, "constable" means a police officer.*

(3) For the purposes of the said enactments in their application by virtue of this section to Scotland or Northern Ireland, any reference to an approved social worker shall be construed as including a reference–

   (a) in Scotland, to any mental health officer within the meaning of the Mental Health (Scotland) Act 1984;

   (b) in Northern Ireland, to any approved social worker within the meaning of the Mental Health (Northern Ireland) Order 1986.

> **Section 88(3)**
> *The equivalent of an ASW is, in Scotland, a "mental health officer" under the Mental Health (Scotland) Act 1984, and, in Northern Ireland, an "approved social worker" under the Mental Health (Norther Ireland) Order 1986.*

(4) This section does not apply to any person who is subject to guardianship.

> **Section 88(4)**
> *Is self explanatory.*

89. Patients absent from hospitals in the Channel Islands or Isle of Man

(1) Any person who under any provision corresponding to section 18 above or 138 below may be taken into custody in any of the Channel Islands or the Isle of Man may be taken into custody in, and returned to the island in question from, England and Wales by an approved social worker or a constable.

> **Section 89(1)**
> *A patient who has escaped from custody or is absent without leave from hospital in the Channel Islands or the Isle of Man can be taken into custody in England and Wales and returned to the relevant island by an ASW or a police officer.*

(2) This section does not apply to any person who is subject to guardianship.

> **Section 89(2)**
> *Is self explanatory.*

GENERAL

90. Regulations for purposes of Part VI

Section 32 above shall have effect as if references in that section to Part II of this Act included references to this Part of this Act and to Part VII of the Mental Health (Scotland) Act 1984, so far as those Parts apply to patients removed to England and Wales thereunder.

> **Section 90**
> *Gives the Secretary of State for Health power to make any regulations necessary for giving full effect to provisions under Part VI relating to patients moved to England and Wales.*[55]
>
> ---
>
> [55] See the Mental Health (Hospital, Guardianship and Consent to Treatment) Regulations 1983, S.I. 1983 No. 893.

91. General provisions as to patients removed from England and Wales

(1) Subject to subsection (2) below, where a patient liable to be detained or subject to guardianship by virtue of an application, order or direction under Part II or III of this Act (other than section 35, 36 or 38 above) is removed from England and Wales in pursuance of arrangements under this Part of this Act, the application, order or direction shall cease to have effect when he is duly received into a hospital or other institution, or placed under guardianship, in pursuance of those arrangements.

> **Section 91(1)**
> *Except where a patient moved from England and Wales was originally detained for reports on his/her mental condition, for treatment, or under an interim hospital order, any application, order or direction will cease to have effect when s/he arrives at his/her destination.*

(2) Where the Secretary of State exercises his powers under section 86(2) above in respect of a patient who is detained pursuant to a hospital order under section 37 above and in respect of whom a restriction order is in force, those orders shall continue in force so as to apply to the patient if s/he returns to England and Wales at any time before the end of the period for which those orders would have continued in force.

> **Section 91(2)**
> *Where a patient, who is not entitled to live in the United Kingdom and is subject to a hospital order and a restriction order, is transferred to another country, the orders will continue in force so that they will apply if s/he returns to England and Wales before their expiry date.*

92. Interpretation of Part VI

(1) References in this Part of this Act to a hospital, being a hospital in England and Wales, shall be construed as references to a hospital within the meaning of Part II of this Act.

Section 92(1)
Is self explanatory.

(2) Where a patient is treated by virtue of this Part of this Act as if he had been removed to a hospital in England and Wales in pursuance of a direction under Part III of this Act, that direction shall be deemed to have been given on the date of his reception into the hospital.

Section 92(2)
Is self explanatory.

(3) A patient removed to England and Wales under this Part of this Act or under Part VII of the Mental Health (Scotland) Act 1984 shall be treated for the purposes of this Act as suffering from such form of mental disorder as may be recorded in his case in pursuance of regulations made by virtue of section 90 above, and references in this Act to the form or forms of mental disorder specified in the relevant application, order or direction shall be construed as including references to the form or forms of mental disorder so recorded.

Section 92(3)
When a patient is moved to England and Wales the RMO must as soon as reasonably practicable make a record of the form of mental disorder from which the patient is suffering. For all purposes under this Act, his/her mental disorder will then be that so recorded.

(4) Sections 80 to 85A above shall have effect as if–

(a) any hospital direction under section 45A above were a transfer direction under section 47 above; and

(b) any limitation direction under section 45A above were a restriction direction under section 49 above.

Section 92(4)

For the purposes of the transfer provisions in s.80 to s.85A a patient subject to a hybrid order under s.45A will be dealt with as if he were subject to a s.47 transfer direction and a s.49 restriction direction.

(5) Sections 80(5), 81(6) and 85(4) above shall have effect as if any reference to a transfer direction given while a patient was serving a sentence of imprisonment imposed by a court included a reference to a hospital direction given by a court after imposing a sentence of imprisonment on a patient.

Section 92(5)

References to transfer directions in s.80(5), s.81(6) and s.85(4) are deemed to include hospital directions made after sentencing to a term of imprisonment.

PART VII

MANAGEMENT OF PROPERTY AND AFFAIRS OF PATIENTS

93. Judicial authorities and Court of Protection

(1) The Lord Chancellor shall from time to time nominate one or more judges of the Supreme Court (in this Act referred to as "nominated judges") to act for the purposes of this Part of this Act.

Section 93(1)

Is self explanatory.

Note: the judges nominated to act in relation to the Court of Protection come from the Chancery Division of the High Court.

(2) There shall continue to be an office of the Supreme Court, called the Court of Protection, for the protection and management, as provided by this Part of this Act, of the property and affairs of persons under disability; and there shall continue to be a Master of the Court of Protection appointed by the Lord Chancellor under section 89 of the Supreme Court Act 1981.

Section 93(2)

The Court of Protection manages and protects the property and affairs of those who are, because of mental disorder, unable to do so for themselves.

Note: most of the work under this Part of the Act is done by non-judicial officers of the Court, under the overall direction of the Master.

(3) The Master of the Court of Protection shall take the oath of allegiance and judicial oath in the presence of the Lord Chancellor; and the Promissory Oaths Act 1868 shall have effect as if the officers named in the Second Part of the Schedule to that Act included the Master of the Court of Protection.

Section 93(3)
Is self explanatory.

Note: the Master must be a barrister or solicitor of at least 10 years' experience (or the Deputy Master).

(4) The Lord Chancellor may nominate other officers of the Court of Protection (in this Part of this Act referred to as "nominated officers") to act for the purposes of this Part of this Act.

Section 93(4)
Is self explanatory.

94. Exercise of the judge's functions: "the patient"

(1) Subject to subsection (1A) below the functions expressed to be conferred by this Part of this Act on the judge shall be exercisable by the Lord Chancellor or by any nominated judge, and shall also be exercisable by the Master of the Court of Protection, by the Public Trustee or by any nominated officer, but–

   (a) in the case of the Master, the Public Trustee or any nominated officer, subject to any express provision to the contrary in this Part of this Act or any rules made under this Part of this Act,

   (aa) in the case of the Public Trustee, subject to any directions of the Master and so far only as may be provided by any rules made under this Part of this Act or (subject to any such rules) by directions of the Master,

   (b) in the case of any nominated officer, subject to any directions of the Master and so far only as may be provided by the instrument by which he is nominated;

   and references in this Part of this Act to the judge shall be construed accordingly.

> **Section 94(1)**
> *Functions of the judge can be exercised by the Lord Chancellor or any nominated judge. Some functions may also be exercised by the Master of the Court of Protection, the Public Trustee and any nominated officer. The term "the judge" in this Part covers all of these people.*

(1A) In such cases or circumstances as may be prescribed by any rules under this Part of this Act or (subject to any such rules) by directions of the Master, the functions of the judge under this Part of this Act shall be exercised by the Public Trustee (but subject to any directions of the Master as to their exercise).

> **Section 94(1A)**
> *The Public Trustee's performance of the judge's functions is governed by rules made under s.106 and by directions of the Master.*

(2) The functions of the judge under this Part of this Act shall be exercisable where, after considering medical evidence, he is satisfied that a person is incapable, by reason of mental disorder, of managing and administering his property and affairs; and a person as to whom the judge is so satisfied is referred to in this Part of this Act as a patient.

> **Section 94(2)**
> *The judge in the Court of Protection has power where (on medical evidence) a person is incapable of looking after his/her property and affairs. The Court has exclusive jurisdiction over all aspects of the patient's property and affairs, but not over the management and care of the patient's person.*
>
> Note: there is no requirement that the medical evidence referred to be provided by a s.12 approved doctor.

95. General functions of the judge with respect to property and affairs of patient

(1) The judge may, with respect to the property and affairs of a patient, do or secure the doing of all such things as appear necessary or expedient–

    (a) for the maintenance or other benefit of the patient,

    (b) for the maintenance or other benefit of members of the patient's family,

    (c) for making provision for other persons or purposes for whom or which the patient might be expected to provide if he were not mentally disordered, or

    (d) otherwise for administering the patient's affairs.

> **Section 95(1)**
> *The judge will manage the patient's property and affairs for him/her with the four prescribed purposes in mind.*

(2) In the exercise of the powers conferred by this section regard shall be had first of all to the requirements of the patient, and the rules of law which restricted the enforcement by a creditor of rights against property under the control of the judge in lunacy shall apply to property under the control of the judge; but, subject to the foregoing provisions of this subsection, the judge shall, in administering a patient's affairs, have regard to the interests of creditors and also to the desirability of making provision for obligations of the patient notwithstanding that they may not be legally enforceable.

> **Section 95(2)**
> *The judge must first have regard to the patient's needs but, provided there are sufficient funds available for the patient's maintenance, s/he must consider the claims of creditors and also the desirability of making provision for those to whom the patient has non-legal obligations.*

96. Powers of the judge as to patient's property and affairs

(1) Without prejudice to the generality of section 95 above, the judge shall have power to make such orders and give such directions and authorities as he thinks fit for the purposes of that section and in particular may for those purposes make orders or give directions or authorities for–

   (a) the control (with or without the transfer or vesting of property or the payment into or lodgment in the Supreme Court of money or securities) and management of any property of the patient;

   (b) the sale, exchange, charging or other disposition of or dealing with any property of the patient;

   (c) the acquisition of any property in the name or on behalf of the patient;

   (d) the settlement of any property of the patient, or the gift of any property of the patient to any such persons or for any such purposes as are mentioned in paragraphs (b) and (c) of section 95(1) above;

   (e) the execution for the patient of a will making any provision (whether by way of disposing of property or exercising a power or otherwise) which could be made by a will executed by the patient if he were not mentally disordered;

   (f) the carrying on by a suitable person of any profession, trade or business of the patient;

(g) the dissolution of a partnership of which the patient is a member;

(h) the carrying out of any contract entered into by the patient;

(i) the conduct of legal proceedings in the name of the patient or on his behalf;

(j) the reimbursement out of the property of the patient, with or without interest, of money applied by any person either in payment of the patient's debts (whether legally enforceable or not) or for the maintenance or other benefit of the patient or members of his family or in making provision for other persons or purposes for whom or which he might be expected to provide if he were not mentally disordered;

(k) the exercise of any power (including a power to consent) vested in the patient, whether beneficially, or as guardian or trustee, or otherwise.

Section 96(1)

Lists the powers a judge has when managing a patient's property and affairs. The judge may buy, sell and manage the patient's property, or even give it away (for the benefit of the patient's family or others whom the patient might be expected to provide for.) S/he may execute a will, make arrangements for a suitable person to take over the patient's business, dissolve a partnership and arrange for the patient's contracts to be fulfilled. S/he may also conduct legal proceedings on the patient's behalf, settle debts and carry out any legal obligations the patient may have e.g. as a guardian or trustee.

This list is not exhaustive.

(2) If under subsection (1) above provision is made for the settlement of any property of a patient, or the exercise of a power vested in a patient of appointing trustees or retiring from a trust, the judge may also make as respects the property settled or trust property such consequential vesting or other orders as the case may require, including (in the case of the exercise of such a power) any order which could have been made in such a case under Part IV of the Trustee Act 1925.

Section 96(2)

Some actions in relation to settlement of property, appointing of trustees and retiring from trusts necessitate the making of further orders: the judge may make whatever consequential orders are necessary.

(3) Where under this section a settlement has been made of any property of a patient, and the Lord Chancellor or a nominated judge is satisfied, at any time before the death of the patient, that any material fact was not disclosed when the settlement was made, or that there has been any substantial change in circumstances, he may by order vary the settlement in such manner as he thinks fit, and give any consequential directions.

Section 96(3)
The Lord Chancellor and nominated judges have power, up until the patient's death, to make changes to settlements of the patient's property where relevant facts were not disclosed at the time or where there has been a change of circumstances.

(4) The power of the judge to make or give an order, direction or authority for the execution of a will for a patient–

  (a) shall not be exercisable at any time when the patient is a minor, and

  (b) shall not be exercised unless the judge has reason to believe that the patient is incapable of making a valid will for himself.

Section 96(4)
The judge cannot make a will unless the patient is aged 18 or over. S/he need only have <u>reason to believe</u> that the patient doesn't have capacity to make his/her own will.

(5) The powers of a patient as patron of a benefice shall be exercisable by the Lord Chancellor only.

Section 96(5)
Only the Lord Chancellor can exercise a patient's power to grant a living from a Church office.

97. Supplementary provisions as to wills executed under s 96

(1) Where under section 96(1) above the judge makes or gives an order, direction or authority requiring or authorising a person (in this section referred to as "the authorised person") to execute a will for a patient, any will executed in pursuance of that order, direction or authority shall be expressed to be signed by the patient acting by the authorised person, and shall be–

  (a) signed by the authorised person with the name of the patient, and with his own name, in the presence of two or more witnesses present at the same time, and

  (b) attested and subscribed by those witnesses in the presence of the authorised person, and

  (c) sealed with the official seal of the Court of Protection.

Section 97(1)
Sets out the necessary formalities where a will has been made on the patient's behalf and is self explanatory.

(2) The Wills Act 1837 shall have effect in relation to any such will as if it were signed by the patient by his own hand, except that in relation to any such will–

(a) section 9 of that Act (which makes provision as to the signing and attestation of wills) shall not apply, and

(b) in the subsequent provisions of that Act any reference to execution in the manner required by the previous provisions of that Act shall be construed as a reference to execution in the manner required by subsection (1) above.

Section 97(2)
The usual statutory requirements as to signing a will in the presence of two witnesses do not apply to wills made on the patient's behalf.

(3) Subject to the following provisions of this section, any such will executed in accordance with subsection (1) above shall have the same effect for all purposes as if the patient were capable of making a valid will and the will had been executed by him in the manner required by the Wills Act 1837.

Section 97(3)
Where the formalities of this section are complied with the will shall be dealt with as if it had been properly made by the patient.

(4) So much of subsection (3) above as provides for such a will to have effect as if the patient were capable of making a valid will–

(a) shall not have effect in relation to such a will in so far as it disposes of any immovable property, other than immovable property in England and Wales, and

(b) where at the time when such a will is executed the patient is domiciled in Scotland or Northern Ireland or in a country or territory outside the United Kingdom, shall not have effect in relation to that will in so far as it relates to any other property or matter, except any property or matter in respect of which, under the law of his domicile, any question of his testamentary capacity would fall to be determined in accordance with the law of England and Wales.

Section 97(4)

Provides for the effect of wills made under s.96 on a patient's behalf. If the will purports to dispose of immovable property outside England and Wales, that part of it will have no effect.

Where at the time the will is executed the patient lives in Scotland or Northern Ireland or outside the United Kingdom and the will relates to any other property or matter, it will have no effect unless and to the extent that the patient's capacity to make a will in respect of that property or matter falls to be determined under the law of England and Wales.

98. Judge's powers in cases of emergency

Where it is represented to the judge, and he has reason to believe, that a person may be incapable, by reason of mental disorder, of managing and administering his property and affairs, and the judge is of the opinion that it is necessary to make immediate provision for any of the matters referred to in section 95 above, then pending the determination of the question whether that person is so incapable the judge may exercise in relation to the property and affairs of that person any of the powers conferred on him in relation to the property and affairs of a patient by this Part of this Act so far as is requisite for enabling that provision to be made.

Section 98

In an emergency the judge may act where s/he has reason to believe that a person may be incapable of looking after his/her affairs.

99. Power to appoint receiver

(1) The judge may by order appoint as receiver for a patient a person specified in the order or the holder for the time being of an office so specified.

Section 99(1)

The judge may appoint a receiver for the patient.

(2) A person appointed as receiver for a patient shall do all such things in relation to the property and affairs of the patient as the judge, in the exercise of the powers conferred on him by sections 95 and 96 above, orders or directs him to do and may do any such thing in relation to the property and affairs of the patient as the judge, in the exercise of those powers, authorises him to do.

Section 99(2)
The judge determines the extent of the receiver's powers and obligations in relation to the patient's property and affairs.

(3) A receiver appointed for any person shall be discharged by order of the judge on the judge being satisfied that that person has become capable of managing and administering his property and affairs, and may be discharged by order of the judge at any time if the judge considers it expedient to do so; and a receiver shall be discharged (without any order) on the death of the patient.

Section 99(3)
A receiver must be discharged if the judge is satisfied that the patient has become capable of looking after his/her property and affairs and may be discharged when the judge considers it appropriate for the patient that the receiver be discharged. Receivership automatically ceases when the patient dies.

100. Vesting of stock in curator appointed outside England and Wales

(1) Where the judge is satisfied–

(a) that under the law prevailing in a place outside England and Wales a person has been appointed to exercise powers with respect to the property or affairs of any other person on the ground (however formulated) that that other person is incapable, by reason of mental disorder, of managing and administering his property and affairs, and

(b) that having regard to the nature of the appointment and to the circumstances of the case it is expedient that the judge should exercise his powers under this section,

the judge may direct any stock standing in the name of the said other person or the right to receive the dividends from the stock to be transferred into the name of the person so appointed or otherwise dealt with as requested by that person, and may give such directions as the judge thinks fit for dealing with accrued dividends from the stock.

(2) In this section "stock" includes shares and also any fund, annuity or security transferable in the books kept by any body corporate or unincorporated company or society, or by an instrument of transfer either alone or accompanied by the formalities, and "dividends" shall be construed accordingly.

Section 100

Where an appointment has been made outside England and Wales for someone to look after a person's affairs because that person is incapable, a judge here may, if appropriate, transfer stock and the right to receive dividends to the appointed person.

101. Preservation of interests in patient's property

(1) Where any property of a person has been disposed of under this Part of this Act, and under his will or his intestacy, or by any gift perfected or nomination taking effect on his death, any other person would have taken an interest in the property but for the disposal–

    (a) he shall take the same interest, if and so far as circumstances allow, in any property belonging to the estate of the deceased which represents the property disposed of; and

    (b) if the property disposed of was real property any property representing it shall so long as it remains part of his estate be treated as if it were real property.

(2) The judge, in ordering, directing or authorising under this Part of this Act any disposal of property which apart from this section would result in the conversion of personal property into real property, may direct that the property representing the property disposed of shall, so long as it remains the property of the patient or forms part of his estate, be treated as if it were personal property.

(3) References in subsections (1) and (2) above to the disposal of property are references to–

    (a) the sale, exchange, charging or other dealing (otherwise than by will) with property other than money,

    (b) the removal of property from one place to another,

    (c) the application of money in acquiring property, or

    (d) the transfer of money from one account to another;

and references to property representing property disposed of shall be construed accordingly and as including the result of successive disposals.

(4) The judge may give such directions as appear to him necessary or expedient for the purpose of facilitating the operation of subsection (1) above, including the carrying of money to a separate account and the transfer of property other than money.

(5) Where the judge has ordered, directed or authorised the expenditure of money for the carrying out of permanent improvements on, or otherwise for the permanent benefit of, any property of the patient, he may order that the whole or any part of the money expended or to be expended shall be a charge upon the property,

whether without interest or with interest at a specified rate; and an order under this subsection may provide for excluding or restricting the operation of subsection (1) above.

(6) A charge under subsection (5) above may be made in favour of such person as may be just, and in particular, where the money charged is paid out of the patient's general estate, may be made in favour of a person as trustee for the patient; but no charge under that subsection shall confer any right of sale or foreclosure during the lifetime of the patient.

Section 101

Makes provision for those who would have received an interest in property on the patient's death if that property had not been dealt with under this Part of the Act. For analysis of the details of this section, which is beyond the scope of this book, see Court of Protection Practice, *Heywood and Massey (12th ed., 1991).*

102. Lord Chancellor's Visitors

(1) There shall continue to be the following panels of Lord Chancellor's Visitors of patients constituted in accordance with this section, namely–

 (a) a panel of Medical Visitors;

 (b) a panel of Legal Visitors; and

 (c) a panel of General Visitors (being Visitors who are not required by this section to possess either a medical or legal qualification for appointment).

Section 102(1)

There are three panels of "Lord Chancellor's Visitors": medical, legal and general.

(2) Each panel shall consist of persons appointed to it by the Lord Chancellor, the appointment of each person being for such term and subject to such conditions as the Lord Chancellor may determine.

Section 102(2)

Is self explanatory.

(3) A person shall not be qualified to be appointed–

 (a) to the panel of Medical Visitors unless he is a registered medical practitioner who appears to the Lord Chancellor to have special knowledge and experience of cases of mental disorder;

(b) to the panel of Legal Visitors unless he has a 10 year general qualification, within the meaning of section 71 of the Courts and Legal Services Act 1990.

Section 102(3)

A Medical Visitor must be a doctor with special knowledge and experience of patients with mental disorder. A Legal Visitor must be a barrister or solicitor of at least 10 years' standing who has a right of audience in relation to any class of proceedings in any part of the Supreme Court, or all proceedings in county courts or magistrates' courts.

(4) If the Lord Chancellor so determines in the case of any Visitor appointed under this section, he shall be paid out of money provided by Parliament such remuneration and allowances as the Lord Chancellor may, with the concurrence of the Treasury, determine.

Section 102(4)

Visitors may be paid fees and allowances with the agreement of the Treasury.

103. Functions of Visitors

(1) Patients shall be visited by Lord Chancellor's Visitors in such circumstances, and in such manner, as may be prescribed by directions of a standing nature given by the Master of the Court of Protection with the concurrence of the Lord Chancellor.

Section 103(1)

The Master of the Court of Protection gives standing directions as to the visiting of patients.

Note: it is a criminal offence under s.129 (below) to obstruct such a visit.

(2) Where it appears to the judge in the case of any patient that a visit by a Lord Chancellor's Visitor is necessary for the purpose of investigating any particular matter or matters relating to the capacity of the patient to manage and administer his property and affairs, or otherwise relating to the exercise in relation to him of the functions of the judge under this Part of this Act, the judge may order that the patient shall be visited for that purpose.

Section 103(2)

Where the judge considers it necessary, particularly for investigating the patient's capacity to look after his/her own affairs, s/he may order that the patient be visited.

(3) Every visit falling to be made under subsection (1) or (2) above shall be made by a General Visitor unless, in a case where it appears to the judge that it is in the circumstances essential for the visit to be made by a Visitor with medical or legal qualifications, the judge directs that the visit shall be made by a Medical or a Legal Visitor.

Section 103(3)
Visits are usually made by General Visitors, unless the judge considers it essential to order that a medical or legal visit be made.

(4) A Visitor making a visit under this section shall make such report on the visit as the judge may direct.

Section 103(4)
Is self explanatory.

(5) A Visitor making a visit under this section may interview the patient in private.

Section 103(5)
Is self explanatory.

Note: it is a criminal offence under s.129 for a person to insist on being present when required to leave by a Visitor who wishes to interview the patient in private.

(6) A Medical Visitor making a visit under this section may carry out in private a medical examination of the patient and may require the production of and inspect any medical records relating to the patient.

Section 103(6)
Is self explanatory.

Note: it is a criminal offence under s.129 for a person to refuse to allow a medical examination by a Visitor or to refuse to produce medical records.

(7) The Master of the Court of Protection may visit any patient for the purpose mentioned in subsection (2) above and may interview the patient in private.

> ### Section 103(7)
> *Is self explanatory.*
>
> Note: obstruction of the Master by any person will be an offence under s.129.

(8) A report made by a Visitor under this section, and information contained in such a report, shall not be disclosed except to the judge and any person authorised by the judge to receive the disclosure.

> ### Section 103(8)
> *Is self-explanatory.*

(9) If any person discloses any report or information in contravention of subsection (8) above, he shall be guilty of an offence and liable on summary conviction to imprisonment for a term not exceeding three months or to a fine not exceeding level 3 on the standard scale or both.

> ### Section 103(9)
> *Unauthorised disclosure of the contents of a Visitor's report is a criminal offence punishable with up to three months' imprisonment or a fine or both.*

(10) In this section references to patients include references to persons alleged to be incapable, by reason of mental disorder, of managing and administering their property and affairs.

> ### Section 103(10)
> *"Patient" in this section means anyone who is <u>or is alleged to be</u> incapable through mental disorder or managing his/her property and affairs.*

104. General powers of the judge with respect to proceedings

(1) For the purposes of any proceedings before him with respect to persons suffering or alleged to be suffering from mental disorder, the judge shall have the same powers as are vested in the High Court in respect of securing the attendance of witnesses and the production of documents.

Section 104(1)

The judge in the Court of Protection has the ordinary powers of a High Court judge to compel witnesses to attend or to compel the production at court of documents.

(2) Subject to the provisions of this section, any act or omission in the course of such proceedings which, if occurring in the course of proceedings in the High Court would have been a contempt of the Court, shall be punishable by the judge in any manner in which it could have been punished by the High Court.

Section 104(2)

A High Court judge, or the Lord Chancellor, sitting in the Court of Protection has the same powers to punish a contempt of court as a judge sitting in the High Court.

(3) Subsection (2) above shall not authorise the Master, or any other officer of the Court of Protection to exercise any power of attachment or committal, but the Master or officer may certify any such act or omission to the Lord Chancellor or a nominated judge, and the Lord Chancellor or judge may upon such certification inquire into the alleged act or omission and take any such action in relation to it as he could have taken if the proceedings had been before him.

Section 104(3)

Where the Master or another officer of the Court of Protection wishes to deal with a contempt they may refer it to the Lord Chancellor or a nominated judge, who can then take action as if the contempt had occurred before him/her.

(4) Subsections (1) to (4) of section 36 of the Supreme Court Act 1981 (which provides a special procedure for the issue of writs of subpoena ad testificandum and duces tecum so as to be enforceable throughout the United Kingdom) shall apply in relation to proceedings under this Part of this Act with the substitution for references to the High Court of references to the judge and for references to such writs of references to such document as may be prescribed by rules under this Part of this Act for issue by the judge for securing the attendance of witnesses or the production of documents.

Section 104(4)

The usual rules of the High Court for compelling witnesses to attend court or for compelling the production at court of documents will apply to proceedings in the Court of Protection.

105. Appeals

(1) Subject to and in accordance with rules under this Part of this Act, an appeal shall lie to a nominated judge from any decision of the Master of the Court of Protection or any nominated officer.

> **Section 105(1)**
>
> *Decisions of the Master or a nominated officer may be appealed to a nominated judge.*
>
> Note: the judge considers the matter afresh: s/he does not simply review the decision of the Master or officer.

(2) The Court of Appeal shall continue to have the same jurisdiction as to appeals from any decision of the Lord Chancellor or from any decision of a nominated judge, whether given in the exercise of his original jurisdiction or on the hearing of an appeal under subsection (1) above, as they had immediately before the coming into operation of Part VIII of the Mental Health Act 1959 as to appeals from orders in lunacy made by the Lord Chancellor or any other person having jurisdiction in lunacy.

> **Section 105(2)**
>
> *Decisions of the Lord Chancellor or a nominated judge may be appealed to the Court of Appeal.*

106. Rules of procedure

(1) Proceedings before the judge with respect to persons suffering or alleged to be suffering from mental disorder (in this section referred to as "proceedings") shall be conducted in accordance with the provisions of rules made under this Part of this Act.

(2) Rules under this Part of this Act may make provision as to–
    (a) the carrying out of preliminary or incidental inquiries;
    (b) the persons by whom and manner in which proceedings may be instituted and carried on;
    (c) the persons who are to be entitled to be notified of, to attend, or to take part in proceedings;
    (d) the evidence which may be authorised or required to be given in proceedings and the manner (whether on oath or otherwise and whether orally or in writing) in which it is to be given;
    (e) the administration of oaths and taking of affidavits for the purposes of proceedings; and
    (f) the enforcement of orders made and directions given in proceedings.

(3) Without prejudice to the provisions of section 104(1) above, rules under this Part of this Act may make provision for authorising or requiring the attendance and examination of persons suffering or alleged to be suffering from mental disorder, the furnishing of information and the production of documents.

(4) Rules under this Part of this Act may make provision as to the termination of proceedings, whether on the death or recovery of the person to whom the proceedings relate or otherwise, and for the exercise, pending the termination of the proceedings, of powers exercisable under this Part of this Act in relation to the property or affairs of a patient.

(5) Rules under this Part of this Act made with the consent of the Treasury may–
   (a) make provision as to the scale of costs, fees and percentages payable in relation to proceedings, and as to the manner in which and funds out of which such costs, fees and percentages are to be paid;
   (b) contain provision for charging any percentage upon the estate of the person to whom the proceedings relate and for the payment of costs, fees and percentages within such time after the death of the person to whom the proceedings relate or the termination of the proceedings as may be provided by the rules; and
   (c) provide for the remission of fees and percentages.

(6) A charge upon the estate of a person created by virtue of subsection (5) above shall not cause any interest of that person in any property to fail or determine or to be prevented from recommencing.

(7) Rules under this Part of this Act may authorise the making of orders for the payment of costs to or by persons attending, as well as persons taking part in, proceedings.

Section 106
Permits the creation of rules of procedure for the Court of Protection.[56]

[56] See the Mental Health (Hospital, Guardianship and Consent to Treatment) Regulations 1983, S.I. 1983 No. 893.

107. Security and accounts

(1) Rules under this Part of this Act may make provision as to the giving of security by a receiver and as to the enforcement and discharge of the security.

Section 107(1)
Is self explanatory.[57]

[57] See the Court of Protection Rules 1994, rr 58-68, and *Court of Protection Practice*, Heywood and Massey.

(2) It shall be the duty of a receiver to render accounts in accordance with the requirements of rules under this Part of this Act, as well after his discharge as during his receivership; and rules under this Part of this Act may make provision for the rendering of accounts by persons other than receivers who are ordered, directed or authorised under this Part of this Act to carry out any transaction.

Section 107(2)
Receivers must produce accounts in accordance with the Court of Protection Rules.

108. General provisions as to rules under Part VII

(1) Any power to make rules conferred by this Part of this Act shall be exercisable by the Lord Chancellor.

(2) Rules under this Part of this Act may contain such incidental and supplemental provisions as appear requisite for the purposes of the rules.

Section 108
Is self explanatory.

109. Effect and proof of orders, etc

(1) Section 204 of the Law of Property Act 1925 (by which orders of the High Court are made conclusive in favour of purchasers) shall apply in relation to orders made and directions and authorities given by the judge as it applies in relation to orders of the High Court.

Section 109(1)
Provides for certain orders made and directions and authorities given in the Court of Protection to be deemed conclusive in favour of purchasers of property.

(2) Office copies of orders made, directions or authorities given or other instruments issued by the judge and sealed with the official seal of the Court of Protection shall be admissible in all legal proceedings as evidence of the originals without any further proof.

Section 109(2)
Is self explanatory.

110. Reciprocal arrangements in relation to Scotland and Northern Ireland as to exercise of powers

(1) This Part of this Act shall apply in relation to the property and affairs in Scotland or Northern Ireland of a patient in relation to whom powers have been exercised under this Part of this Act, or a person as to whom powers are exercisable and have been exercised under section 98 above as it applies in relation to his property and affairs in England and Wales unless–

  (a) in Scotland, a curator bonis, tutor or judicial factor has been appointed for him; or

  (b) in Northern Ireland, he is a patient in relation to whom powers have been exercised under Part VIII of the Mental Health (Northern Ireland) Order 1986, or a person as to whom powers are exercisable and have been exercised under Article 97(2) of that Order.

> **Section 110(1)**
> *Where the Court of Protection is acting for a patient in England and Wales who has "property and affairs" in Scotland or Northern Ireland, the Court will also have jurisdiction over them unless, in Scotland, a person has been appointed to perform those functions or, in Northern Ireland, powers under the corresponding Northern Irish legislation have been exercised.*

(2) Where under the law in force in Scotland . . . with respect to the property and affairs of persons suffering from mental disorder a curator bonis, tutor, or judicial factor has been appointed for any person, the provisions of that law shall apply in relation to that persons's property and affairs in England and Wales unless he is a patient in relation to whom powers have been exercised under this Part of this Act, or a person as to whom powers are exercisable and have been exercised under section 98 above.

> **Section 110(2)**
> *Where someone has been appointed in Scotland to look after the property and affairs of a patient, and the Court of Protection has not exercised its powers in relation to him/her in England and Wales, the Scottish appointee will have jurisdiction under the Scottish law over any of his/her property and affairs in England and Wales.*

(2A) Part VIII of the Mental Health (Northern Ireland) Order 1986 shall apply in relation to the property and affairs in England and Wales of a patient in relation to whom powers have been exercised under that Part, or a person as to whom powers are exercisable and have been exercised under Article 97(2) of that Order as it applies in relation to his property and affairs in Northern Ireland unless he is a patient in relation to whom powers have been exercised under this Part of this Act, or a person as to whom powers are exercisable and have been exercised under section 98 above.

Section 110(3)

Where a patient's property and affairs are being managed under Northern Irish provisions, and where the Court of Protection has not exercised its powers in relation to him/her in England and Wales, any of his/her property and affairs in England and Wales may also be managed under the Northern Irish provisions.

(3) Nothing in this section shall affect any power to execute a will under section 96(1)(e) above or Article 99(1)(e) of the Mental Health (Northern Ireland) Order 1986 or the effect of any will executed in the exercise of such a power.

Section 110(4)

This section does not affect the power, either of the Court of Protection or under the corresponding Northern Irish provisions, to execute a will on a patient's behalf.

(4) In this section references to property do not include references to land or interests in land but this subsection shall not prevent the receipt of rent or other income arising from land or interests in land.

Section 110(5)

The powers in this section are exercisable in relation to the receipt of income or rent from land, but not exercisable in relation to land itself or interests in land.

111. Construction of references in other Acts to judge or authority having jurisdiction under Part VII

(1) The functions expressed to be conferred by any enactment not contained in this Part of this Act on the judge having jurisdiction under this Part of this Act shall be exercisable by the Lord Chancellor or by a nominated judge.

Section 111(1)

Where a statutory provision other than this Act gives functions to a judge of the Court of Protection, those functions are to be performed only by the Lord Chancellor or by a nominated judge.

(2) Subject to subsection (3) and (3A) below, the functions expressed to be conferred by any such enactment on the authority having jurisdiction under this Part of this Act shall, subject to any express provision to the contrary, be exercisable by the Lord Chancellor, a nominated judge, the Master of the Court of Protection, by the Public Trustee or a nominated officer.

Section 111(2)
Where a statutory provision other than this Act gives functions to an "authority having jurisdiction under Part VII" of this Act, those functions may be performed by the Lord Chancellor, a nominated judge, the Master of the Court of Protection, the Public Trustee or by a nominated officer (unless expressly excluded).

(2A) The exercise of the functions referred to in subsection (2) above by the Public Trustee shall be subject to any directions of the Master and they shall be exercisable so far only as may be provided by any rules made under this Part of this Act or (subject to any such rules) by directions of the Master.

Section 111(2A)
The Public Trustee's performance of any such functions is governed by rules made under s.106 and by directions of the Master.

(3) The exercise of the functions referred to in subsection (2) above by a nominated officer shall be subject to any directions of the Master and they shall be exercisable so far only as may be provided by the instrument by which the officer is nominated.

Section 111(3)
A nominated officer's performance of any such functions is governed by directions of the Master and limited by the terms of the officer's nomination.

(3A) In such cases or circumstances as may be prescribed by any rules under this Part of this Act or (subject to any such rules) by directions of the Master, the functions referred to in subsection (2) above shall be exercised by the Public Trustee (but subject to any directions of the Master as to their exercise).

Section 111(3A)
The Public Trustee's performance of any such functions is governed by rules made under s.106 and by directions of the Master.

(4) Subject to the foregoing provisions of this section–

(a) references in any enactment not contained in this Part of this Act to the judge having jurisdiction under this Part of this Act shall be construed as references to the Lord Chancellor or a nominated judge, and

(b) references in any such enactment to the authority having jurisdiction under this Part of this Act shall be construed as references to the Lord Chancellor, a nominated judge, the Master of the Court of Protection or a nominated officer.

Section 111(4)
Is self explanatory.

112. Interpretation of Part VII

In this Part of this Act, unless the context otherwise requires–

"nominated judge" means a judge nominated in pursuance of subsection (1) of section 93 above;

"nominated officer" means an officer nominated in pursuance of subsection (4) of that section;

"patient" has the meaning assigned to it by section 94 above;

"property" includes any thing in action, and any interest in real or personal property;

"the judge" shall be construed in accordance with section 94 above;

"will" includes a codicil.

Section 112

"Nominated judge"	*Nominated by the Lord Chancellor, from the Chancery Division of the High Court.*
"Nominated officer"	*Officer of the Court of Protection nominated by the Lord Chancellor.*
"Patient"	*Person who is unable, because of mental or disorder, to look after his/her own property and affairs (except in s.103, where it includes a person who is <u>alleged</u> to be so incapable).*
"The judge"	*Functions of the judge can be exercised by the Lord Chancellor or any nominated judge: some functions may also be exercised by the Master of the Court of Protection, the Public Trustee and any nominated officer. The term "the judge" in this Part covers all of these people.*

113. Disapplication of certain enactments in relation to persons within the jurisdiction of the judge

The provisions of the Acts described in Schedule 3 to this Act which are specified in the third column of that Schedule, so far as they make special provision for persons suffering from mental disorder, shall not have effect in relation to patients and to persons as to whom powers are exercisable and have been exercised under section 98 above.

Section 113
The Acts referred to are dated between 1773 and 1894. The specified provisions do not apply to persons who are unable, because of mental disorder, to look after their own property and affairs, nor to those whom there is reason to believe may fall into this category and in respect of whom the judge has exercised emergency powers under s.98.

PART VIII

MISCELLANEOUS FUNCTIONS OF LOCAL AUTHORITIES AND THE SECRETARY OF STATE

APPROVED SOCIAL WORKERS

Note: for the purposes of Part VIII, "hospital" does not include a registered mental nursing home, because s.34(2) does not apply.

114. Appointment of approved social workers

(1) A local social services authority shall appoint a sufficient number of approved social workers for the purpose of discharging the functions conferred on them by this Act.

Section 114(1)
The local authority must ensure that sufficient ASWs are appointed to perform all of the functions under the Act.

(2) No person shall be appointed by a local social services authority as an approved social worker unless he is approved by the authority as having appropriate competence in dealing with persons who are suffering from mental disorder.

Section 114(2)
An ASW must be approved as competent in dealing with persons suffering from mental disorder.

(3) In approving a person for appointment as an approved social worker a local social services authority shall have regard to such matters as the Secretary of State may direct.

> ### Section 114(3)
> *The Secretary of State for Health can specify matters that the local social services authority must take into consideration in appointing ASWs.*

115. Powers of entry and inspection

An approved social worker of a local social services authority may at all reasonable times after producing, if asked to do so, some duly authenticated document showing that he is such a social worker, enter and inspect any premises (not being a hospital) in the area of that authority in which a mentally disordered patient is living, if he has reasonable cause to believe that the patient is not under proper care.

> ### Section 115
> *Where an ASW has good reason to believe that a patient is not being properly cared for s/he may enter and inspect the place where the patient lives, including a registered mental nursing home. This must be done at time that is reasonable in the circumstances and s/he must be able to show a document to prove that s/he is an ASW.*
>
> Note: there is no provision for using force if entry is denied. However, under s.135 the ASW may apply to a magistrate, who can give a warrant allowing a police officer to enter by force and remove the patient if appropriate.

VISITING PATIENTS

116. Welfare of certain hospital patients

(1) Where a patient to whom this section applies is admitted to a hospital or nursing home in England and Wales (whether for treatment for mental disorder or for any other reason) then, without prejudice to their duties in relation to the patient apart from the provisions of this section, the authority shall arrange for visits to be made to him on behalf of the authority, and shall take such other steps in relation to the patient while in the hospital or nursing home as would be expected to be taken by his parents.

> ### Section 116(1)
> *The local authority has a duty to visit certain patients in hospital or nursing homes, whatever they are there for, and to take any other steps that parents would be expected to take.*

(2) This section applies to–

    (a) a child or young person–

        (i) who is in the care of a local authority by virtue of a care order within the meaning of the Children Act 1989, or

        (ii) in respect of whom the rights and powers of a parent are vested in a local authority by virtue of section 16 of the Social Work (Scotland) Act 1968;

    (b) a person who is subject to the guardianship of a local social services authority under the provisions of this Act or the Mental Health (Scotland) Act 1984; or

    (c) a person the functions of whose nearest relative under this Act or under the Mental Health (Scotland) Act 1984 are for the time being transferred to a local social services authority.

> **Section 116(2)**
> *The patients referred to under this section are:*
>
> *(a)   patients under the age of 18 for whom the local authority has responsibility under a care order; ((ii) applies only in Scotland);*
>
> *(b)   persons under guardianship of the local authority; and*
>
> *(c)   persons for whom the local authority acts as nearest relative under the Act.*

AFTER-CARE

117. After-care

(1) This section applies to persons who are detained under section 3 above, or admitted to a hospital in pursuance of a hospital order made under section 37 above, or transferred to a hospital in pursuance of a hospital direction made under section 45A above or a transfer direction made under section 47 or 48 above, and then cease to be detained and (whether or not immediately after so ceasing) leave hospital.

> **Section 117(1)**
> *The duty to provide after-care under this section applies to certain people who cease to be detained and leave hospital. The categories of people are:*
>
> *(i)   those admitted for treatment under s.3 or pursuant to a hospital order under s.37; and*
>
> *(ii)   those detained in hospital under hybrid orders (see s.45A) or transferred to hospital from prison for treatment under s.47 or s.48.*
>
> Note: the Code of Practice (1999 ed.) gives guidance on after-care in Chapter 27.

(2) It shall be the duty of the Health Authority and of the local social services authority to provide, in co-operation with relevant voluntary agencies, after-care services for any person to whom this section applies until such time as the Health Authority and the local social services authority are satisfied that the person concerned is no longer in need of such services; but they shall not be so satisfied in the case of a patient who is subject to after-care under supervision at any time while he remains so subject.

Section 117(2)

Health authorities <u>and</u> local authorities are obliged to provide after-care services for each patient until s/he no longer needs them. Where a patient's after-care is supervised, it cannot be determined that s/he doesn't need the services any more: the supervision must first be discharged.

Note: although subsection (1) refers to a patient who leaves hospital, it is clear that the duty does not arise only on the patient's discharge[58] but that the after-care services must be planned and arranged before the patient leaves hospital. Indeed, an after-care plan should be prepared and put before the Mental Health Review Tribunal for its consideration. If an authority is unable to make the necessary arrangements it must try to obtain them from another authority and if arrangements still cannot be made the case must be referred back to a Mental Health Review Tribunal through the Secretary of State.

[58] See *R v Ealing District Health Authority ex parte Fox* [1993] 3 All ER 170 and *R v Mental Health Review Tribunal & others ex p Russell Hall* [1999] Lloyd's Rep Med 274 and subsequent appeal to the Court of Appeal on 30th July 1999 (unreported at the time of publishing, but due to be reported in Lloyd's Rep Med).

(2A)   It shall be the duty of the Health Authority to secure that at all times while a patient is subject to after-care under supervision–

   (a) a person who is a registered medical practitioner approved for the purposes of section 12 above by the Secretary of State as having special experience in the diagnosis or treatment of mental disorder is in charge of the medical treatment provided for the patient as part of the after-care services provided for him under this section; and

   (b) a person professionally concerned with any of the after-care services so provided is supervising him with a view to securing that he receives the after-care services so provided.

Section 117(2A)

Where a patient's after-care is under supervision, the Health Authority must ensure that:

(a)   a s.12 approved doctor is in charge of the patient's medical treatment which is given as after-care; and

(b)   an appropriate professional connected with the after-care services is working to ensure that s/he receives them.

(2B) Section 32 above shall apply for the purposes of this section as it applies for the purposes of Part II of this Act.

Section 117(2B)

Gives the Secretary of State for Health power to make any regulations necessary for giving full effect to s.117.

(3) In this section "the Health Authority" means the Health Authority, and "the local social services authority" means the local social services authority, for the area in which the person concerned is resident or to which he is sent on discharge by the hospital in which he was detained.

Section 117(3)

The health authority and local social services authority with the duty under this section are those for the area in which the patient lives or to which s/he has been sent on discharge.

Where the patient is not going to live in the area in which s/he was resident before his/her admission, the local authority for that area will still have a duty under this section until a new authority accepts responsibility for him/her.[59]

[59] See *R v Mental Health Review Tribunal & others ex p Russell Hall* [1999] Lloyd's Rep Med 274.

FUNCTIONS OF THE SECRETARY OF STATE

118. Code of practice

(1) The Secretary of State shall prepare, and from time to time revise, a code of practice–

(a) for the guidance of registered medical practitioners, managers and staff of hospitals and mental nursing homes and approved social workers in relation to the admission of patients to hospitals and mental nursing homes under this Act and to guardianship and after-care under supervision under this Act; and

(b) for the guidance of registered medical practitioners and members of other professions in relation to the medical treatment of patients suffering from mental disorder.

Section 118(1)
The most recent Code of Practice was published in March 1999. By virtue of subsection (b) the advice in the Code is not limited to the treatment of hospital or detained patients.

Note: the Code is advisory and does not have the force of law. However, as with other such codes of practice issued pursuant to legislation, it is expected that it will be followed and the courts are likely to have considerable regard for its provisions, for example in assessing whether a practitioner has been negligent.

(2) The code shall, in particular, specify forms of medical treatment in addition to any specified by regulations made for the purposes of section 57 above which in the opinion of the Secretary of State give rise to special concern and which should accordingly not be given by a registered medical practitioner unless the patient has consented to the treatment (or to a plan of treatment including that treatment) and a certificate in writing as to the matters mentioned in subsection (2)(a) and (b) of that section has been given by another registered medical practitioner, being a practitioner appointed for the purposes of this section by the Secretary of State.

Section 118(2)
The Code may be used to add medical treatments of concern to those already covered by the protection of s.57.

Note: no additional forms of treatment are currently specified in the Code.

(3) Before preparing the code or making any alteration in it the Secretary of State shall consult such bodies as appear to him to be concerned.

Section 118(3)
The Secretary of State for Health must consult with appropriate bodies before preparing or altering the Code.

(4) The Secretary of State shall lay copies of the code and of any alteration in the code before Parliament; and if either House of Parliament passes a resolution requiring the code or any alteration in it to be withdrawn the Secretary of State shall withdraw the code or alteration and, where he withdraws the code, shall prepare a code in substitution for the one which is withdrawn.

Section 118(4)
The Code is subject to the approval of Parliament.

(5) No resolution shall be passed by either House of Parliament under subsection (4) above in respect of a code or alteration after the expiration of the period of 40 days beginning with the day on which a copy of the code or alteration was laid before that House; but for the purposes of this subsection no account shall be taken of any time during which Parliament is dissolved or prorogued or during which both Houses are adjourned for more than four days.

Section 118(5)
If either the House of Commons or the House of Lords is to object to the Code, or to any alteration, it must do so within 40 days of a copy having been put before that House.

(6) The Secretary of State shall publish the code as for the time being in force.

Section 118(6)
Is self explanatory.

119. Practitioners approved for Part IV and section 118

(1) The Secretary of State may make such provision as he may with the approval of the Treasury determine for the payment of remuneration, allowances, pensions or gratuities to or in respect of registered medical practitioners appointed by him for the purposes of Part IV of this Act and section 118 above and to or in respect of other persons appointed for the purposes of section 57(2)(a) above.

Section 119(1)
"Second opinion approved doctors", doctors approved for the purpose of giving certification under s.118 and persons approved by the Mental Health Act Commission for the purpose of Part IV may be paid or have their expenses provided for.

(2) A registered medical practitioner or other person appointed by the Secretary of State for the purposes of the provisions mentioned in subsection (1) above may, for the purpose of exercising his functions under those provisions, at any reasonable time–

(a) visit and interview and, in the case of a registered medical practitioner, examine in private any patient detained in a mental nursing home; and

(b) require the production of and inspect any records relating to the treatment of the patient in that home.

Section 119(2)

Those mentioned in subsection (1) above may visit and interview in private a patient detained in a mental nursing home, at a time that is reasonable in the circumstances, and may see any records relating to the patient's treatment. A doctor may also examine the patient in private.

Note: it is a criminal offence (under s.129) to refuse to allow an approved person to visit, interview or examine a patient, to refuse to produce documents, to insist on being present when told to leave by an approved person, or to obstruct in any other way.

120. General protection of detained patients

(1) The Secretary of State shall keep under review the exercise of the powers and the discharge of the duties conferred or imposed by this Act so far as relating to the detention of patients or to patients liable to be detained under this Act and shall make arrangements for persons authorised by him in that behalf–

    (a) to visit and interview in private patients detained under this Act in hospitals and mental nursing homes; and

    (b) to investigate–
        (i) any complaint made by a person in respect of a matter that occurred while he was detained under this Act in a hospital or mental nursing home and which he considers has not been satisfactorily dealt with by the managers of that hospital or mental nursing home; and
        (ii) any other complaint as to the exercise of the powers or the discharge of the duties conferred or imposed by this Act in respect of a person who is or has been so detained.

Section 120(1)

The Secretary of State for Health is obliged to review the powers and duties in relation to detained patients and to arrange for visits to be made to patients detained in hospitals and mental nursing homes and for patients' complaints, or complaints made on their behalf, to be investigated. At the visits patients are to be interviewed in private.

(2) The arrangements made under this section in respect of the investigation of complaints may exclude matters from investigation in specified circumstances and shall not require any person exercising functions under the arrangements to undertake or continue with any investigation where he does not consider it appropriate to do so.

Section 120(2)
If the appointed person considers it inappropriate to do so, s/he need not investigate a patient's complaint.

(3) Where any such complaint as is mentioned in subsection (1)(b)(ii) above is made by a Member of Parliament and investigated under the arrangements made under this section the results of the investigation shall be reported to him.

Section 120(3)
An MP making a complaint on a patient's behalf must be given a report on the results of any investigation.

(4) For the purpose of any such review as is mentioned in subsection (1) above or of carrying out his functions under arrangements made under this section any person authorised in that behalf by the Secretary of State may at any reasonable time–

  (a) visit and interview and, if he is a registered medical practitioner, examine in private any patient in a mental nursing home; and

  (b) require the production of and inspect any records relating to the detention or treatment of any person who is or has been detained in a mental nursing home.

Section 120(4)
For the purpose of a review, visit or investigation under subsection (1) above any person authorised by the Secretary of State for Health may visit and interview in private a patient detained in a hospital or mental nursing home, at a time that is reasonable in the circumstances, and may see any records relating to the patient's detention or treatment. A doctor may also examine the patient in private.

It is a criminal offence to refuse to allow an authorised person to visit, interview or examine a patient, to refuse to produce documents, to insist on being present when told to leave by an authorised person, or to obstruct in any other way (see s.129).

(5) ...

Section 120(5)
Has been repealed.

(6) The Secretary of State may make such provision as he may with the approval of the Treasury determine for the payment of remuneration, allowances, pensions or

gratuities to or in respect of persons exercising functions in relation to any such review as is mentioned in subsection (1) above or functions under arrangements made under this section.

Section 120(6)

Authorised persons under this section may be paid fees and expenses with the approval of the Treasury.

(7) The powers and duties referred to in subsection (1) above do not include any power or duty conferred or imposed by Part VII of this Act.

Section 120(7)
The Secretary of State for Health does not under this section have to review powers and duties in connection with the Court of Protection.

121. Mental Health Act Commission

(1) Without prejudice to section 126(3) of the National Health Service Act 1977 (power to vary or revoke orders or directions) there shall continue to be a ... Special Health Authority known as the Mental Health Act Commission established under section 11 of that Act.

Section 121(1)
Is self explanatory.

(2) Without prejudice to the generality of his powers under section 13 of that Act, the Secretary of State shall direct the Commission to perform on his behalf-

   (a) the function of appointing registered medical practitioners for the purposes of Part IV of this Act and section 118 above and of appointing other persons for the purposes of section 57(2)(a) above; and
   (b) the functions of the Secretary of State under sections 61 and 120(1) and (4) above.

Section 121(2)

The Secretary of State for Health has a general power to direct a special health authority to exercise functions on his/her behalf. This section specifies that s/he must delegate certain functions to the Mental Health Act Commission. Those functions are:

(a) *appointing second opinion approval doctors, persons to give certification under s.57(2) and doctors to give certification under s.118;*

(b) *reviewing s.57 and s.58 treatments;*

(c) *reviewing powers and duties in relation to detained patients, visiting and interviewing detained patients and investigating complaints in relation to the detention of patients.*

(3) The registered medical practitioners and other persons appointed for the purposes mentioned in subsection (2)(a) above may include members of the Commission.

Section 121(3)

The Mental Health Act Commission may appoint its own members to be SOAD's, doctors able to give certificates under s.118 and other persons able to give certificates under s.57(2).

(4) The Secretary of State may, at the request of or after consultation with the Commission and after consulting such other bodies as appear to him to be concerned, direct the Commission to keep under review the care and treatment, or any aspect of the care and treatment, in hospitals and mental nursing homes of patients who are not liable to be detained under this Act.

Section 121(4)

The Secretary of State for Health may extend the Commission's responsibilities to include the review of non-detained patients in hospitals or mental nursing homes.

Note: as yet this has not been done, but the Code of Practice applies to all patients by virtue of s.118(1)(b).

(5) For the purpose of any such review as is mentioned in subsection (4) above any person authorised in that behalf by the Commission may at any reasonable time-

(a) visit and interview and, if he is a registered medical practitioner, examine in private any patient in a mental nursing home; and
(b) require the production of and inspect any records relating to the treatment of any person who is or has been a patient in a mental nursing home.

Section 121(5)

For the purpose of a review under subsection (4) any person authorised by the Mental Health Act Commission may visit and interview in private a non-detained patient in a hospital or mental nursing home, at a time that is reasonable in the circumstances, and may see any records relating to the patient's treatment. A doctor may also examine the patient in private.

Note: any obstruction of a person performing these functions would be an offence under s.129.

(6) The Secretary of State may make such provision as he may with the approval of the Treasury determine for the payment of remuneration, allowances, pensions or gratuities to or in respect of persons exercising functions in relation to any such review as is mentioned in subsection (4) above.

Section 121(6)

The Secretary of State for Health may pay persons performing these functions.

(7) The Commission shall review any decision to withhold a postal packet (or anything contained in it) under subsection (1)(b) or (2) of section 134 below if any application in that behalf is made-

(a) in a case under subsection (1)(b), by the patient; or
(b) in a case under subsection (2), either by the patient or by the person by whom the postal packet was sent;

and any such application shall be made within six months of the receipt by the applicant of the notice referred to in subsection (6) of that section.

Section 121(7)

Under s.134, a patient may have post that s/he sends or receives withheld; the patient, and sender of the item if applicable, must be notified within 7 days that this has happened. Within six months of notice being given they may apply for a review of that decision, which must be conducted by the Mental Health Act Commission.

(8) On an application under subsection (7) above the Commission may direct that the postal packet which is the subject of the application (or anything contained in it) shall not be withheld and the managers in question shall comply with any such direction.

Section 121(8)
On a review the Commission can overrule the hospital managers' decision to withhold post and have the item delivered.

(9) The Secretary of State may by regulations make provision with respect to the making and determination of applications under subsection (7) above, including provision for the production to the Commission of any postal packet which is the subject of such an application.

Section 121(9)
The Secretary of State for Health has power to make regulations about applications to the Commission in respect of the withholding of postal items.[60]

[60] Regulation 18, Mental Health (Hospital, Guardianship and Consent to Treatment) Regulations 1983, S.I. 1983 No. 893.

(10) The Commission shall in the second year after its establishment and subsequently in every second year publish a report on its activities; and copies of every such report shall be sent by the Commission to the Secretary of State who shall lay a copy before each House of Parliament.

Section 121(10)
The Mental Health Act Commission must publish a biennial report into its activities. This report will be sent to the Secretary of State for Health and laid before Parliament.

(11) Paragraph 9 of Schedule 5 to the said Act of 1977 (pay and allowances for chairmen and members of . . . Special Health Authorities) shall have effect in relation to the Mental Health Act Commission as if references in sub-paragraphs (1) and (2) to the chairman included references to any member and as if the reference to a member in sub-paragraph (4) included a reference to the chairman.

Section 121(11)
The Chairman and members of the Commission will be paid in accordance with the National Health Service Act 1977.

122. Provision of pocket money for in-patients in hospital

(1) The Secretary of State may pay to persons who are receiving treatment as in-patients (whether liable to be detained or not) in special hospitals or other hospitals

being hospitals wholly or mainly used for the treatment of persons suffering from mental disorder, such amounts as he thinks fit in respect of their occasional personal expenses where it appears to him that they would otherwise be without resources to meet those expenses.

> ### Section 122(1)
> *Where a patient receiving treatment in a hospital would otherwise have no money to spend on occasional personal expenses, the Secretary of State for Health can give him/her money for this purpose.*

(2) For the purposes of the National Health Service Act 1977, the making of payments under this section to persons for whom hospital services are provided under that Act shall be treated as included among those services.

> ### Section 122(2)
> *Is self explanatory.*

123. Transfers to and from special hospitals

(1) Without prejudice to any other provisions of this Act with respect to the transfer of patients, any patient who is for the time being liable to be detained in a special hospital under this Act (other than under section 35, 36 or 38 above) may, upon the directions of the Secretary of State, at any time be removed into any other special hospital.

> ### Section 123(1)
> *A patient detained in a special hospital may be moved to another special hospital, unless s/he is there for reports under s.35, for treatment under s.36 or under a s.37 interim hospital order.*

(2) Without prejudice to any such provision, the Secretary of State may give directions for the transfer of any patient who is for the time being liable to be so detained into a hospital which is not a special hospital.

> ### Section 123(2)
> *A patient detained in a special hospital may be moved to a hospital other than a special hospital.*

(3) Subsections (2) and (4) of section 19 above shall apply in relation to the transfer or removal of a patient under this section as they apply in relation to the transfer or removal of a patient from one hospital to another under that section.

Section 123(3)
The patient will be dealt with as if s/he had been admitted to the second hospital on the date of admission to the first hospital.

124. Default Powers of Secretary of State

Repealed by NHS and Community Care Act 1990.

125. Inquiries

(1) The Secretary of State may cause an inquiry to be held in any case where he thinks it advisable to do so in connection with any matter arising under this Act.

Section 125
Is self explanatory.

(2) Subsections (2) to (5) of section 250 of the Local Government Act 1972 shall apply to any inquiry held under this Act, except that no local authority shall be ordered to pay costs under subsection (4) of that section in the case of any inquiry unless the authority is a party to the inquiry.

Section 125(2)
Any inquiry ordered by the Secretary of State will have power to compel witnesses to attend to give evidence on oath and to require the production of documents. Any person failing to attend, or to give evidence, or to produce documents when required to do so will commit an offence. A local authority will only be ordered to pay costs in relation to an inquiry if it is a party to the inquiry.

PART IX

OFFENCES

126. Forgery and False statements

This section makes it a criminal offence to forge documents or make false statements in applications and recommendations under the Act or to make use of the false statements of others.

(1) Any person who without lawful authority or excuse has in his custody or under his control any document to which this subsection applies, which is, and which he knows or believes to be, false within the meaning of Part I of the Forgery and Counterfeiting Act 1981, shall be guilty of an offence.

Section 126(1)

It is a criminal offence for a person knowingly to have a false document (of the type identified in subsection 3 below) without lawful authority or excuse.

Note: s.9 of the Forgery and Counterfeiting Act 1981 describes a false document as one which purports to be made (or authorised) in the form or terms in which it is made by someone who did not make (or authorise) it in that form or those terms.

(2) Any person who without lawful authority or excuse makes, or has in his custody or under his control, any document so closely resembling a document to which subsection (1) above applies as to be calculated to deceive shall be guilty of an offence.

Section 126(2)

It is a criminal offence for anyone to have a forged document (of the type identified in subsection 3 below) which is calculated to induce someone to believe that a false thing is true without lawful authority or excuse.

(3) The documents to which subsection (1) above applies are any documents purporting to be-

  (a) an application under Part II of this Act;
  (b) a medical or other recommendation or report under this Act; and
  (c) any other document required or authorised to be made for any of the purposes of this Act.

Section 126(3)

Identifies the relevant documents for this section of the Act and is self explanatory.

(4) Any person who-

  (a) wilfully makes a false entry or statement in any application, recommendation, report, record or other document required or authorised to be made for any of the purposes of this Act; or
  (b) with intent to deceive, makes use of any such entry or statement which he knows to be false,

shall be guilty of an offence.

126(4)

It is a criminal offence for a person to either:

(a)   intentionally make an untrue entry or statement in any document used for the purposes of the Act; or

(b)   make use of a statement in a document which s/he knows to be untrue with the intention of inducing another to believe it is true.

Note: a statement can be false because of an omission even if its contents are true as far as they go.

(5) Any person guilty of an offence under this section shall be liable-

   (a) on summary conviction, to imprisonment for a term not exceeding six months or to a fine not exceeding the statutory maximum, or to both;
   (b) on conviction on indictment, to imprisonment for a term not exceeding two years or to a fine of any amount, or to both.

Section 126(5)
A person convicted of an offence under this section may be imprisoned for a maximum of six months, if tried by magistrates, or two years, if tried in the Crown Court. A fine may be imposed as an addition or as an alternative.

127. Ill treatment of patients

This section makes it a criminal offence for those responsible for the care of a patient to ill-treat or intentionally neglect the patient. The section protects not only all in-patients but also those under guardianship or subject to supervised discharge.

(1) It shall be an offence for any person who is an officer on the staff of or otherwise employed in, or who is one of the managers of, a hospital or mental nursing home-

   (a) to ill-treat or wilfully to neglect a patient for the time being receiving treatment for mental disorder as an in-patient in that hospital or home; or
   (b) to ill-treat or wilfully to neglect, on the premises of which the hospital or home forms part, a patient for the time being receiving such treatment there as an out-patient.

Section 127(1)

It is an offence for an employee or manager of a hospital or nursing home to deliberately ill treat or neglect a patient whilst:

(a)   s/he is receiving treatment for a mental disorder as an in-patient in that hospital or nursing home; or

(b)   s/he is receiving treatment as an out-patient on the hospital or nursing home premises.

Note: this section applies to all patients being treated for mental disorder (as defined in s.1(2)) there is no requirement that the person is or has been detained under the Act.

(2) It shall be an offence for any individual to ill-treat or wilfully to neglect a mentally disordered patient who is for the time being subject to his guardianship under this Act or otherwise in his custody or care (whether by virtue of any legal or moral obligation or otherwise).

Section 127(2)

It is an offence for a person to deliberately ill treat or neglect a patient subject to his/her guardianship or in his/her care. This section includes those with no formal or professional obligations to the patient, such as relatives, friends and other carers.

(2A)   It shall be an offence for any individual to ill-treat or wilfully to neglect a mentally disordered patient who is for the time being subject to after-care under supervision.

Section 127(2A)

It is a criminal offence for a person to deliberately ill-treat or neglect a patient subject to after-care under supervision.

(3) Any person guilty of an offence under this section shall be liable-
  (a) on summary conviction, to imprisonment for a term not exceeding six months or to a fine not exceeding the statutory maximum, or to both;
  (b) on conviction on indictment, to imprisonment for a term not exceeding two years or to a fine of any amount, or to both.

Section 127(3)

A person convicted of an offence under this section of the Act may be imprisoned for a maximum of six months if tried by magistrates, or for two years if tried in the Crown Court. A fine may be imposed in addition or as an alternative.

(4) No proceedings shall be instituted for an offence under this section except by or with the consent of the Director of Public Prosecutions.

Section 127(4)
Is self explanatory.

128. Assisting patients to abscond or avoid recapture

(1) Where any person induces or knowingly assists another person who is liable to be detained in a hospital within the meaning of Part II of this Act or is subject to guardianship under this Act to absent himself without leave he shall be guilty of an offence.

Section 128(1)
It is a criminal offence for a person to knowingly help a patient who is detained under Part II or Part III of the Act or is subject to guardianship to absent him/herself without leave or abscond.

(2) Where any person induces or knowingly assists another person who is in legal custody by virtue of section 137 below to escape from such custody he shall be guilty of an offence.

Section 128(2)
It is a criminal offence for a person to knowingly help a patient who is in legal custody (as defined in s.137) to escape.

Note: s.137 states that a person is to be in legal custody whilst required to be conveyed to any place or detained at or conveyed to a place of safety under the Act.

(3) Where any person knowingly harbours a patient who is absent without leave or is otherwise at large and liable to be retaken under this Act or gives him any assistance with intent to prevent, hinder or interfere with his being taken into custody or returned to the hospital or other place where he ought to be he shall be guilty of an offence.

Section 128(3)
It is a criminal offence for a person to knowingly hide or assist in preventing the recapture of a patient who is absent without leave or has escaped from legal custody.

(4) Any person guilty of an offence under this section shall be liable-

(a) on summary conviction, to imprisonment for a term not exceeding six months or to a fine not exceeding the statutory maximum, or to both;

(b) on conviction on indictment, to imprisonment for a term not exceeding two years or to a fine of any amount, or to both.

> **Section 128(4)**
>
> *A person convicted of an offence under this section of the Act may be imprisoned for a maximum of six months if tried by magistrates, or for two years if tried in the Crown Court. A fine may be imposed in addition or as an alternative.*
>
> Note: s.18 and s.138 set out provisions relating to the retaking of patients absent without leave or who have escaped from legal custody.

129. Obstruction

> *This section makes it a criminal offence to obstruct those exercising their functions under the Act.*

(1) Any person who without reasonable cause-

   (a) refuses to allow the inspection of any premises; or
   (b) refuses to allow the visiting, interviewing or examination of any person by a person authorised in that behalf by or under this Act [or to give access to any person to a person so authorised]; or
   (c) refuses to produce for the inspection of any person so authorised any document or record the production of which is duly required by him; or
   (d) otherwise obstructs any such person in the exercise of his functions, shall be guilty of an offence.

> **Section 129(1)**
>
> *It is an offence for anyone without good reason to refuse to:*
>
> *(a)   allow inspection of premises;*
>
> *(b)   allow visiting, interviewing or examining of a patient or access to a patient;*
>
> *(c)   produce a document for authorised inspection; or*
>
> *(d)   to obstruct a person who is conducting their authorised functions under the Act.*

(2) Without prejudice to the generality of subsection (1) above, any person who insists on being present when required to withdraw by a person authorised by or under this Act to interview or examine a person in private shall be guilty of an offence.

Section 129(2)

It is an offence for anyone, having been requested to leave whilst a private interview or examination of a person for the purposes of the Act is conducted, to refuse to do so.

Note: doctors have a right to request a private interview by virtue of s.24(1) and s.76(1) but social workers do not. However, a person who refuses to leave and disrupts an ASW's interview of a patient may nevertheless still be committing an offence by virtue of s.129(1)(d).

(3) Any person guilty of an offence under this section shall be liable on summary conviction to imprisonment for a term not exceeding three months or to a fine not exceeding level 4 on the standard scale or to both.

Section 129(3)

A person convicted of an offence under this section of the Act may be imprisoned for a maximum of three months or fined or both. Any trial under this section would be in a magistrates court.

130. Prosecutions by Local Authorities

A local social services authority may institute proceedings for any offence under this Part of this Act, but without prejudice to any provision of this Part of this Act requiring the consent of the Director of Public Prosecutions for the institution of such proceedings.

Section 130

Prosecutions under this part of the Act may be brought by a local social services authority save that prosecutions for ill-treatment of patients (s.127) must be either brought by the Director of Public Prosecutions (DPP) or commenced with the DPP's consent.

PART X

MISCELLANEOUS AND SUPPLEMENTARY

MISCELLANEOUS PROVISIONS

131. Informal admission of patients

(1) Nothing in this Act shall be construed as preventing a patient who requires treatment for mental disorder from being admitted to any hospital or mental nursing home in pursuance of arrangements made in that behalf and without any application, order or direction rendering him liable to be detained under this Act, or from remaining in any hospital or mental nursing home in pursuance of such arrangements after he has ceased to be so liable to be detained.

Section 131 (1)

Patients can be admitted to a hospital or nursing home informally for treatment of their mental disorder and there is no need for such treatment to be under the Mental Health Act.

Patients may also remain in hospital or in a nursing home informally after a period of detention under the Mental Health Act ends.

Note: this includes both 'voluntary' patients who have consented to be in hospital and 'informal' patients who lack the capacity to consent to treatment but who nevertheless make no request or attempt to leave[61] Treatment of incapable 'informal' patients is lawful by virtue of the common law doctrine of necessity, providing that any treatment given is in the patient's best interests.

Such incapable 'informal' and capable 'voluntary' patients are not subject to the consent to treatment provisions of Part IV (save for s.57 - surgical interventions).

[61] Rv Bournewood Mental Health NHS Trust, ex parte L [1998] 3 W.L.R. 107.

(2) In the case of a minor who has attained the age of 16 years and is capable of expressing his own wishes, any such arrangements as are mentioned in subsection (1) above may be made, carried out and determined even though there are one or more persons who have parental responsibility for him (within the meaning of the Children Act 1989).

Section 131 (2)

A person of 16 or 17 years old who has capacity can informally admit him/herself to hospital without the need for consent of his/her parents or those responsible for him/her.

Note: a competent person under 18 years old retains an independent right to consent to treatment. However should s/he refuse to give that consent a parent (or someone with parental responsibility) can give the consent instead. A parent may not however veto the valid consent of their child.

Chapter 31 of the Code of Practice (1999 ed.) gives further guidance on issues affecting children.

132. Duty of managers of hospitals to give information to detained patients

(1) The managers of a hospital or mental nursing home in which a patient is detained under this Act shall take such steps as are practicable to ensure that the patient understands-

(a) under which of the provisions of this Act he is for the time being detained and the effect of that provision; and

(b) what rights of applying to a Mental Health Review Tribunal are available to him in respect of his detention under that provision;

and those steps shall be taken as soon as practicable after the commencement of the patient's detention under the provision in question.

Section 132 (1)

As soon as a patient is detained the hospital or nursing home managers must take all practicable steps to ensure that s/he understands:

(a)   the sections of the Act which have been applied to detain him/her and the practical effect of those sections; and

(b)   his/her rights to apply to a MHRT.

---

(2) The managers of a hospital or mental nursing home in which a patient is detained as aforesaid shall also take such steps as are practicable to ensure that the patient understands the effect, so far as relevant in his case, of sections 23, 25, 56 to 64, 66(1)(g), 118 and 120 above and section 134 below; and those steps shall be taken as soon as practicable after the commencement of the patient's detention in the hospital or nursing home.

Section 132 (2)

As soon as possible after a patient's detention begins the hospital or nursing home managers must take all practicable steps to ensure that s/he understands the effects of the following sections, where relevant:

(a) s.23   - discharge of patients;

(b) s.25   - restrictions on discharge by a nearest relative;

(c) s.56 to s.64   - consent to treatment provisions;

(d) s.66(1)(g)   - right to apply to a MHRT if the RMO bars a nearest relative's order of discharge;

(e) s.118   - the code of practice;

(f) s.120   - general protection of detained patients;

(g) s.134   - withholding correspondence of patients.

Note: chapter 14 of the Code of Practice (1999 ed.) gives further guidance on information to be given to patients, those subject to guardianship and their nearest relatives.

---

(3) The steps to be taken under subsections (1) and (2) above shall include giving the requisite information both orally and in writing.

Section 132(3)
Is self explanatory.

(4) The managers of a hospital or mental nursing home in which a patient is detained as aforesaid shall, except where the patient otherwise requests, take such steps as are practicable to furnish the person (if any) appearing to them to be his nearest relative with a copy of any information given to him in writing under subsections (1) and (2) above; and those steps shall be taken when the information is given to the patient or within a reasonable time thereafter.

Section 132(4)
A nearest relative must (as far as is practicable) be given the same information as that given to the detained patient unless the patient asks that this should not be done.

This should be done at the same time as, or soon after the patient is given the information.

133. Duty of managers of hospitals to inform nearest relatives of discharge

(1) Where a patient liable to be detained under this Act in a hospital or mental nursing home is to be discharged otherwise than by virtue of an order for discharge made by his nearest relative, the managers of the hospital or mental nursing home shall, subject to subsection (2) below, take such steps as are practicable to inform the person (if any) appearing to them to be the nearest relative of the patient; and that information shall, if practicable, be given at least seven days before the date of discharge.

Section 133(1)
If a patient is to be discharged from a hospital or nursing home the managers must take all practicable steps to ensure that his/her nearest relative is informed.

This should be done at least seven days before discharge occurs (if practicable) but is not necessary where the discharge is following a nearest relative's own order.

(2) Subsection (1) above shall not apply if the patient or his nearest relative has requested that information about the patient's discharge should not be given under this section.

Section 133(2)
It is also unnecessary where the patient or his/her nearest relative has requested that the nearest relative is not told about the discharge.

134. Correspondence of patients

(1) A postal packet addressed to any person by a patient detained in a hospital under this Act and delivered by the patient for dispatch may be withheld from the Post Office-

(a) if that person has requested that communications addressed to him by the patient should be withheld; or

(b) subject to subsection (3) below, if the hospital is a special hospital and the managers of the hospital consider that the postal packet is likely-

---

Section 134(1)

Permits withholding of mail sent by a detained patient if:

(a)   the intended recipient has asked not to receive mail from the patient (by writing to either the hospital managers, the RMO or the Secretary of State for Health); or

(b)   In a Special Hospital, it is deemed by the managers that the mail is likely to cause danger to anyone or distress to anyone other than hospital staff.

Note: this section does not apply to informal patients.

---

(2) Subject to subsection (3) below, a postal packet addressed to a patient detained in a special hospital under this Act may be withheld from the patient if, in the opinion of the managers of the hospital, it is necessary to do so in the interests of the safety of the patient or for the protection of other persons.

Section 134(2)

Permits withholding of mail sent to a detained special hospital patient if this is considered by the managers to be necessary in the interests of the safety of the patient or for the protection of others.

Note: the MHAC can review decisions to withhold incoming or outgoing mail under s.121(7) above if applications are made within six months of receiving notice of the hospital managers' actions.

---

(3) Subsections (1)(b) and (2) above do not apply to any postal packet addressed by a patient to, or sent to a patient by or on behalf of-

(a) any Minister of the Crown or Member of either House of Parliament or of the Northern Ireland Assembly;

(b) the Master or any other officer of the Court of Protection or any of the Lord Chancellor's Visitors;

(c) the Parliamentary Commissioner for Administration,the Welsh Administration Ombudsman, the Health Service Commissioner for England, the Health Service Commissioner for Wales or a Local Commissioner within the meaning of Part III of the Local Government Act 1974;

(d) a Mental Health Review Tribunal;

(e) a Health Authority or Special Health Authority, a local social services authority, a Community Health Council or a probation committee (within the meaning of the Probation Service Act 1993);

(f) the managers of the hospital in which the patient is detained;

(g) any legally qualified person instructed by the patient to act as his legal adviser; or the European Commission of Human Rights or the European Court of Human Rights.

Section 134(3)

Prohibits the withholding of mail under s.134(1) and (2) sent to or by certain categories of people or bodies and is self explanatory.

(4) The managers of a hospital may inspect and open any postal packet for the purposes of determining-

(a) whether it is one to which subsection (1) or (2) applies, and

(b) in the case of a postal packet to which subsection (1) or (2) above applies, whether or not it should be withheld under that subsection;

and the power to withhold a postal packet under either of those subsections includes power to withhold anything contained in it.

Section 134(4)

Allows hospital managers to open and inspect mail and withhold any part of it in exercising their powers in s.134(1) and (2) above.

Note: this section does not permit selected censorship of documents but does permit the removal a document in its entirety from a postal packet.

There is no power to require return of mail sent by a Special Hospital patient once it has reached its destination.[62]

[62] Broadmoor Hospital Authority v Robinson [1999] QB 957.

(5) Where a postal packet or anything contained in it is withheld under subsection (1) or (2) above the managers of the hospital shall record that fact in writing.

Section 134(5)

If mail or part of it is withheld this must be recorded in writing by the hospital managers.

Note: the regulations require that a special register is kept for this purpose[63].

[63] Mental Health (Hospital, Guardianship and Consent to Treatment) Regulations 1983, (S.I. 1983/893), reg. 17.

(6) Where a postal packet or anything contained in it is withheld under subsection (1)(b) or (2) above the managers of the hospital shall within seven days give notice of that fact to the patient and, in the case of a packet withheld under subsection (2) above, to the person (if known) by whom the postal packet was sent; and any such notice shall be given in writing and shall contain a statement of the effect of section 121(7) and (8) above.

> **Section 134(6)**
>
> *If mail or part of it is withheld the hospital managers must inform the patient and the sender of the mail (if known) within seven days of the fact of withholding of mail and the Mental Health Act Commission's power to review that decision.*
>
> Note: the regulations also require that, where mail has been inspected but not withheld, a record of the packet having been opened must be placed within the packet before resealing.[64]
>
> ---
> [64] Mental Health (Hospital, Guardianship and Consent to Treatment) Regulations 1983, (S.I. 1983/893), reg. 17.

(7) The functions of the managers of a hospital under this section shall be discharged on their behalf by a person on the staff of the hospital appointed by them for that purpose and different persons may be appointed to discharge different functions.

> **Section 134(7)**
>
> *Permits delegation of the hospital managers' functions under this section to one or more members of hospital staff.*

(8) the Secretary of State may make regulations with respect to the exercise of the powers conferred by this section.

> **Section 134(8)**
>
> *Is self explanatory.*

(9) In this section "hospital" has the same meaning as in Part II of this Act, "postal packet" has the same meaning as in the Post Office Act 1953 and the provisions of this section shall have effect notwithstanding anything in section 56 of that Act.

> **Section 134(9)**
>
> *"Postal packet" includes a letter, postcard, printed packet, telegram and any packet or article transmissible by post.*

135. Warrant to search for and remove patients

(1) If it appears to a justice of the peace, on information on oath laid by an approved social worker, that there is reasonable cause to suspect that a person believed to be suffering from mental disorder-

  (a) has been, or is being, ill-treated, neglected or kept otherwise than under proper control, in any place within the jurisdiction of the justice, or
  (b) being unable to care for himself, is living alone in any such place,

the justice may issue a warrant authorising any constable . . . to enter, if need be by force, any premises specified in the warrant in which that person is believed to be, and, if thought fit, to remove him to a place of safety with a view to the making of an application in respect of him under Part II of this Act, or of other arrangements for his treatment or care.

> **Section 135**
>
> *A magistrate may issue a warrant authorising any police officer to enter any premises, using as much force as is reasonably necessary, and take a person to a place of safety from where arrangements can be made for his/her treatment and care or for an application for admission or guardianship to be made.*
>
> *To issue the warrant it must appear to the magistrate, on the basis of information on oath provided by an ASW, that a person who suffers with mental disorder is:*
>
> *(a) being ill treated or neglected or is not under proper control ; or*
>
> *(b) is unable to care for him/herself and lives alone.*
>
> Note: the premises to be entered must be specified on the warrant, although the person's name may be unknown.
>
> 'Place of safety' is defined in s.135(6) below.

(2) If it appears to a justice of the peace, on information on oath laid by any constable or other person who is authorised by or under this Act or under section 83 of the Mental Health (Scotland) Act 1984 to take a patient to any place, or to take into custody or retake a patient who is liable under this Act or under the said section 83 to be so taken or retaken-

  (a) that there is reasonable cause to believe that the patient is to be found on premises within the jurisdiction of the justice; and
  (b) that admission to the premises has been refused or that a refusal of such admission is apprehended,

the justice may issue a warrant authorising any constable . . . to enter the premises, if need be by force, and remove the patient.

Mental Health Act 1983

Section 135(2)

If it appears to a magistrate, on the basis of information provided on oath by a police officer or anyone authorised to detain a patient unlawfully at large (under s.18):

(a)   that a person is likely to be on a specific premises; and

(b)   admission to that premises has been or is likely to be refused,

the magistrate may issue a warrant authorising any police officer to enter any premises, using as much force as is reasonably necessary and remove the patient.

Note: the premises to be entered and the patient's name must be specified on the warrant.

(3) A patient who is removed to a place of safety in the execution of a warrant issued under this section may be detained there for a period not exceeding 72 hours.

Section 135(3)

The 72 hours permitted detention begins on arrival at the place of safety and not on execution of the warrant.

(4) In the execution of a warrant issued under subsection (1) above, a constable shall be accompanied by an approved social worker and by a registered medical practitioner, and in the execution of a warrant issued under subsection (2) above a constable may be accompanied-

(a) by a registered medical practitioner;
(b) by any person authorised by or under this Act or under section 83 of the Mental Health (Scotland) Act 1984 to take or retake the patient.

Section 135(4)

A police officer executing a warrant under s.135(1) must be accompanied by an ASW and a doctor.

A police officer executing a warrant under s.135(2) may be accompanied by a doctor and anyone authorised to retake the absconded patient (including those persons authorised to retake patients who have absconded from Scotland).

(5) It shall not be necessary in any information or warrant under subsection (1) above to name the patient concerned.

Section 135(5)

Is self explanatory.

251

(6) In this section "place of safety" means residential accommodation provided by a local social services authority under Part III of the National Assistance Act 1948 . . ., a hospital as defined by this Act, a police station, a mental nursing home or residential home for mentally disordered persons or any other suitable place the occupier of which is willing temporarily to receive the patient.

Section 135(6)

A 'place of safety' can be:

    (i)   *social services residential accommodation*

    (ii)   *a hospital;*

    (iii) *a police station;*

    (iv) *a mental nursing/residential care home;*

    (v)   *any suitable place which the occupier will allow to be used as such (eg a relative's home).*

Note: the Code of Practice advises that 'as a general rule' it is preferable that hospital rather than a police station is used as the place of safety.

Should the person be detained at a police station the provisions of the Police and Criminal Evidence Act 1984 (PACE) Code of Practice, Part C, will apply.[65]

---

[65] Police and Criminal Evidence Act 1984 (s.60(1)(a) and s.66) Codes of Practice Revised Edition (1999), London. The Stationery Office.

136. Mentally disordered persons found in public places

(1) If a constable finds in a place to which the public have access a person who appears to him to be suffering from mental disorder and to be in immediate need of care or control, the constable may, if he thinks it necessary to do so in the interests of that person or for the protection of other persons, remove that person to a place of safety within the meaning of section 135 above.

Section 136(1)

A police officer who comes across a person who appears to the police officer to be suffering with mental disorder and who immediately needs to be either cared for or controlled (whether in their own interests or to protect others) may, without a warrant, apprehend the person and take him/her to a place of safety.

This power can only be exercised in a place where the public have access.

Note: a 'place where the public have access' is not limited to public places such as streets and parks but would include privately owned places where the public enter with or without a fee (such as a shop or a zoo) and public parts of private buildings (such as the balcony of a block of flats). An officer can not enter a private dwelling house under this section and even if the permission of the occupier to enter a private dwelling were given there would be no power to remove the mentally disordered person from that place.

(2) A person removed to a place of safety under this section may be detained there for a period not exceeding 72 hours for the purpose of enabling him to be examined by a registered medical practitioner and to be interviewed by an approved social worker and of making any necessary arrangements for his treatment or care.

Section 136(2)

The 72 hours potential detention period begins on arrival at the place of safety and not when apprehended. The purpose of detention must be to allow assessment by a doctor and ASW. Thus a person ought not to be detained under s.136 simply to give them time to 'sober up' etc.

Note: the Divisional Court has stated that detention under s.136 gives rise to an obligation on the police to call a doctor to assess the mental state of the detainee.[66]

[66] Francis v DPP [1997] RTR 113.

---

137. Provisions as to custody, conveyance and detention

(1) Any person required or authorised by or by virtue of this Act to be conveyed to any place or to be kept in custody or detained in a place of safety or at any place to which he is taken under section 42(6) above shall, while being so conveyed, detained or kept, as the case may be, be deemed to be in legal custody.

Section 137(1)

Whilst detained or conveyed under the Act a person is to be considered as being in legal custody.

Note: it is a criminal offence (under s.128(2)) for a person knowingly to help a patient who is in legal custody to escape.

---

(2) A constable or any other person required or authorised by or by virtue of this Act to take any person into custody, or to convey or detain any person shall, for the purposes of taking him into custody or conveying or detaining him, have all the powers, authorities, protection and privileges which a constable has within the area for which he acts as constable.

Section 137(2)

A police officer or any other person who is required or authorised to have a person in legal custody has all the powers of a constable when s/he is acting in this capacity.

---

(3) In this section "convey" includes any other expression denoting removal from one place to another.

Section 137(3)
Is self explanatory

138. Retaking of patients escaping from custody

(1) If any person who is in legal custody by virtue of section 137 above escapes, he may, subject to the provisions of this section, be retaken-

(a) in any case, by the person who had his custody immediately before the escape, or by any constable or approved social worker;

(b) if at the time of the escape he was liable to be detained in a hospital within the meaning of Part II of this Act, or subject to guardianship under this Act, by any other person who could take him into custody under section 18 above if he had absented himself without leave.

Section 138(1)
Anyone who escapes from legal custody may be retaken:

(a) by the person s/he escapes from, any police officer or any ASW;

(b) if the escapee is subject to guardianship or a detained patient, by any of those authorised in s.18 to take absconding patients into custody.

(2) A person to whom paragraph (b) of subsection (1) above applies shall not be retaken under this section after the expiration of the period within which he could be retaken under section 18 above if he had absented himself without leave on the day of the escape unless he is subject to a restriction order under Part III of this Act or an order or direction having the same effect as such an order; and subsection (4) of the said section 18 shall apply with the necessary modifications accordingly.

Section 138(2)
Patients who escape from legal custody are to treated as if absent without leave for the purposes of calculating time limits on re-capture. Unrestricted patients may only be retaken if the time limits within which they would be liable to be retaken under s.18 have not expired.

(3) A person who escapes while being taken to or detained in a place of safety under section 135 or 136 above shall not be retaken under this section after the expiration of the period of 72 hours beginning with the time when he escapes or the period during which he is liable to be so detained, whichever expires first.

Section 138(3)
A person who escapes from legal detention under s.135 or s.136 may not be taken after 72 hours.

The 72 hours will begin on escape or arrival at the place of safety whichever is earlier.

(4) This section, so far as it relates to the escape of a person liable to be detained in a hospital within the meaning of Part II of this Act, shall apply in relation to a person who escapes-

   (a) while being taken to or from such a hospital in pursuance of regulations under section 19 above, or of any order, direction or authorisation under Part III or VI of this Act (other than under section 35, 36, 38, 53, 83 or 85) or under section 123 above; or
   (b) while being taken to or detained in a place of safety in pursuance of an order under Part III of this Act (other than under section 35, 36 or 38 above) pending his admission to such a hospital,

as if he were liable to be detained in that hospital and, if he had not previously been received in that hospital, as if he had been so received.

Section 138(4)
The provisions regarding retaking of escapees will apply to those detained patients under Parts III and VI who escape whilst being conveyed to or from hospital or escape from a place of safety whilst awaiting admission to hospital.

(5) In computing for the purposes of the power to give directions under section 37(4) above and for the purposes of sections 37(5) and 40(1) above the period of 28 days mentioned in those sections, no account shall be taken of any time during which the patient is at large and liable to be retaken by virtue of this section.

Section 138(5)
Time spent unlawfully at large does not count towards the 28 day time limits set in s.37(5) and s.40(1) (relating to conveyance to hospital pursuant to a hospital order).

(6) Section 21 above shall, with any necessary modifications, apply in relation to a patient who is at large and liable to be retaken by virtue of this section as it applies in relation to a patient who is absent without leave and references in that section to section 18 above shall be construed accordingly.

Section 138(6)
The provisions of s.21 for extending time limits in respect of s.18 (return of those absent without leave) also apply to escapees.

139. Protection for acts done in pursuance of this Act

(1) No person shall be liable, whether on the ground of want of jurisdiction or on any other ground, to any civil or criminal proceedings to which he would have been liable apart from this section in respect of any act purporting to be done in pursuance of this Act or any regulations or rules made under this Act, or in, or in pursuance of anything done in, the discharge of functions conferred by any other enactment on the authority having jurisdiction under Part VII of this Act, unless the act was done in bad faith or without reasonable care.

Section 139(1)
Provides immunity from both civil and criminal liability for actions in pursuance of the Act (or its subsidiary regulations and rules) unless the actions complained of arise from bad faith or lack of reasonable care.

(2) No civil proceedings shall be brought against any person in any court in respect of any such act without the leave of the High Court; and no criminal proceedings shall be brought against any person in any court in respect of any such act except by or with the consent of the Director of Public Prosecutions.

Section 139(2)
Even where an action complained of is said to arise from bad faith or lack of reasonable care no proceedings can be brought without first obtaining the leave of the High Court (in civil actions) or the consent of the DPP (in criminal cases).

(3) This section does not apply to proceedings for an offence under this Act, being proceedings which, under any other provision of this Act, can be instituted only by or with the consent of the Director of Public Prosecutions.

Section 139(3)
This section does not apply to offences of ill treatment or neglect under s.127.

(4) This section does not apply to proceedings against the Secretary of State or against a Health Authority or Special Health Authorityor against a National Health

Service trust established under the National Health Service and Community Care Act 1990.

(5) In relation to Northern Ireland the reference in this section to the Director of Public Prosecutions shall be construed as a reference to the Director of Public Prosecutions for Northern Ireland.

Section 139(4) and (5)
Are self explanatory.

140. Notification of hospitals having arrangements for reception of urgent cases

It shall be the duty of every Health Authority to give notice to every local social services authority for an area wholly or partly comprised within the Health Authority's area specifying the hospital or hospitals administered by or otherwise available to the Health Authority in which arrangements are from time to time in force for the reception, in case of special urgency, of patients requiring treatment for mental disorder.

Section 140
Health Authorities must notify any social services authority local to the areas they serve of their arrangements for emergency admission of patients with mental disorders.

141. Members of Parliament suffering from mental illness

(1) Where a member of the House of Commons is authorised to be detained on the ground (however formulated) that he is suffering from mental illness, it shall be the duty of the court, authority or person on whose order or application, and of any registered medical practitioner upon whose recommendation or certificate, the detention was authorised, and of the person in charge of the hospital or other place in which the member is authorised to be detained, to notify the Speaker of the House of Commons that the detention has been authorised.

Section 141(1)
If an M.P. is compulsorily detained on the grounds of mental illness the Speaker of the House of Commons must be informed of this by:
  (i)   *the court, authority or person who made the application; and*
  (ii) *any doctor who authorised or provided a report in support of detention; and*
  (iii) *the person in charge of the place where the M.P. is detained.*
Note: this section does not apply where an M.P. is suffering with psychopathic disorder or (severe) mental impairment.

(2) Where the Speaker receives a notification under subsection (1) above, or is notified by two members of the House of Commons that they are credibly informed that such an authorisation has been given, the Speaker shall cause the member to whom the notification relates to be visited and examined by two registered medical practitioners appointed in accordance with subsection (3) below.

(3) The registered medical practitioners to be appointed for the purposes of subsection (2) above shall be appointed by the President of the Royal College of Psychiatrists and shall be practitioners appearing to the President to have special experience in the diagnosis or treatment of mental disorders.

Section 141(2)

On receipt of this notification (or on being so informed by two other M.P.s) the Speaker must arrange for examination of the detained M.P. by two doctors.

Section 141(3)

The two doctors authorised to examine an M.P. will be so appointed by the President of the Royal College of Psychiatrists.

(4) The registered medical practitioners appointed in accordance with subsection (3) above shall report to the Speaker whether the member is suffering from mental illness and is authorised to be detained as such.

(5) If the report is to the effect that the member is suffering from mental illness and authorised to be detained as aforesaid, the Speaker shall at the expiration of six months from the date of the report, if the House is then sitting, and otherwise as soon as may be after the House next sits, again cause the member to be visited and examined by two such registered medical practitioners as aforesaid, and the registered medical practitioners shall report as aforesaid.

(6) If the second report is that the member is suffering from mental illness and authorised to be detained as mentioned in subsection (4) above, the Speaker shall forthwith lay both reports before the House of Commons, and thereupon the seat of the member shall become vacant.

Section 141(4) to (6)

If the two doctors report on two occasions at least six months apart that the M.P. is suffering with mental illness and is a detained patient the Speaker will inform the House of Commons and the M.P.s seat will be vacated.

(7) Any sums required for the payment of fees and expenses to registered medical practitioners acting in relation to a member of the House of Commons under this section shall be defrayed out of moneys provided by Parliament.

Section 141(7)
Is self explanatory.

(8) This section also has effect in relation to members of the Scottish Parliament but as if-

    (a) any references to the House of Commons or the Speaker were references to the Scottish Parliament or (as the case may be) the Presiding Officer, and

    (b) subsection (7) were omitted.

(9) This section also has effect in relation to members of the National Assembly for Wales but as if-

    (a) references to the House of Commons were to the Assembly and references to the Speaker were to the presiding officer, and

    (b) in subsection (7), for "defrayed out of moneys provided by Parliament" there were substituted "paid by the National Assembly for Wales".

Sections 141(8) and (9)
Apply this section to the Parliaments of Scotland and Wales.

Note: There is provision not yet in force to apply this section to the Northern Ireland Assembly.

142. Pay, pensions, etc, of mentally disordered persons

(1) Where a periodic payment falls to be made to any person by way of pay or pension or otherwise in connection with the service or employment of that or any other person, and the payment falls to be made directly out of moneys provided by Parliament or the Consolidated Fund, or other moneys administered by or under the control or supervision of a government department, the authority by whom the sum in question is payable, if satisfied after considering medical evidence that the person to whom it is payable (referred to in this section as "the patient") is incapable by reason of mental disorder of managing and administering his property and affairs, may, instead of paying the sum to the patient, apply it in accordance with subsection (2) below.

(2) The authority may pay the sum or such part of it as they think fit to the institution or person having the care of the patient, to be applied for his benefit and may pay the remainder (if any) or such part of the remainder as they think fit-

    (a) to or for the benefit of persons who appear to the authority to be members of the patient's family or other persons for whom the patient might be expected to provide if he were not mentally disordered, or

(b) in reimbursement, with or without interest, of money applied by any person either in payment of the patient's debts (whether legally enforceable or not) or for the maintenance or other benefit of the patient or such persons as are mentioned in paragraph (a) above.

Section 142(1) and (2)
Where a person is incapable by reason of mental disorder of managing his/her property and affairs and is due monies from the government provision may be made for any monies to be paid to:

the institution or person caring for the person, for their own benefit;

their family or others they would have provided for;

others persons to whom they owe debts or who have maintained their family or any others they would have provided for.

(3) In this section "government department" does not include a Northern Ireland department.

Section 142(3)
Is self explanatory.

SUPPLEMENTAL

143. General provisions as to regulations, orders and rules

(1) Any power of the Secretary of State or the Lord Chancellor to make regulations, orders or rules under this Act shall be exercisable by statutory instrument.

(2) Any order in Council under this Act or any order made under section 54A or 65 above and any statutory instrument containing regulations or rules made under this Act shall be subject to annulment in pursuance of a resolution of either House of Parliament.

(3) No order shall be made under section 45A(10), 68(4) or 71(3) above unless a draft of it has been approved by a resolution of each House of Parliament.

Section 143(1) (2) & (3)
Are self explanatory.

144. Power to amend local Acts

Her Majesty may by Order in Council repeal or amend any local enactment so far as appears to Her Majesty to be necessary in consequence of this Act.

Section 144
Is self explanatory.

145. Interpretation

(1) In this Act, unless the context otherwise requires-

"absent without leave" has the meaning given to it by section 18 above and related expressions shall be construed accordingly;

"application for admission for assessment" has the meaning given in section 2 above;

"application for admission for treatment" has the meaning given in section 3 above;

"approved social worker" means an officer of a local social services authority appointed to act as an approved social worker for the purposes of this Act;

"Health Authority" means a Health Authority established under section 8 of the National Health Service Act 1977;

"hospital" means-

(a) any health service hospital within the meaning of the National Health Service Act 1977; and

(b) any accommodation provided by a local authority and used as a hospital by or on behalf of the Secretary of State under that Act;

and "hospital within the meaning of Part II of this Act" has the meaning given in section 34 above;

"hospital direction" has the meaning given in section 45A(3)(a) above;

"hospital order" and "guardianship order" have the meanings respectively given in section 37 above;

"interim hospital order" has the meaning given in section 38 above;

"limitation direction" has the meaning given in section 45A(3)(b) above;

"local social services authority" means a council which is a local authority for the purpose of the Local Authority Social Services Act 1970;

"the managers" means-

(a) in relation to a hospital vested in the Secretary of State for the purposes of his functions under the National Health Service Act 1977, and in relation to any accommodation provided by a local authority and used as a hospital by or on behalf of the Secretary of State under that Act, the Health Authority or Special Health Authority responsible for the administration of the hospital;

(b) in relation to a special hospital, the Secretary of State;

(bb) in relation to a hospital vested in a National Health Service trust, the trust;

(c) in relation to a mental nursing home registered in pursuance of the Registered Homes Act 1984 the person or persons registered in respect of the home;

and in this definition "hospital" means a hospital within the meaning of Part II of this Act;

"medical treatment" includes nursing, and also includes care, habilitation and rehabilitation under medical supervision;

"mental disorder", "severe mental impairment", "mental impairment" and "psychopathic disorder" have the meanings given in section 1 above;

"mental nursing home" has the same meaning as in the Registered Homes Act 1984;

"nearest relative", in relation to a patient, has the meaning given in Part II of this Act;

"patient" (except in Part VII of this Act) means a person suffering or appearing to be suffering from mental disorder;

"the responsible after-care bodies" has the meaning given in section 25D above;

"restriction direction" has the meaning given to it by section 49 above;

"restriction order" has the meaning given to it by section 41 above;

"Special Health Authority" means a Special Health Authority established under section 11 of the National Health Service Act 1977;

"special hospital" has the same meaning as in the National Health Service Act 1977;

"supervision application" has the meaning given in section 25A above;

"transfer direction" has the meaning given to it by section 47 above.

(1A) References in this Act to a patient being subject to after-care under supervision (or to after-care under supervision) shall be construed in accordance with section 25A above.

(2) . . .

Section 145(1)(1A)

Provide definitions of terms used within the Act and are self explanatory.[67]

Note: "medical treatment" is very broadly defined and thus covers any nursing or management of the patient under medical supervision.[68]

---

[67] s.145(2) was repealed by the Statute Law (Repeals) Act 1993.

[68] B v Croydon Health Authority (1995)1 All ER 683.

---

(3) In relation to a person who is liable to be detained or subject to guardianship by virtue of an order or direction under Part III of this Act (other than under section 35, 36 or 38), any reference in this Act to any enactment contained in Part II of this Act or in section 66 or 67 above shall be construed as a reference to that enactment as it applies to that person by virtue of Part III of this Act.

Section 145(3)
Where a person is detained or under guardianship under Part III of the Act and a reference in relation to them is made to a provision of Part II of the Act (or s.66 and s.67) any such references should be construed in a way which makes that Part II (or s.66 and s.67) provision applicable to Part III patients.

146. Application to Scotland

Sections 42(6), 80, 88 (and so far as applied by that section sections 18, 22 and 138), 104(4), 110 (and so much of Part VII of this Act as is applied in relation to Scotland by that section), 116, 122, 128 (except so far as it relates to patients subject to guardianship), 137, 139(1), 141, 142, 143 (so far as applicable to any Order in Council extending to Scotland) and 144 above shall extend to Scotland together with any amendment or repeal by this Act of or any provision of Schedule 5 to this Act relating to any enactment which so extends; but, except as aforesaid and except so far as it relates to the interpretation or commencement of the said provisions, this Act shall not extend to Scotland.

Section 146
Provides for limited application of the Act to Scotland in respect of those sections mentioned.

147. Application to Northern Ireland

Sections 81, 82, 86, 87, 88 (and so far as applied by that section sections 18, 22 and 138), 104(4), 110 (and so much of Part VII as is applied in relation to Northern Ireland by that section), section 128 (except so far as it relates to patients subject to guardianship), 137, 139, 141, 142, 143 (so far as applicable to any Order in Council extending to Northern Ireland) and 144 above shall extend to Northern Ireland together with any amendment or repeal by this Act of or any provision of Schedule 5 to this Act relating to any enactment which so extends; but except as aforesaid and except so far as it relates to the interpretation or commencement of the said provisions, this Act shall not extend to Northern Ireland.

Section 147
Provides for limited application of the Act to Northern Ireland in respect of those sections mentioned.

148. Consequential and transitional provisions and repeals

(1) Schedule 4 (consequential amendments) and Schedule 5 (transitional and saving provisions) to this Act shall have effect but without prejudice to the operation of sections 15 to 17 of the Interpretation Act 1978 (which relate to the effect of repeals).

(2) Where any amendment in Schedule 4 to this Act affects an enactment amended by the Mental Health (Amendment) Act 1982 the amendment in Schedule 4 shall come into force immediately after the provision of the Act of 1982 amending that enactment.

(3) The enactments specified in Schedule 6 to this Act are hereby repealed to the extent mentioned in the third column of that Schedule.

149. Short title, commencement and application to Scilly Isles

(1) This Act may be cited as the Mental Health Act 1983.

(2) Subject to subsection (3) below and Schedule 5 to this Act, this Act shall come into force on 30th September 1983.

(3) Sections 35, 36, 38 and 40(3) above shall come into force on such day (not being earlier than the said 30th September) as may be appointed by the Secretary of State and a different day may be appointed for each of those sections or for different purposes of any of those sections.

(4) Section 130(4) of the National Health Service Act 1977 (which provides for the extension of that Act to the Isles of Scilly) shall have effect as if the references to that Act included references to this Act.

Section 148 & 149
Make provision for the Act coming into force and in so far as they are not self explanatory are now of little relevance.

SCHEDULES

SCHEDULE 1

SECTIONS 40(4), 41(3),(5), 55(4)

APPLICATION OF CERTAIN PROVISIONS TO PATIENTS SUBJECT TO HOSPITAL AND GUARDIANSHIP ORDERS

PART I

Patients Not Subject to Special Restrictions

1. Sections 9, 10, 17, 21 to 21B, 24(3) and (4), 25C to 28, 31, 32, 34, 67 and 76 shall apply in relation to the patient without modification.

2. Sections 16, 18, 19, 20, 22, 23, 25A, 25B and 66 shall apply in relation to the patient with the modifications specified in paragraphs 3 to 9 below.

3. In section 16(1) for references to an application for admission or a guardianship application there shall be substituted references to the order or direction under Part III of this Act by virtue of which the patient is liable to be detained or subject to guardianship.

4. In section 18 subsection (5) shall be omitted.

5. In section 19(2) for the words from "as follows" to the end of the subsection there shall be substituted the words "as if the order or direction under Part III of this Act by virtue of which he was liable to be detained or subject to guardianship before being transferred were an order or direction for his admission or removal to the hospital to which he is transferred, or placing him under the guardianship of the authority or person into whose guardianship he is transferred, as the case may be".

6. In section 20-

   (a) in subsection (1) for the words from "day on which he was" to "as the case may be" there shall be substituted the words "date of the relevant order or direction under Part III of this Act"; and

   (b) in subsection (9) for the words "the application for admission for treatment or, as the case may be, in the guardianship application, that application" there shall be substituted the words "the relevant order or direction under Part III of this Act, that order or direction".

7. In section 22 for references to an application for admission or a guardianship application there shall be substituted references to the order or direction under Part III of this Act by virtue of which the patient is liable to be detained or subject to guardianship.

8. In section 23(2)-

   (a) in paragraph (a) the words "for assessment or" shall be omitted; and

   (b) in paragraphs (a) and (b) the references to the nearest relative shall be omitted.

8A. In sections 25A(1)(a) and 25B(5)(a) for the words "in pursuance of an application for admission for treatment" there shall be substituted the words "by virtue of an order or direction for his admission or removal to hospital under Part III of this Act".

9. In section 66-

   (a) in subsection (1), paragraphs (a),(b),(c),(g) and (h), the words in parenthesis in paragraph (i) and paragraph (ii) shall be omitted; and

   (b) in subsection (2), paragraphs (a),(b),(c) and (g), and in paragraph (d) ",(g)", shall be omitted.

PART II

Patients Subject to Special Restrictions

1. Sections 24(3) and (4), 32 and 76 shall apply in relation to the patient without modification.

2. Sections 17 to 19, 22, 23 and 34 shall apply in relation to the patient with the modifications specified in paragraphs 3 to 8 below.

3. In section 17-

   (a) in subsection (1) after the word "may" there shall be inserted the words "with the consent of the Secretary of State";

   (b) in subsection (4) after the words "the responsible medical officer" and after the words "that officer" there shall be inserted the words "or the Secretary of State"; and

   (c) in subsection (5) after the word "recalled" there shall be inserted the words "by the responsible medical officer", and for the words from "he has ceased" to the end of the subsection there shall be substituted the words "the expiration of the period of twelve months beginning with the first day of his absence on leave".

4. In section 18 there shall be omitted-

   (a) in subsection (1) the words "subject to the provisions of this section"; and

   (b) subsections (3),(4) and (5).

5. In section 19-

   (a) in subsection (1) after the word "may" in paragraph (a) there shall be inserted the words "with the consent of the Secretary of State", and the words from "or into" to the end of the subsection shall be omitted; and

(b) in subsection (2) for the words from "as follows" to the end of the subsection there shall be substituted the words "as if the order or direction under Part III of this Act by virtue of which he was liable to be detained before being transferred were an order or direction for his admission or removal to the hospital to which he is transferred"; and

(c) in subsection (3) after the words "may at any time" there shall be inserted the words ", with the consent of the Secretary of State,".

6. In section 22 subsection (1) and paragraph (a) of subsection (2) shall not apply.

7. In section 23-

(a) in subsection (1) references to guardianship shall be omitted and after the word "made" there shall be inserted the words "with the consent of the Secretary of State and"; and

(b) in subsection (2)-
(i) in paragraph (a) to the words "for assessment or" and "or by the nearest relative of the patient" shall be omitted; and
(ii) paragraph (b) shall be omitted.

8. In section 34, in subsection (1) the definition of "the nominated medical attendant" and subsection (3) shall be omitted.

SCHEDULE 2

SECTION 65(2)

MENTAL HEALTH REVIEW TRIBUNALS

1. Each of the Mental Health Review Tribunals shall consist of-

(a) a number of persons (referred to in this Schedule as "the legal members") appointed by the Lord Chancellor and having such legal experience as the Lord Chancellor considers suitable;

(b) a number of persons (referred to in this Schedule as "the medical members") being registered medical practitioners appointed by the Lord Chancellor after consultation with the Secretary of State; and

(c) a number of persons appointed by the Lord Chancellor after consultation with the Secretary of State and having such experience in administration, such knowledge of social services or such other qualifications or experience as the Lord Chancellor considers suitable.

2. Subject to paragraph 2A below the members of Mental Health Review Tribunals shall hold and vacate office under the terms of the instrument under which they are appointed, but may resign office by notice in writing to the Lord Chancellor; and any such member who ceases to hold office shall be eligible for re-appointment.

2A. A member of a Mental Health Review Tribunal shall vacate office on the day on which he attains the age of 70 years; but this paragraph is subject to section 26(4) to (6) of the Judicial Pensions and Retirement Act 1993 (power to authorise continuance in office up to the age of 75 years).

3. One of the legal members of each Mental Health Review Tribunal shall be appointed by the Lord Chancellor as chairman of the Tribunal.

4. Subject to rules made by the Lord Chancellor under section 78(2)(c) above, the members who are to constitute a Mental Health Review Tribunal for the purposes of any proceedings or class or group of proceedings under this Act shall be appointed by the chairman of the tribunal or, if for any reason he is unable to act, by another member of the tribunal appointed for the purpose by the chairman; and of the members so appointed-

   (a) one or more shall be appointed from the legal members;

   (b) one or more shall be appointed from the medical members; and

   (c) one or more shall be appointed from the members who are neither legal nor medical members.

5. A member of a Mental Health Review Tribunal for any area may be appointed under paragraph 4 above as one of the persons to constitute a Mental Health Review Tribunal for any other area for the purposes of any proceedings or class or group of proceedings; and for the purposes of this Act, a person so appointed shall, in relation to the proceedings for which he was appointed, be deemed to be a member of that other tribunal.

6. Subject to any rules made by the Lord Chancellor under section 78(4)(a) above, where the chairman of the tribunal is included among the persons appointed under paragraph 4 above, he shall be president of the tribunal; and in any other case the president of the tribunal shall be such one of the members so appointed (being one of the legal members) as the chairman may nominate.

SCHEDULE 3

Section 113

Enactments Disapplied in Respect of Persons Within Jurisdiction Under Part VII

Session and Chapter	Short Title	Enactments
13 Geo. 3. c. 81.	The Inclosure Act 1773.	Sections 22 and 24.
7 Geo. 4. c. 16.	The Chelsea and Kilmainham Hospitals Act 1826.	Sections 44 to 48.
2 & 3 Will. 4. c. 80.	The Ecclesiastical Corporations Act 1832.	Section 3.
1 & 2 Vict. c. 106.	The Pluralities Act 1838.	Section 127.
4 & 5 Vict. c. 38.	The School Sites Act 1841.	Section 5.
5 & 6 Vict. c. 26.	The Ecclesiastical Houses of Residence Act 1842.	Section 12.
5 & 6 Vict. c. 108.	The Ecclesiastical Leasing Act 1842.	Section 24.
8 & 9 Vict. c. 16.	The Companies Clauses Consolidation Act 1845.	Section 79.
8 & 9 Vict. c. 18.	The Lands Clauses Consolidation Act 1845.	Section 9.
8 & 9 Vict. c. 118.	The Inclosure Act 1845.	Sections 20, 133, 134 and 137.
9 & 10 Vict. c. 73.	The Tithe Act 1846.	Sections 5, 9 and 10.
17 & 18 Vict. c. 112.	The Literary and Scientific Institutions Act 1854.	Section 5.
25 & 26 Vict. c. 53.	The Land Registry Act 1862.	Section 116.
27 & 28 Vict. c. 114.	The Improvement of Land Act 1864.	Section 24.
29 & 30 Vict. c. 122.	The Metropolitan Commons Act 1866.	Section 28.
31 & 32 Vict. c. 109.	The Compulsory Church Rate Abolition Act 1868.	Section 7
36 & 37 Vict. c. 50.	The Places of Worship Sites Act 1873.	Sections 1 and 3.
57 & 58 Vict. c. 60.	The Merchant Shipping Act 1894.	In section 55, subsection (1).

SCHEDULE 4

SECTION 148

CONSEQUENTIAL AMENDMENTS

(This Schedule contains amendments only.)

SCHEDULE 5

SECTION 148

TRANSITIONAL AND SAVING PROVISIONS

1. Where any period of time specified in an enactment repealed by this Act is current at the commencement of this Act, this Act shall have effect as if the corresponding provision of this Act had been in force when that period began to run.

2. Nothing in this Act shall affect the interpretation of any provision of the Mental Health Act 1959 which is not repealed by this Act and accordingly sections 1 and 145(1) of this Act shall apply to any such provision as if it were contained in this Act.

3. Where, apart from this paragraph, anything done under or for the purposes of any enactment which is repealed by this Act would cease to have effect by virtue of that repeal it shall have effect as if it had been done under or for the purposes of the corresponding provision of this Act.

4.- (1) (Is spent)

(2) Any appointment of a person as a mental welfare officer for the purposes of the Mental Health Act 1959 or this Act shall terminate at the expiration of the period mentioned in sub-paragraph (1) above but without prejudice to anything previously done by that person or to the continuation by an approved social worker of anything which is then in process of being done by that person.

5. (Is spent)

6. This Act shall apply in relation to any authority for the detention or guardianship of a person who was liable to be detained or subject to guardianship under the Mental Health Act 1959 immediately before 30th September 1983 as if the provisions of this Act which derive from provisions amended by sections 1 or 2 of the Mental Health (Amendment) Act 1982 and the amendments in Schedule 3 to that Act which are consequential on those sections were included in this Act in the form the provisions from which they derive would take if those amendments were disregarded but this provision shall not apply to any renewal of that authority on or after that date.

7. This Act shall apply to any application made before 30th September 1983 as if the provisions of this Act which derive from provisions amended by sections 3 to 5 of the Mental Health (Amendment) Act 1982 and the amendments in Schedule 3 to that Act which are consequential on those sections were included in this Act in the form the provisions from which they derive would take if those amendments were disregarded.

8.- (1) Where on 30th September 1983 a person who has not attained the age of sixteen years is subject to guardianship by virtue of a guardianship application the authority for his guardianship shall terminate on that day.

(2) Section 8(1) of this Act has effect (instead of section 34(1) of the Mental Health Act 1959) in relation to a guardianship application made before the coming into force of this Act as well as in relation to one made later.

9.- (1) Section 20(1) of this Act shall have effect in relation to any application for admission for treatment and to any guardianship application made before 1st October 1983 with the substitution for the words "six months" of the words "one year".

(2) Section 20(2) of this Act shall have effect in relation to any authority renewed before 1st October 1983 with the substitution for the words "six months" of the words "one year" and for the words "one year" in both places they occur of the words "two years".

(3) Where an authority has been renewed on or before 30th September 1983 for a period of two years of which less than 16 months has expired on that date that period shall expire at the end of 18 months from the date on which it began.

10. Section 23(2)(a) of this Act shall have effect in relation to a patient liable to be detained in pursuance of an application under section 25 of the Mental Health Act 1959 made before 30th September 1983 as if the reference to the nearest relative of the patient were omitted.

11. Where at any time before 30th September 1983 an application to a Mental Health Review Tribunal has been made by a person who at that time was the patient's nearest relative and the application has not then been determined and by reason of the coming into force of section 26 of this Act that person ceased to be the patient's nearest relative on that date, that person shall nevertheless be treated for the purposes of the application as continuing to be his nearest relative.

12. A person-

   (a) who was admitted to hospital in pursuance of an application for admission for treatment; or

   (b) in respect of whom a guardianship application was accepted; or

   (c) in respect of whom a hospital order was made,

before 30th September 1983 may make an application to a tribunal under section 66 of this Act in the cases mentioned in subsection (1)(b) and (c) of that section and under section 69(1)(b) of this Act within the period of six months beginning with the day on which he attains the age of 16 years if that period is later than that which would otherwise apply to an application in his case.

13. Subsection (1) of section 68 of this Act does not apply to any patient admitted or transferred to hospital more than six months before 30th September 1983; and subsection (2) of that section applies only in relation to a renewal of authority for detention after that date.

14. Section 69(1)(b) of this Act shall have effect in relation to patients liable to be detained immediately before 30th September 1983 as if after the words "in respect of a patient" there were inserted the words "admitted to a hospital in pursuance of a hospital order or".

15. The provisions of this Act which derive from sections 24 to 27 of the Mental Health (Amendment) Act 1982 shall have effect in relation to a transfer direction given before 30th September 1983 as well as in relation to one given later, but where, apart from this paragraph, a transfer direction given before 30th September 1983 would by virtue of the words in section 50(3) of this Act which are derived from section 24(3) of the Mental Health (Amendment) Act 1982 have ceased to have effect before that date it shall cease to have effect on that date.

16. The words in section 42(1) of this Act which derive from the amendment of section 66(1) of the Mental Health Act 1959 by section 28(1) of the Mental Health (Amendment) Act 1982 and the provisions of this Act which derive from section 28(3) of and Schedule 1 to that Act have effect in relation to a restriction order or, as the case may be, a restriction direction made or given before 30th September 1983 as well as in relation to one made or given later, but-

    (a) any reference to a tribunal under section 66(6) of the said Act of 1959 in respect of a patient shall be treated for the purposes of subsections (1) and (2) of section 77 of this Act in their application to sections 70 and 75(2) of this Act as an application made by him; and

    (b) sections 71(5) and 75(1)(a) of this Act do not apply where the period in question has expired before 30th September 1983.

17. Section 91(2) of this Act shall not apply in relation to a patient removed from England and Wales before 30th September 1983.

18.- (1) Subsection (3) of section 58 of this Act shall not apply to any treatment given to a patient in the period of six months beginning with the 30th September 1983 if-

    (a) the detention of the patient began before the beginning of that period; and

    (b) that subsection has not been complied with in respect of any treatment previously given to him in that period.

(2) The Secretary of State may by order reduce the length of the period mentioned in sub-paragraph (1) above.

19. In the case of a patient who is detained at the time when section 132 of this Act comes into force, the steps required by that section shall be taken as soon as practicable after that time.

20. The repeal by the Mental Health (Amendment) Act 1982 of section 77 of the Mental Health Act 1959 does not affect subsection (4) of that section in its application to a transfer direction given before 30th September 1983, but after the coming into force of this Act that subsection shall have effect for that purpose as if for the references to subsection (6) of section 60, Part IV of that Act and the provisions of that Act there were substituted respectively references to section 37(8), Part II and the provisions of this Act.

21. Section 46(3) of this Act shall apply to any direction to which section 71(4) of the Mental Health Act 1959 applied immediately before the commencement of this Act.

22. Notwithstanding the repeal by this Act of section 53(5) of the Mental Health Act 1959, the discharge or variation under that section of an order made under section 52 of that Act shall not affect the validity of anything previously done in pursuance of the order.

23. For any reference in any enactment, instrument, deed or other document to a receiver under Part VIII of the Mental Health Act 1959 there shall be substituted a reference to a receiver under Part VII of this Act.

24. Nothing in this Act shall affect the operation of the proviso to section 107(5) of the Mental Health Act 1959 in relation to a charge created before the commencement of this Act under that section.

25. Nothing in this Act shall affect the operation of subsection (6) of section 112 of the Mental Health Act 1959 in relation to a charge created before the commencement of this Act by virtue of subsection (5) of that section.

26. If the person who is the Master of the Court of Protection at the commencement of this Act has before that time duly taken the oaths required by section 115(1) of the Mental Health Act 1959 he shall not be obliged to take those oaths again by virtue of section 93(3) of this Act.

27. Nothing in this Act shall affect the operation of section 116 of the Mental Health Act 1959 in relation to orders made, directions or authorities given or other instruments issued before the commencement of this Act.

28. References to applications, recommendations, reports and other documents in section 126 of this Act shall include those to which section 125 of the Mental Health Act 1959 applied immediately before the commencement of this Act and references in section 139 of this Act to the Acts to which that section applies shall include those to which section 141 of the said Act of 1959 applied at that time.

29. The repeal by the Mental Health Act 1959 of the Mental Treatment Act 1930 shall not affect any amendment effected by section 20 of that Act in any enactment not repealed by the said Act of 1959.

30. The repeal by the Mental Health Act 1959 of the provisions of the Lunacy Act 1890 and of the Mental Deficiency Act 1913 relating to the superannuation of officers or employees shall not affect any arrangements for the payment of allowances or other benefits made in accordance with those provisions and in force on 1st November 1960.

31.- (1) Any patient who immediately before the commencement of this Act was liable to be detained in a hospital or subject to guardianship by virtue of paragraph 9 of Schedule 6 to the Mental Health Act 1959 shall unless previously discharged continue to be so liable for the remainder of the period of his treatment current on 1st November 1960.

(2) The patient may before the expiration of the period of treatment referred to in sub-paragraph (1) above apply to a Mental Health Review Tribunal.

32. Any patient who immediately before the commencement of this Act was liable to be detained or subject to guardianship by virtue of an authority which had been renewed under paragraph 11 of Schedule 6 to the Mental Health Act 1959 shall unless previously discharged continue to be so liable during the period for which that authority was so renewed.

33.- (1) This paragraph applies to patients who at the commencement of this Act are liable to be detained or subject to guardianship by virtue of paragraph 31 or 32 above.

(2) Authority for the detention or guardianship of the patient may on the expiration of the relevant period, unless the patient has previously been discharged, be renewed for a further period of two years.

(3) Sections 20(3) to (10) and 66(1)(f) of this Act shall apply in relation to the renewal of authority for the detention or guardianship of a patient under this paragraph as they apply in relation to the renewal of authority for the detention or guardianship of the patient under section 20(2).

(4) In this paragraph "the relevant period" means-

(a) in relation to a patient liable to be detained or subject to guardianship by virtue of the said paragraph 31, the period of his treatment referred to in that paragraph;

(b) in relation to a patient detained by virtue of the said paragraph 32, the period for which authority for the detention or guardianship of the patient has been renewed under paragraph 11 of Schedule 6 to the 1959 Act;

(c) in relation to a patient the authority for whose detention or guardianship has previously been renewed under this paragraph, the latest period for which it has been so renewed.

34.- (1) Any patient who is liable to be detained in a hospital or subject to guardianship by virtue of paragraph 31 above shall (subject to the exceptions and modifications specified in the following provisions of this paragraph) be treated as if he had been admitted to the hospital in pursuance of an application for admission for treatment under Part II of this Act or had been received into guardianship in pursuance of a guardianship application under the said Part II and had been so admitted or received as a patient suffering from the form or forms of mental disorder recorded under paragraph 7 of Schedule 6 to the Mental Health Act 1959 or, if a different form or forms have been specified in a report under section 38 of that Act as applied by that paragraph, the form or forms so specified.

(2) Section 20 of this Act shall not apply in relation to the patient, but the provisions of paragraph 33 above shall apply instead.

(3) Any patient to whom paragraph 9(3) of Schedule 6 to the Mental Health Act 1959 applied at the commencement of this Act who fell within paragraph (b) of that paragraph shall cease to be liable to be detained on attaining the age of 25 years unless, during the period of two months ending on the date when he attains that age, the responsible medical officer records his opinion under the following provisions of this Schedule that the patient is unfit for discharge.

(4) If the patient was immediately before 1st November 1960 liable to be detained by virtue of section 6, 8(1) or 9 of the Mental Deficiency Act 1913, the power of discharging him under section 23 of this Act shall not be exercisable by his nearest relative, but his nearest relative may make one application in respect of him to a Mental Health Review Tribunal in any period of 12 months.

35. - (1) The responsible medical officer may record for the purposes of paragraph 34(3) above his opinion that a patient detained in a hospital is unfit for discharge if it appears to the responsible medical officer-

(a) that if that patient were released from the hospital he would be likely to act in a manner dangerous to other persons or to himself, or would be likely to resort to criminal activities; or

(b) that that patient is incapable of caring for himself and that there is no suitable hospital or other establishment into which he can be admitted and where he would be likely to remain voluntarily; and where the responsible medical officer records his opinion as aforesaid he shall also record the grounds for his opinion.

(2) Where the responsible medical officer records his opinion under this paragraph in respect of a patient, the managers of the hospital or other persons in charge of the establishment where he is for the time being detained or liable to be detained shall cause the patient to be informed, and the patient may, at any time before the expiration of the period of 28 days beginning with the date on which he is so informed, apply to a Mental Health Review Tribunal.

(3) On any application under sub-paragraph (2) above the tribunal shall, if satisfied that none of the conditions set out in paragraphs (a) and (b) of sub-paragraph (1) above are fulfilled, direct that the patient be discharged, and subsection (1) of section 72 of this Act shall have effect in relation to the application as if paragraph (b) of that subsection were omitted.

36. Any person who immediately before the commencement of this Act was deemed to have been named as the guardian of any patient under paragraph 14 of Schedule 6 to the Mental Health Act 1959 shall be deemed for the purposes of this Act to have been named as the guardian of the patient in an application for his reception into guardianship under Part II of this Act accepted on that person's behalf by the relevant local authority.

37.- (1) This paragraph applies to patients who immediately before the commencement of this Act were transferred patients within the meaning of paragraph 15 of Schedule 6 to the Mental Health Act 1959.

(2) A transferred patient who immediately before the commencement of this Act was by virtue of sub-paragraph (2) of that paragraph treated for the purposes of that Act as if he were liable to be detained in a hospital in pursuance of a direction under section 71 of that Act shall be treated as if he were so liable in pursuance of a direction under section 46 of this Act.

(3) A transferred patient who immediately before the commencement of this Act was by virtue of sub-paragraph (3) of that paragraph treated for the purposes of that Act as if he were liable to be detained in a hospital by virtue of a transfer direction under section 72 of that Act and as if a direction restricting his discharge had been given under section 74 of that Act shall be treated as if he were so liable by virtue of a transfer direction under section 47 of this Act and as if a restriction direction had been given under section 49 of this Act.

(4) Section 84 of this Act shall apply to a transferred patient who was treated by virtue of sub-paragraph (5) of that paragraph immediately before the commencement of this Act as if he had been removed to a hospital under section 89 of that Act as if he had been so removed under the said section 84.

(5) Any person to whom sub-paragraph (6) of that paragraph applied immediately before the commencement of this Act shall be treated for the purposes of this Act as if he were liable to be detained in a hospital in pursuance of a transfer direction given under section 48 of this Act and as if a restriction direction had been given under section 49 of this Act, and he shall be so treated notwithstanding that he is not suffering from a form of mental disorder mentioned in the said section 48.

38. Any patient who immediately before the commencement of this Act was treated by virtue of sub-paragraph (1) of paragraph 16 of Schedule 6 to the Mental Health Act 1959 as if he had been conditionally discharged under section 66 of that Act shall be treated as if he had been conditionally discharged under section 42 of this Act and any such direction as is mentioned in paragraph (b) of that sub-paragraph shall be treated as if it had been given under the said section 42.

39. Upon a restriction direction in respect of a patient who immediately before the commencement of this Act was a transferred patient, within the meaning of paragraph 15 of Schedule 6 to the Mental Health Act 1959, ceasing to have effect, the responsible medical officer shall record his opinion whether the patient is suffering from mental illness, severe mental impairment, psychopathic disorder or mental impairment, and references in this Act to the form or forms of mental disorder specified in the relevant application, order or direction shall be construed as including references to the form or forms of mental disorder recorded under this paragraph or under paragraph 17 of the said Schedule 6.

40. A person who immediately before the commencement of this Act was detained by virtue of paragraph 19 of Schedule 6 to the Mental Health Act 1959 may continue to be detained until the expiration of the period of his treatment current on 1st November 1960 or until he becomes liable to be detained or subject to guardianship under this Act, whichever occurs first, and may be so detained in any place in which he might have been detained under that paragraph.

41. Any opinion recorded by the responsible medical officer under the foregoing provisions of this Schedule shall be recorded in such form as may be prescribed by regulations made by the Secretary of State.

42.- (1) In the foregoing provisions of this Schedule-

(a) references to the period of treatment of a patient that was current on 1st November 1960 are to the period for which he would have been liable to be detained or subject to guardianship by virtue of any enactment repealed or excluded by the Mental Health Act 1959, or any enactment repealed or replaced by any such enactment as aforesaid, being a period which began but did not expire before that date; and

(b) "the responsible medical officer" means-

(i) in relation to a patient subject to guardianship, the medical officer authorised by the local social services authority to act (either generally or in any particular case or for any particular purpose) as the responsible medical officer;

(ii) in relation to any other class of patient, the registered medical practitioner in charge of the treatment of the patient.

(2) Subsection (2) of section 34 of this Act shall apply for the purposes of the foregoing provisions of this Schedule as it applies for the purposes of Part II of this Act.

(3) The sentence or other period of detention of a person who was liable to be detained or subject to guardianship immediately before 1st November 1960 by virtue of an order under section 9 of the Mental Deficiency Act 1913 shall be treated for the purposes of the foregoing provisions of this Schedule as expiring at the end of the period for which that person would have been liable to be detained in a prison or other institution if the order had not been made.

(4) For the purposes of the foregoing provisions of this Schedule, an order sending a person to an institution or placing a person under guardianship made before 9th March 1956 on a petition presented under the Mental Deficiency Act 1913 shall be deemed to be valid if it was so deemed immediately before the commencement of this Act by virtue of section 148(2) of the Mental Health Act 1959.

43.- (1) Any order or appointment made, direction or authority given, or thing done which by virtue of paragraph 25 of Schedule 6 to the Mental Health Act 1959 had effect immediately before the commencement of this Act as if made, given or done under any provision of Part VIII of that Act shall have effect as if made, given or done under Part VII of this Act.

(2) Where at the commencement of this Act Part VIII of the Mental Health Act 1959 applied in any person's case by virtue of paragraph 25 of Schedule 6 to that Act as if immediately after the commencement of that Act it had been determined that he was a patient within the meaning of the said Part VIII, Part VII of this Act shall apply in his case as if immediately after the commencement of this Act it had been determined that he was a patient within the meaning of the said Part VII.

44. Where a person who immediately before 1st November 1960 was the committee of the estate of a person of unsound mind so found by inquisition was immediately before the commencement of this Act deemed by virtue of paragraph 26 of Schedule 6 to the Mental Health Act 1959 to be a receiver appointed under section 105 of that Act for that person, he shall be deemed to be a receiver appointed under section 99 of this Act for that person and shall continue to have the same functions in relation to that person's property and affairs as were exercisable by him immediately before the commencement of that Act as committee of the estate and references in any document to the committee of the estate of that person shall be construed accordingly.

45. Section 101(1) of this Act shall apply in relation to any disposal of property (within the meaning of that section) of a person living on 1st November 1960, being a disposal effected under the Lunacy Act 1890 as it applies in relation to the disposal of property of a person effected under Part VII of this Act.

SCHEDULE 6

Section 148(3)

REPEALS

(This Schedule contains repeals only.)

Index

suspension 79
termination 77–9
ward of court 92
Air Force Act 1955 s.116 127
alien patients
removal 195–6
application for admission *see* admission
application
application for warrant to search for and
remove patients 29
application of Act 3–4
applications
county court procedure 90
general provisions 22–4
appropriate body, meaning 50
appropriate medical officer, definition 34
Approved Social Worker (ASW)
appointment 223–4
assessment application 6
duty to make applications 28–30
emergency application for assessment 9
entry and inspection powers 224
guardianship application 16
Northern Ireland 198
Scotland 198
treatment application 8
warrant application 224
Arbitration Act 1996 Part I 178
Armed Forces Act 1996 Sch.7 Pt.III 128
Army Act 1955 s.116 127
assessment
admission for *see* admission for
assessment
ASW *see* Approved Social Worker

B v Croydon Health Authority [1995] 1 All
ER 683 152, 262
*Barker v Barking Havering & Brentwood
Community Healthcare NHS Trust* [1999]
Lloyd's Rep Med 101 35, 38, 43
brain tissue 146
*Briscoe, Re (Application for habeus corpus ad
subjiciendum)* [1998] C.O.D. 402, QBD 23

Broadmoor Hospital Authority v Robinson
[1999] QB 957 248

Channel Islands
removal from 192–4
removal to 190–1
removal to E&W of insane offenders
191–2
responsibility transferred from
194–5
return of absent patients to 198
transfer of responsibility to 191
Children Act 1989 84, 244
children and young persons
local authority care, nearest relative 84
presumption of age 145
Children and Young Persons Act 1933
s.99 145
s.107(1) 143
civil liability 256
civil prisoner
meaning 131, 143
notification of entitlement to discharge
171
transfer direction 130–2, 140
Civil Procedure Rules 1999 90
Code of Practice 1993
after-care under supervision 56
Code of Practice 1999 228
absent without leave 36–9
accused person report 96, 97, 100
admission for assessment 6
admission for treatment 8
after-care guidance 56, 225
Approved Social Worker 6, 8, 30
children 244
emergency admissions 10
guardianship 17
hospital and limitation direction 122
hospital manager
powers of discharge 52
information to patients 245–6
leave of absence 35

acting 85–90
children and young persons in care 84
definition 82–3
determination 83–4
discharge and variation of orders under
s.29 88–90
duty of hospital managers to inform of
discharge 246
minor under guardianship 84–5
notice of intention to discharge 55
power of discharge 53–6
necessity test 6
neglect 256
NHS (Functions of Health Authorities and
Administrations) Regulations 1996 25
nominated judge 201
meaning 203, 222
nominated medical attendant, meaning 92
nominated officer 220–2
meaning 202, 222
non-molestation order breach 95, 103, 106
Northern Ireland
application of Act to 263
patient's property and affairs
reciprocal arrangements 219–20
patients absent without leave 196–7
reciprocal arrangements 219–20
removal to 183–5
removal to E&W from 187–9
transfer of responsibility to 186
transfer of responsibility to E&W
189–90
Northern Ireland Assembly
mental illness of member 259
nurse
detention application 13
written record of detention 12

obstruction 242–3
occupation order breach 95, 103, 106
order for discharge 52
orders
general provisions 260

patient
absent without leave *see* absent without
leave
alien 196
assisting to abscond or avoid recapture
241–2
correspondence *see* postal packet
detained in custody by court order 50–1
discharge 52–6, 166–73, 246
escorted leave 35–6
ill treatment 239–41, 256
informal admission 243–4
interests in property, preservation
210–11
leave of absence from hospital 34–6
mail *see* postal packet
meaning 262
monies from government department
259–60
pay and pension 259–60
pocket money provision 235–6
property and affairs management *see*
Court of Protection
reclassification 32–3
relatives *see* relative of patient
removal to Scotland *see* Scotland
restricted *see* restricted patient
sentenced to imprisonment 50–1
subject to detention or guardianship
32–4
visit and examination by doctor 53–5
visit and interview 229–30, 231
voluntary 244
warrant 250–2
pension 259–60
person liable to be detained 262–3
person serving a sentence of imprisonment,
meaning 130, 144
place of safety 96, 99, 104, 107, 124
meaning 143, 252
permitted detention period 252, 253
removal to 251–3
retaking of escapee 254–5